Counseling
Victims of
Violence

Sandra L. Brown

AMERICAN
COUNSELING
ASSOCIATION

5999 Stevenson Avenue
Alexandria, VA 22304-3300

(AACD became the American Counseling Association on July 1, 1992)

American Counseling Association
5999 Stevenson Avenue
Alexandria, VA 22304

Cover design by Sarah Jane Valdez

Library of Congress Cataloging-in-Publication Data

Brown, Sandra L., 1957–
    Counseling victims of violence / by Sandra L. Brown.
        p. cm.
    Includes bibliographical references.
    ISBN 1-55620-083-8
    1. Victims of crimes—Counseling of—United States.   2. Violence—
United States—Psychological aspects.   3. Post-traumatic stress disorder—Treatment—United States.   4. Crisis intervention (Psychiatry)—
United States.   I. American Association for Counseling and Development.   II. Title.
    HV6250.3.U5B76   1991
    362.88—dc20   91-16795
                                                                        CIP

Printed in the United States of America (Third Printing)

This book is dedicated to those victims and survivors of violence who have bravely chosen the option of healing, and in loving memory to my father, Frankie Brown, who was murdered May 13, 1983.

I love you and miss you, Dad.

Contents

Foreword

Robert H. Rencken

Over the past 15 or 20 years, counselors have been thrust into the front line of defense against violent, abusive, and exploitive behavior. Although other professionals are also involved in that defense, counselors have found that their training and skills have proved more effective than those of practitioners in some more established professions in this relatively new, complex, and crucial arena. This book is certainly applicable to different disciplines, but it is counselors, specialists or not, who will benefit from the information.

The problem of violence is not new, of course, but it has grown to encompass us all. In my work in sexual abuse, I emphasize the extent of the problem by telling both professional and lay audiences that *every one* of them *will* be affected by sexual abuse. If we are fortunate enough not to experience sexual abuse in our own family, we know a friend, neighbor, relative, or colleague who has been touched by the problem. If this example is true for sexual abuse, it is obviously true for the broader category of violence. All of us will either be victims of violence or know someone who is. Counselors, regardless of the setting, are faced with assisting those who have been hurt, traumatized, and, even, devastated by the violent behavior of others.

We live in a society that deals ambivalently, at best, with underlying issues of violence. We continue to glorify violent solutions to problems, from the gunfights of the Western frontier to our "war" on drugs to

Robert H. Rencken is a mental health counselor and clinical sexologist in private practice in Tucson, Arizona. He is the author of *Intervention Strategies for Sexual Abuse* (AACD, 1989).

our technologically advanced ''victory'' in the Persian Gulf. We ignore conditions of poverty, inequity, and illiteracy and then respond minimally to those who are hurt by the violence that results from these conditions. This book contributes to our understanding of the complex problems resulting from violence and suggests methods that counselors can use to try to solve them.

Counselors deal with victims of violence in many settings such as schools, mental health offices, hospitals, and prisons. They also deal with a widely disparate population—children, adults, families, and groups. The information provided in this volume can be adapted easily to each of these settings and populations. The book is, unfortunately, timely and necessary.

The perspective Sandra Brown offers comes from experience both as a surviving victim and as one who has extensive contact with a variety of victims. Despite the title and its clear focus on victimization, the book is more about survival and survivors, those who have struggled out of the bonds of victimization. This survivor-centered approach enables us to be critical helpers in the process of empowerment and control. We certainly have to deal with those who are still victims, but we also need to realize that, with time, it is possible for these victims to become survivors. Our skill can both shorten the time needed for this recovery and allow it to be more complete.

The skills needed are not simple and the task of applying them is frequently neither easy nor appreciated. This is an era in which short-term treatment, personal growth emphases, and monetary reward for counselors are stressed. Working with victims and survivors of violence frequently involves months of intense and frustrating therapy, interaction with less-than-ideal bureaucratic systems, and limited financial remuneration. Counselors are often content with the eventual appreciation of their clients. For these counselors, the material discussed in this book may be both helpful and validating.

Those who are not used to confronting the complexity of the issues of violence may be somewhat disappointed that this book is not, and cannot be, a ''cookbook.'' In my experience with workshops and presentations across the country, counselors and therapists are indeed hungry for specific ''how-to'' techniques. By the end of a workshop, however, they are more likely to see the advantages of a more holistic, strategic, and integrated perspective. By reading about the various kinds of violence, their unique and common effects, and the levels and duration of intervention, counselors are able to gain a much better understanding of how to respond to these concerns in a more integrated and effective manner.

The techniques described are essentially developmental intervention strategies, an approach familiar to most counselors. Not only is trauma healed in this approach, but clients are empowered to deal more effectively with their circumstances. It is a process of education, awareness, and realistic optimism. This optimism is present even when the victims/survivors are severely impaired with dissociative patterns and multiple personality disorders.

It is also essential to consider these counseling strategies as integrative. Our work in sexual abuse with children and adult survivors has emphasized both the treatment team and multimodal therapy. The counselor of victims of violence must be prepared to implement support networks, understand the criminal justice system, coordinate individual and group therapy, and heal various family systems. Interventions may include crisis intervention, suicide prevention, relationship counseling, and intense anger work. Professionals must possess flexibility and varied skills as well as the ability to create a treatment team that will bring the most expertise to bear on each case.

Knowing when to bring other professionals into a treatment team underscores the importance of recognizing one's limitations. These limitations are manifest in the strategies presented in this book. They are related to skills and psychological impact. This book should increase awareness of counselors struggling with this problem. We have to recognize our own boundaries and accept the need for referral of clients to other team members, ongoing supervision with a specialist in the field, and continuing education.

The psychological impact on counselors is too often ignored. Anyone who works in this field knows that each case demands a tremendous investment of time, physical energy, and spirit. Although this investment pays off in treatment successes, it also promotes burnout in the most intense way. Very few counselors are able to work in this field for extended periods without shifting focus, renewing personal lives, or taking time off. (An interesting tangent is to notice the burnout rate of police officers/detectives who are assigned to sex crimes and other violent crimes described in this book.) This pressure should be noted and addressed by the readers.

There is one other indirect message to be received from Sandra's work: "Above all else, do no harm"! This admonition, traditionally directed at physicians, is critically important in working with the highly vulnerable population of victims/survivors. The potential for harm by inexperienced and unsupervised professionals is indeed great. The harm can range from simple ineffectiveness that reinforces the client's problems (e.g., a reaction of pity from the counselor that I call "co-whining behavior") to an underestimation of the fragility of a client in a dissociative state. This book will have done a great service if it conveys the message that, despite the optimism noted above, these victims/survivors deserve our most cautious care.

There are at least five specific topics in this volume that, I believe, deserve particular attention:

Secondary victimization. In describing her work with Dede, Sandra points out the problems of secondary victimizaton. We are probably aware of this issue in rape (as this is written, the dramatic principles associated with the Smith rape case in Florida come to mind). Secondary victimization is also a pervasive concern in sexual abuse (removal of a child, court testimony, mandatory sentencing), robbery (ineffective law enforcement), and ritual abuse (incredulity and scorn). As counselors, we must be aware of these effects and provide strategies to counteract or soften the reactions to them through cooperation with "the system," client advocacy, and empowerment.

The encodement process. The section in chapter 2 on the information processing of trauma provides a helpful base for understanding both the intensity and complexity of victimization. It is particularly useful to understand the multisensory nature of trauma encodement. The behavior of victims/survivors has frequently been considered perplexing because of their unexplained reactions to auditory, olfactory, or kinesthetic stimuli. The causes of these reactions are often buried in the subconscious, and extra skill is required to bring them to awareness and to create new, controlled options for handling these reactions. This is a particularly sensitive concern when dealing with sexuality and sexual relationships, where sensual stimuli and reactions are likely to be profound.

Holistic approaches. Not only is it necessary to provide integrated and multimodal treatment, but also to emphasize the spiritual dimension. Although some of us do not feel adequately trained in or comfortable with issues of religion and spirituality, it is a dimension that can add tremendously to the recovery process. Long ago, Alcoholics Anonymous demonstrated the effectiveness of including a "higher power" as a part of recovery. That perspective can be added either within or outside of the counseling relationship, taking care, however, not to foster overdependence. Because the effects of victimization are so pervasive and "holistic" in their destructiveness, it certainly makes sense that treatment also be holistic.

Long-term counseling. One of the greatest differences between "typical" counseling and victim/survivor counseling is the frequent need for long-term treatment. This may include actual long-term therapy of 1 to 2 years and even longer monitoring, follow-up, and occasional "patch" work. The duration can be important because time is a great ally in the healing process. Even the most intense and effective treatment may be only partially successful without sufficient time for healing to occur. We can do the best job in the world of putting a broken leg in a cast or suturing a wound, but time (and protection) is necessary to achieve a real cure.

Ritual abuse. Nothing that counselors have addressed can equal the incredulity involved in the issue of ritual abuse. We simply do not believe (or choose not to believe) that these practices occur. We cannot fathom the possibility of sanctioned abuse, torture, and murder that survivors of ritualized episodes report. Research clearly does not provide helpful data on the true incidence or damage in this area. We are now, like we once were in the area of intrafamilial sexual abuse, relying on anecdotal information and the sharing of clinical experiences. It is plain that the reports are true, frightening, and very difficult to accept. We need to address this issue and confront it with the intensity that we have devoted to other issues of violence.

Sandra Brown provides us with a look at the effects of violence and offers strategies for assisting victims/survivors of that violence to cope, recover, and grow. This book should provide a renewed focus on the need for the counseling profession to render quality care, vigilant advocacy, and diligent concern.

Acknowledgments

I wish to thank those who have faithfully given of themselves at Bridgework. I thank Terry Owens for his outstanding dedication to this work and the women we counsel. I thank Pat Christensen, who has lovingly held each of these women in her heart and stood with them through crises and victories, and for the priceless and precious gift of her friendship to me; Elaine Arnold, who has broadened not only the women's but my own vision of healing; Dr. Ben Keyes, who has patiently guided, taught, and supervised our staff and who has been a kind friend and personal therapist; Randy Evans and Camille Regan, who have compassionately assisted with our groups; and Laurie Hill, who has been a mountain of encouragement to me and shares the challenges of working with MPD victims.

I also wish to acknowledge those who have personally touched my life in many ways and have believed in our work—Steve Coker, who shared his heart and wisdom and kept me focused on the One who is larger than I; my dear friend, Ruth Pierson, who taught me that I can have and should expect to find my "miracle a day"; Rev. Dick Christensen, who has been a mentor of integrity, courage, and strength to me; and my pastor, Rev. John Lloyd, who has compassionately and paternally molded and shaped my Christian development and encouraged me many times when I wanted to quit. I thank all of you because you have added richly to my life, each of you weaving part of yourself into the tapestry that is then passed on through the work done at Bridgework. Bridgework would not have touched the lives it has without each of you.

I thank my husband Ken and daughters Lindsay and Lauren, who have sacrificed much to enable me to work in this field; my mother, Joyce, who encourages me by her fortitude and gentle character, and who always believes in me; and my sister, Linda, who has lived through the same difficult victimizations and survived.

I thank four special friends—Gayle, who helps me stay centered on my own recovery and brings great personal revelation to the work done at Bridgework; Kevin, who has walked with me through 18 years of victimizations and recovery, always believing that I would heal; Judy, who has continued to support and encourage me and share her healing with me; and Margaret, who began much of our work by bringing the first multiple personality disordered woman to me.

But most of all, my heartfelt thanks go to all the women and children from Bridgework, who taught me and afforded me the privilege to be part of their healing process. The ways in which you have touched my life ensure I will never be the same. I commend your commitment to healing and to life.

Hope deferred makes the heart sick, but a longing fulfilled is a tree of life.
                                                            —Proverbs 13:12

About the Author

Sandra L. Brown is the founder and executive director of Bridgework Ministries, Inc., an educational and counseling resource concerned with victims of violence. The educational program offers 16-hour Master Conferences to train professionals how to meet the needs of victims of violence. Bridgework also offers a counseling program designed to meet the needs of sexually abused women and children and other types of victims of violence. This program includes individual and group counseling, as well as wilderness retreats and other expressive therapies.

Sandra Brown produced an award-winning cable television show, "A Voice for Victims." She is also president of the board of directors of Attention Home, Inc., which is a residential treatment home for sexually abused boys in Clearwater, Florida. She has taught victimology at private and state colleges and has lectured nationwide on issues of traumatology.

She is a survivor of numerous victimizations, including sexual abuse and homicide. She has come up through grass-roots organizations and is a member of a number of professional victim associations.

Ms. Brown is a licensed minister, holds a BA in counseling, and is currently working on her master's in counseling, specializing in dissociative and multiple personality disorders.

Patricia S. Gerard, MA, is currently the director of the Spouse Abuse Shelter of Religious Community Services in Clearwater, Florida. Ms. Gerard began her work with battered women as a victim advocate for the city of Largo, Florida, Police Department. She has worked with the problem of domestic violence for the past 7 years and has extensive experience in training law enforcement officers, counselors, and social service providers in the dynamics of domestic violence. She has a bachelor's degree in psychology and a master's degree in rehabilitation counseling from the University of South Florida, serves on the Governor's Coordinating Council for Victim Rights and Services for the State of Florida, and is a member of the Crime Victim Rights Committee of the Florida Bar. She is also a formerly battered woman.

Prologue

It is much easier to tell a person what to do with his problem than to stand with him in his pain.

—*David Augusburger*

I come from what is popularly known as a "dysfunctional family." Although, growing up as a child, I didn't know what that was. I was a child of a celebrity. That is not all that glamorous, although many would not consider that to be a victimization. My father was a famous jazz musician who traveled with Duke Ellington, Woody Herman, Sinatra, Jr., and just about any of the pops and jazz greats. He was a famous kind of guy, having been noted as the World's Youngest Coronet Soloist. He started playing the horn at age 2½ and was on vaudeville professionally by age 5, supporting the family.

I didn't know how hard it was to be a child of a celebrity until I tried to figure out who I was aside from "Frankie Brown's daughter." I didn't have a first name, an identity, or self-esteem. I was known only for whom I belonged to, from whose loins my "untapped potential" came, and whose shadow I stood in. As I grew up and my "untapped potential" revealed itself more purely as "nontalent," the title of "castrated musician" or "impotent artist" became an unspoken assault. Nonetheless, I loved my daddy as any little girl does and saw much loneliness and pain in his eyes. I always wanted to comfort him. I always wanted to be there for him.

At age 6 I was sexually molested by a family member. I didn't tell anyone until I was a teenager. I decided that it wasn't abuse if everyone knew about it and did nothing. To my horror, my story of abuse became dinner table conversation for new friends and guests. The story was repeated often. It wasn't until I was almost 30 that I realized that I had been abused.

In 1981 I ended a seriously damaging marriage. I had fled into a relationship of convenience. However, the convenience became incarceration. A son of an alcoholic father and a mentally ill mother, my husband soon became an alcoholic and manic-depressive. He monitored the mileage in the car, what I wore to work, whom I talked to; he went through my purse and searched my panty drawer. Shopping, tennis, and friends were prohibited. After being placed on Lithium, he began drinking and soon was suicidal. On some days when I would return home he would be in a fetal position. I left with our 18-month-old daughter, and he was committed and administered shock treatments.

In May 1982, my boyfriend was killed in a DUI crash when the car hit a tree and flipped; he was thrown from the car and the car landed on top of him, crushing him to death.

While I was still trying to recover from his loss, in May 1983 (almost an exact year to the day) my father was murdered. He was stabbed to death outside his jazz club by a motorcycle gang man. His death was a violent, bloody mess. When I arrived the following day, I was taken to the murder scene in which I viewed his blood dramatically sprayed over cars, curbs, sidewalks, and buildings. That scene was a haunting heritage of pain for me for many years.

For 2 years I remained emotionally comatose. I would work for a few months and go to bed for a few months. Suicide seemed a likely option. I would go from being numb to being hysterical. Soon, severe neurological problems emerged and I was diagnosed with M.S. (multiple sclerosis). I would be only blocks from home and not know where I was. I had chronic vertigo and remained bedridden.

My family had fallen apart since my father's murder, and I no longer was in contact with three fourths of my family. The murder had taken more than my father. . .it had taken the rest of my family, my health, my sanity.

Two and a half years following the murder, I stumbled across a pilot program of a homicide survivors group. It was a 10-week focal psychotherapy pilot to see if homicide survivors would respond to this type of treatment. By the 6th week, my neurological symptoms were greatly improved. By the 7th week, I was back in church. And by the 10th week, I made a commitment to carry on so that others might know the healing that came through the group. I became president of the organization, worked for 2 years opening an office, writing, obtaining grants, promoting the program nationally, and speaking and teaching at conferences. I also traveled throughout the United States receiving specific training in victimology—child abuse, homicide, sexual abuse, domestic violence, and multiple personality disorders.

When I look in the faces of the wounded women, I remember a day not so long ago that it was me. Although I am not wound-free, I have gone from being a wounded victim to a wounded healer. I love this work with a passion and am amazed at the strength of the victims who take the risk and the courage to heal, and at the heart of a loving God, who paternally holds them close as they chance the first step in healing.

As arduous and laborious as my life has been, I wouldn't trade any of it. There is a richness of wisdom, compassion, and a new zeal for life that could not have been born without much of what I lost. What was lost was given back to me in the form of a heart for humanity, benevolence, and grace. Thank you Michael, Dad, Uncle Bob, and my abuser. . .not for what you did, or what happened to you, but for what God turned it into. May I forever be a vessel of healing for others. . .if not in this work, in my friendship to others, my desire to see healing, and my advocacy for victims of violence.

—Sandra L. Brown

Introduction

Since the late 1980s, the needs of victims of violence have gained increasing attention. Because of the dramatic increase of violence, all counselors must arm themselves with the necessary tools for counseling victims of violence.

We, as mental health professionals, are becoming increasingly aware of crime and its impact. National statistics from the U.S. Department of Justice (1988) show us that one out of four people has been a victim of some sort of crime. What does that mean to us as counselors? What kinds of crime? How many victims? For example:

- One out of four girls has been or will be sexually molested by the age of 18.
- One out of seven boys has been or will be sexually molested by the age of 18.
- There was one forcible rape every 6 minutes in 1988.
- Violence will occur at least once in two thirds of all marriages.
- A murder occurs every 25 minutes.
  (National Victim Center, 1990)

These statistics disclose only the surface. For instance, rape professionals indicate that only 1 in 10 rapes is reported, and if all rapes were reported, it would reveal an increase in rape that bypasses the nation's population growth ("The Hunt for Crime Starts," 1989).

Rape on campus has grown faster than other classifications of rape. Campuses are having to find new and creative ways of ensuring safety for women. Even as I write this, the tragedy of the Gainesville serial murders was just revealed 2 days ago at the University of Florida. This apparent Ted Bundy serial copycat murderer has promoted the nation's fear of further off-campus violence through his brutal mutilation of the victims' bodies. Bundy was infamous for the murder of campus sorority girls in Tallahassee, Florida.

Since 1933, the rape rate in the United States has increased by over 700%. Murder has increased 233% in the past 20 years (FBI, 1989). The mental health field must respond to this increase by educating its practitioners to serve the byproduct of crime—the victims. It has been suggested that "victims compose a presumably large yet underserved population" (Norris, Kaniasty, & Scheer, 1990).

The victims' rights movement grew consistently stronger throughout the 1970s and 1980s. The services and help to victims increased proportionately. But there still remain gaping areas where no services or too few services exist. It is hoped that this book will assist mental health professionals in reponding to these unmet victim needs.

The victim population must rely largely on the mental health community for recovery. In the past, in the absence of trained mental health professionals, victims sought solace from peers and other victims. Self-help support groups such as MADD (Mothers Against Drunk Driving) have been instrumental in assisting grieving victims. Yet in a recent study, "it has been suggested (Coates & Winston, 1983, pp. 169–194; Coates, Wortman, & Abbey, 1979, pp. 21–52) that naturally occurring social resources, typically useful for coping with stress, may be relatively ineffective in alleviating the distress accompanying victimization." Taken together, the presence of high distress and low informal support implies that many victims would benefit from professional psychological services (Norris, Kaniasty, & Scheer, 1990, pp. 538–547). Additionally the study by Norris et al. "suggests that about 1 in 8 victims of crime may be expected to seek professional mental health assistance within the first few months of the incident, an estimate that expands to 1 in 6 victims when the entire first postvictimization year is considered."

Various elements have assisted victims in working through their pain and trauma. Assistance has come through state and local victim advocacy programs, self-help groups, clergy, and the mental health field. Yet many who could help are untrained and unfamiliar with victim issues.

This book, *Counseling Victims of Violence*, is designed as a handbook and guide to victim issues in a wide range of different elements of violence. "Victimization counseling" remains a subspecialty field within counseling. Many counselors specialize in only one or two areas of victimology. Some focus on domestic violence and child violence (physical abuse), whereas others focus only on incest and rape (sexual abuse).

This is a resource for counselors, social workers, therapists, psychologists, psychiatrists, school guidance counselors, RNs and medical staff, victim advocates and legal personnel, clergy, religious counselors, lay/peer counselors, those engaged in support or 12-step programs, and any others who desire to work with the population of victims of violence. This book also will assist caregivers in understanding the needs of victims of violence.

The chapters provide background clinical information on trauma and its encodement, posttraumatic stress and grief, and specific types of victimization. Vignettes of victim cases provide clinical examples. A chapter on therapies for trauma victims lists various types including art therapy, journaling, wilderness retreats, and inner healing.

The book is divided into categories of victimizations that will allow counselors to go directly to the victimization they may need more information about. In the chapter on a particular victimization (chapters 4–10), counselors will find background information aboutthe trauma involved, what skills and issues need to be addressed during the crisis intervention phase and the short-term and long-term counseling stages, what the usual concerns of the victim are at each stage, secondary victimizations, and social services that may be needed to stabilize the victim throughout the three stages of the counseling process.

This will give the counselor enough information to ascertain if a victim will need to be referred out at any of the three stages of the counseling process or if the counselor has the skills to meet the need.

At the conclusion of most of the chapters is a bibliography of recommended reading as well as a list of national victim resources in a particular type of trauma, along with toll-free numbers.

Easy reference charts outline the basics of crisis intervention/short-term/long-term issues, secondary victimizations, and social services. These charts are designed as reminders-at-a-glance, summarizing the chapter contents.

Recovery is not limited to a predetermined posttraumatic stress inventory but is a lifelong process of surges and regressions and of struggles and victories. It is also the process of coming to terms with life's most complicated dichotomies.

Patricia Gerard coauthored chapter 6 in this book. She is not only a mental health worker or an agency director. She was first a victim and is now a survivor who rose above not only the mediocrity that victims often fall into, but above her pain and anger to make an impact in her field and in the lives of the walking wounded.

It is my hope both as a survivor and as a mental health and pastoral counselor that this book will be used as a stepping-stone for those of you who desire to work in the field of victimization. The wounded and the broken thank you. And Pat Gerard and I thank you.

1

A Victim's Story

It is disconcerting to many professionals working with victims of violence that the victim of a crime can fall through the cracks of our mental health system virtually anywhere in the nation. In this age of the mental health boom it is hard to imagine that victims can fall through the cracks so easily. Florida is considered to be on the forefront of victim services in the nation. Yet, daily, victims come to Bridgework who have or are falling through the cracks. These are the all-too-common victims of rape, incest, and other abuse. There are enough loopholes in existing victim services so that if the victim does not meet the exact criteria, services can be and are denied. The loopholes often result from either government restrictions or the services' own interagency laws that determine what types of victims they treat, how victims are selected, what types of victims they do not serve, and how services are offered.

Recently, one of my clients I will call Dede called me from the psychiatric ward of one of our hospitals, where she had been treated off and on for years. Yet this psychiatric ward was never able to detect that she had been and was being sexually abused by her stepfather. During my brief first visit with her, I cut away to the main issues and started asking her about the abuse. It started when she was 6 years old. It had even escalated to the point that the stepfather would drug her, rape her, and put her in a dark closet, telling her that is how she would have to live if she ever told about the abuse. By the time she was 11 she was pregnant with his child. She bore the child and it is now in state custody. The physical and sexual abuse continued for years. She told me that at age 11 she gave up and gave in. She never thought it would get better, she just resigned. After her pregnancy her mother divorced her stepfather, yet he continued to come to the house almost weekly to rape her. No one ever called the police.

Dede weighs 380 pounds. She said she got that way hoping he would leave her alone and stop abusing her sexually. Dede assumed that rape was related to her sexual appeal. No one ever told her that rape was not about sex. She has a progressive bone disease that has eaten away all the bones in her legs, which have been replaced with metal rods, and the disease is now progressing to her arms. She moved from her mother's neighborhood into her own apartment, where her stepfather continued to come almost weekly and rape her. Although the neighbors heard her cries for help, no one called the police for her. Psychologically she had been programmed into believing that she deserved this, that no one would help her or believe her if she asked for help. She had been programmed to believe this since she was 6 years old, so Dede never reached out and asked. She had also been repeatedly taught that disclosure would bring more of the same type of abuse . . . and worse. She feared further abuse and retribution if she disclosed the horrors of her life. Last year she lost his second child at 6 months into the pregnancy from a vicious beating. This year she terminated a pregnancy at the 2nd month, and she called yesterday to tell me her pregnancy test was positive again.

I moved Dede into one of our domestic violence shelters. She lasted one night. Her case was too intense. We moved her to an ACLF (adult congregate living facility) unit while she awaited the clearance to go into another domestic violence shelter. This shelter stated that she was "ineligible" because their program dealt only with victims who were abused by spouses or boyfriends, not family members. Dede was denied. She had been staying in the ACLF and needed to go back to her apartment to get more clothing. Because an ACLF is not set up like a domestic violence shelter and the personnel do not assist the victim as a shelter would, Dede had to do it by herself. She went back for a few minutes to get her clothing and he was there waiting for her. In fact, he had been waiting almost a week. He beat her violently and raped her. She went back to the ACLF and a week later needed to be in the area for a doctor's appointment. He saw her in the neighborhood, pulled her out of the car and beat her so severely she had to go to the emergency room. While she was in the emergency room he went back to her apartment and broke all the windows, resulting in Dede's having to pay a huge bill to her landlord.

Dede is only 20 years old. Dede slipped through the cracks in a number of ways. The mental health service personnel did not recognize nor were trained to detect the psychological indicators of incest. Dede has been receiving counseling from the mental health system for a few years now. Because the incest was not detected, Dede was subjected to years of repeated torture by the abuser, as well as to shock treatments and ineffective counseling. She fell through the cracks of our criminal justice system. No one ever advised Dede that she could place a restraining order on her stepfather when the police were called. No one ever told her that she had rights as a victim. No one ever told her she could prosecute. She fell through the cracks of our shelter protection program. She was not the "right kind" of victim. Her abuser didn't fit the profile. She fell through the cracks of our long-term hospitalization and suicide prevention programs. Her suicide attempts were continuous, yet practitioners treated her for the minimum 14 days and kept releasing her. Dede's arm looked like a road map from constant slashings. She had taken 400 pills at once and put a plastic garbage bag over her head. She fell through the cracks of her church when she told her pastor what happened, and was told that she only wanted attention and that is why she continued to focus on her problem and that all she needed to do was forgive. She fell through the cracks of eating disorders diagnosis. The doctors kept saying, "Dede, do you know you're overweight?"

She fell through the cracks of obstetrics when as an 11-year-old girl she got pregnant and continued to get pregnant and suffered other vaginal disorders and no one reported it. She fell through the cracks of humanity when her neighbors heard her cries and did nothing.

The tragedy of Dede's life is not only the brutal physical and sexual abuse she endured. It is also the lack of intervention by mental health workers, doctors, psychiatrists, mental hospitals, the police, clergy, and shelter protection programs. The tragedy bypasses that of a personal nature and becomes a professional tragedy for which each of us must bear responsibility. Dede is one of millions that continues to fall through cracks while her life continues to be one movies are made of.

I think that there are many Dedes out there who need your personal services. Unfortunately, those of us who work in victim services will always have job security. Crime rates are rising. Disclosure in rape and incest is becoming more common. There is a great harvest of victims awaiting someone to know they have been hurt, even when they are incapable of saying so. They need someone who will anticipate their needs, know what social services they will require, know how to explain to them what they will go through psychologically on their road to recovery, and then help them get there. They need someone to stand with them, to wait with them, to pray with them. We don't just need PhDs, EdDs, or MDs who can do this . . . we need mental health workers in every category on every educational level who are willing and able to bring rest to the violent world of victims.

Will a Dede come to your office, unable to tell you the hell she has endured? If she doesn't tell you, will you still know? Can you cut away to the issues, break the silence that she's praying you will do?

2

Psychodynamics of Trauma

Clinical evidence has suggested that criminal victimization of any sort can be a highly stressful event, causing the victim significant psychological distress (Atkeson, Calhoun, Resick, & Ellis, 1982; Burman et al., 1988; Cook, Smith, & Harrell, 1987; Frieze, Hymer, & Greenberg, 1987; Kahn, 1984; Kilpatrick, Veronen, & Best, 1985).

To assist victims of violence adequately, we as mental health professionals must have a working knowledge not only of trauma, but how we can assess the damage done by that trauma. In this chapter, we will look at how to assess the depth of trauma, how to understand how trauma is encoded in our brain, and why it is important to resurface that trauma so it can be reframed and stored in past memory.

THE ASSESSMENT

As with any counseling, the assessment will direct intervention and treatment. The Triads of Abuse is an assessment tool that is helpful in grasping the intensity of the abuse. In addition, other assessments are useful, such as assessments for background, history, and ego strength that measure and link trauma themes (McCann & Pearlman, 1990). For now, we will look at how the Triads of Abuse can focus the assessment.

The TRIADS was developed by Ann Burgess, University of Pennsylvania, School of Nursing (Burgess, Hartman, & Kelley, 1990). It was designed primarily for use in rape trauma/sexual abuse, but other professionals in victimization have found it can also be applied to various other areas of abuse, such as physical abuse (as seen in domestic violence, ethnic/hate/gay assaults, and child abuse) and ritualistic/cult torture.

"Using the acronym TRIADS, this assessment tool describes *T*ypes of abuse (physical, sexual, psychological), *R*ole relationships between victim and offender (intra vs. extrafamilial), *I*ntensity (number of acts and offenders), *A*ffective state (expressed vs. controlled demeanor), *D*uration (length of time), and *S*tyle of abuse (single, patterned, or ritualistic)."

    I. *T*ype of Abuse
        1. Physical abuse
        2. Sexual abuse
        3. Psychological abuse

   II. *R*ole Relationship of Victim to Offender
        1. Intrafamilial
        2. Extrafamilial
        3. Authority of abuse

  III. *I*ntensity of Abuse
        1. Number of acts
        2. Number of abuses

   IV. *A*ffective State
        1. Expressed style (anxious, angry, sad)
        2. Controlled style (blank, calm, denial)

    V. *D*uration
        1. Length of time

   VI. *S*tyle of Abuse
        1. Blitz style of abuse
        2. Repetitive/patterned abuse
        3. Ritualistic/ceremonial abuse

This assessment helps to understand the depths of trauma that was inflicted on the victim and will help guide treatment. It gives an indication of the length of treatment that may be necessary based on the depth of the abuse.

Under Roman numeral I on the outline previously given, the type of abuse or the combination of the abuse is significant in understanding the behavioral symptomatology or watching for the repetition of the abuse on self or others. Many types of abuse will be combined and some will overlap. Burgess et al. (1990, p. 8) indicated that "all types may be present, but the experience the child initially presents plus the symptoms indicate the dominant abusive experience. It is in the treatment process that shifts are noted in the dominance of one abuse pattern over another.''

Under Roman numeral II on the outline, the role relationship of victim to offender denotes whether the abuse is intrafamilial (within the family unit) or extrafamilial (outside the family unit). This role relationship sets a particular meaning of the abuse to the victim and affects trust, the attachment to the family, and attachment to others outside the family relationship. This role relationship holds personal meaning to children and can give them specific internal messages such as ''I must be to blame or dad wouldn't hurt me this way;'' ''I am wrong or bad because if I blame dad, I will have no one.''

Under Roman numeral III in the outline, the intensity of the abuse includes the age of the victim when the abuse began and ended, the number of times the child was abused, and the number of offenders involved in the abuse. A number of different abusers will have a more damaging effect on the child or the adult in terms of trust, safety, self-esteem, and personal constructs of self.

Under Roman numeral IV, the affective state describes the response of the victim to the abuse. There are two states: Expressed (hyperarousal, anxious, angry, sad) or Controlled (numb, blank, calm, denial). Burgess indicated that affective moods such as depression, hostility, anger, defiance, or rebelliousness may be associated with these states. There can be fearfulness, passivity, timidity, anxiousness, and an inability to protect and defend oneself. During hyperarousal, there could be the presence of stomachaches, startle reflex (jumping in response to loud noise or sudden touch), night terrors, avoiding places and people, crying, and enuresis. Also, there could be attempts at total avoidance by the use of drugs and alcohol, numbing (dissociation), acting out aggressively, sexualized behaviors, and a lack of empathy for others.

Under Roman numeral V, the duration of the abuse is measured in terms of length of time over which the abuse occurred, such as days, weeks, months, or years.

The last Roman numeral, VI, addresses the style of abuse. This denotes the offender's particular techniques. It is predicated that the abuse occurred spontaneously and without anticipation on the part of the victim, or that it had cues that alerted the victim to a series of anticipated acts. The style of abuse also refers to whether the activities to the child were ''blitz'' or spontaneous, repetitively patterned, or ritualistic or ceremonial.

Blitz/spontaneous style of abuse is where the act occurs simply as an expression or reaction to the moment. It seems to happen "out of the blue." In physical abuse, it is a random explosive rage that unleashes an assault. In sexual abuse, the adult exhibits a set of behaviors and spontaneously "sexualizes the child to a set pattern of repetitive sexual acts." In psychological abuse, the adult yells at the child, criticizes particular body parts of the child, and criticizes the child as a person. Often the adult will show some signs of remorse for assaulting the child verbally.

Repetitive/patterned abuse is when the abuse (either physical, sexual, or psychological) occurs as a pattern. The victim may not know specifically when the abuse will happen but once the abuse has begun, specific cues direct and control the victim to behave in certain ways. Burgess indicated, "In this style, the child is incorporated into the activities. For example, the child is forced to select the instrument of physical abuse and go to a specific location for the punishment" (Burgess et al., 1990, p. 11).

Ritualistic or ceremonial abuse is both patterned and also carefully integrated and linked with a symbol of overriding power, authority, and purpose, most commonly a religious or pseudoreligious notion. It is idiosyncratic and assumes characteristics of a ceremony. There may be a spiritual component that directs the nature of the physical abuse, for example, "Your behavior is evil; you should not sin against your father. It is God's will that you be punished in this way" (Burgess et al., 1990, p. 11). Burgess further indicated that in sexual abuse there is a predetermined intent by the offender to convert the victim to a victimizer's role.

Yet, treating the victim through counseling is only the first step we, as counselors, must take. For some victims, retrieving the trauma becomes a focal point of treatment. Many emerge into counseling with an etiology of symptomatology but with no memory to accompany it. Some victims feel it necessary to retrieve some portion of memory to focus on during treatment and also as a means to validate their suspicions of abuse.

INFORMATION PROCESSING OF TRAUMA

Burgess et al. (1990) indicated that once the assessment on the type, role relationship, intensity, affective state, duration, and style of abuse has been completed, an understanding of how the information of the trauma was processed into the memory of the victim is crucial. This processing and memory storage of trauma is referred to as encodement.

Something changes in our brains because of trauma and affects the way we are able to process information. It affects our acute and over-time phase and the coding, storing, and sequencing of events, and it overrides our alarm system. Trauma disrupts the processing of infor-mation and incoming sensory stimuli in the limbic system of our brain. When the brain's limbic system is overriden because of high amounts of stress/trauma, we are unable to handle the stressors and we switch to survival techniques, which is psychological numbing. (For more information on this see Psychobiology of Posttraumatic Stress later in this chapter).

Understanding how information is processed in the victim's mind helps to retrieve stored memories that are not easily accessible. In the beginning stages of our center's work, I noticed that "talk therapy" (cognitive therapy) worked for some sexually abused women but didn't work at all for others. I struggled to understand why resurfacing of memories/trauma in a cognitive approach didn't work for all survivors. When I heard Ann Burgess teach how trauma is stored and encoded in different ways and what counselors can do to resurface it, I began to understand why some of our efforts had been unsuccessful.

Although Burgess was talking about child sexual abuse, her state-ment still enables us to understand how trauma in general is encoded for a victim. Burgess stated:

A trauma learning model describes how child victims think and process in-formation about sexual abuse. Critical to the trauma experience is the encap-sulation process in which a defensive silence insulates the ongoing abuse, holds the event in present (rather than past) memory, depletes the child's psychic energy and interrupts academic, social and self-development of the child. Symptoms and behaviors imply the memory traces and cures from the fear imprinting trauma. The TRIADS survey identifies memory linkages of symptoms at a sensory, perceptual, cognitive and interpersonal level" (Bur-gess et al., 1990, p. 1).

* * *

Bridgework found this to be true with adult survivors of sexual abuse, in cases of child physical abuse, extreme cases of adult domestic violence, and, of course, ritualistic torture. Adult survivors show the same patterns of trauma encodement, they hold events in the present memory and not the past (unresolved material is not settled), and their self-development as adults also is interrupted. Much of the victims' social and emotional self-development stops during the process of abuse.

Burgess equated our processing of trauma to the format a computer uses to store information. The trauma must be resurfaced the same way it was stored in the memory. Therefore, we have to have the correct "password" to retrieve the information to the surface/screen. The password is how the trauma was encoded. Encoding is the transformation of messages into signals (Chaplin, 1972). In the case of abuse, it would be how the abuse was stored in the memory and how that message is translated into memory signals. The information/trauma can be stored:

- Cognitively (and surface verbally)
- Sensorially (stored in taste, smell, touch)
- Visually
- Auditorially
- Interpersonally

This explains why many survivors will resurface memories as a result of being touched in a certain way, smelling a particular cologne, or tasting something that reminds them of the abuse. Likewise, certain phrases or sights may retrieve memory for them.

Burgess, Hartman, and Kelley (1990) further indicated that intervention is directed by the TRIADS assessment and gives insight in dealing with disruption in the cognitive, sensory, visual, auditory, and interpersonal domains. Understanding the abuse, symptoms, and behavior allows for desensitizing the victim to the sensory and perceptual cognitive cues of the abuse, permitting broader areas of disruption to be addressed. These authors indicated that intervention can then focus on these areas of disruption. Disruptions other than those Burgess discussed will now be addressed.

Sensory Disruption

Symptoms of sensory disruption include hyperactivity, nightmares, enuresis, and startle responses. These responses may be amenable to different relaxation techniques as well as psychopharmacology.

Perceptual/Cognitive Disruption

Perceptual disturbances and intrusive mental activity are not uncommon among trauma survivors (McCann & Pearlman, 1990). Symptoms of perceptual/cognitive disruption include both internal and external cues that produce intrusion of images and auditory and kinesthetic information associated with the trauma. These are self-generated attributions related to cause, responsibility, predictability, or future concerns about danger (Burgess et al., 1990). Cognitive disturbances could be flashbacks, nightmares about the event, or dissociation. Putnam (1985) described dissociation as an alteration of consciousness in which experiences and affects are not integrated into memory and awareness. Perceptual/cognitive symptoms may be amenable to strategies such as thought stopping, clarification, reframing beliefs, and linking distress directly to the trauma experience.

Interpersonal Disruption

Symptoms of interpersonal disruption include excessive fear of others, inability to assert and protect oneself, or repetition of aggressive sexualized behavior toward others. Sexual problems have been noted in rape victims, adult survivors of childhood sexual abuse, domestic violence victims, and Vietnam veterans.

The inability to develop intimate emotional relationships with men is common among female rape victims. This inability may also be manifested in increased marital and family problems among those who were sexually abused as children, women who were battered, and Vietnam veterans. Intervention strategies aimed at desensitizing victims to fearful involvement with others, focused role playing to discriminate threatening exploitative behavior in others from safe behavior, and empathy training are all relevant to disruptions in this area (Burgess et al., 1990).

Biological Disruption

McCann and Pearlman (1990) discussed biological disruptions. Physiological hyperarousal is shown by an increase in autonomic nervous system arousal (Blanchard, Kolb, Pallmeyer, & Gerardi, 1982; Giller, 1990; Kolb, 1984). In children and adults who have been physically abused, somatic disturbances can be seen as injuries to the central nervous system and can be associated with a variety of neurobehavorial problems (e.g., Monane, Leichter, & Lewis, 1984). Likewise, increased general somatic disorders have been seen in adult survivors of child abuse, female survivors of domestic violence, children from homes of domestic violence, and those who have developed multiple personality disorders.

Behavioral Response Disruption

McCann and Pearlman (1990) indicated that some victims go on to develop aggressive or antisocial behavior patterns, engage in substance abuse, or display suicidal behavior. These victims can include children of sexual or physical abuse, children living in violent homes, male adults who were abused as children, and some Vietnam veterans.

Impaired social functioning can be seen through social withdrawal and isolation in victims of rape, domestic violence, and other crimes. It is seen in decreased school performance and a lack of peer inter-relating in children who have been physically abused and also those who live in violent homes. It is seen in reduced social adjustment among women who attend college who were also sexually abused. And lastly, it is seen in a reduced ability to attain occupational achievement among Vietnam veterans.

As previously repressed episodes of past trauma surface, they are processed through defense/coping mechanisms. These include:

- Denial
- Dissociation
- Self-fragmentation
- Arousal
- Repression
- Splitting

Denial

Denial can be a powerful defense and coping mechanism. Established early on in the trauma event, denial helps to insulate the victim from the reality of a traumatic event.

Dissociation

Dissociation is an inventive way victims distance themselves from an abusive event. During the abuse itself, victims emotionally remove themselves from the event usually by visualizing themselves as being somewhere safe in order to protect their emotional core. Putnam's (1985) definition of dissociation as an altered state of consciousness including symptoms of depersonalization and derealization well describes the protective function of dissociation.

Self-Fragmentation

In self-fragmentation, victims internalize separate concepts about self and self-construct. They internalize the breaking apart of self through a disharmonious view of themselves.

Arousal

The hyperarousal of victims can be seen in the ways in which they become acutely aware of others, their environment, and their own personal safety schemas.

Repression

Through repression, the victim works subconsciously at keeping the memories from coming to the surface/conscious level. In this way, denial can stay intact and the memories can be held at bay.

Splitting

Splitting allows the victims to divide the abuse into two concepts. For instance, if the perpetrator is the father, the concept of the primary caregiver abusing them is overwhelming to them. Aside from suffering the violation of their physical body, it is psychologically traumatic for children to struggle with the concept of someone they love hurting them in this manner. Therefore, a child will split the abuse into two concepts: my father and the abuser. Often the child will conceptualize: "This is not my father who is doing this to me. This is someone else who looks like my father."

These defense/coping mechanisms alter victims' perception and storage of trauma. While working with victims of traumatic violence who may or may not have readily available memory, it is necessary to resurface the trauma the way in which it was encoded in the memory.

The body retains the trauma that the mind chooses to forget or repress. Most trauma can be resurfaced through understanding how it was encoded and working through the means that will best allow the survivor to experience the trauma in the way it was encoded. This can be attempted through regressions and retrieval that focus on specific ways that memory and parts of a memory were encoded. For instance, some memory may be retrieved by using sensory stimulation (smell, touch, taste, hearing, sight). A particular incident of abuse could be lodged in the memory in a number of different ways. One incident of abuse could be split in the memory between different senses. The victim could retrieve part of the memory through seeing something that triggers part of the memory of the abuse, retrieve another part of the same abuse through a smell trigger, and still another part through a taste trigger. Any image, affect, or verbal fragment related to the traumatic memory may elicit other fragments (McCann & Pearlman, 1990). These authors indicated that "Working through a traumatic memory requires exploring the verbal memory traces as well as the corresponding imagery (visual) and affect" (p. 29).

Survivors often ask why they can't be touched in a certain way, even though they do not have conscious memory. For instance, people who were forced to perform oral sex may not tolerate being touched behind the neck because this is the position in which they were held while the abuse occurred.

In some people, being touched in a certain way may evoke great physical rage, even though they don't know why. Helping survivors understand that the body remembers what the mind chooses to forget/ repress, and that this rage is a testimony to the fact that the trauma still lives in the body, assists them in understanding this phenomenon. Furthermore, explaining that they received trauma not just through the act itself, but through visual and auditory perceptions and verbal and interpersonal messages, allows survivors to see the wide range of possibilities in trauma encodement. Survivors readily accept this explanation of encodement and trauma. It merely puts words and an explanation to what they have already lived through and learned about themselves.

Burgess et al. (1990) further indicated that part of survivors' recovery work is focused on resurfacing events caught in short-term memory that influence their daily living and cause symptomatic responses, and moving the events, after they have been resurfaced, experienced, and defused, to long-term memory. This is a primary reason for doing regression therapy. Regression therapy is a technique for regressing a person back psychologically to the age when trauma occurred. While at this age during the regression, a survivor can experience trapped or regressed affect, retrieve memory, or work on inner child issues. Survivors are often unaware that trapped subconscious memory is affecting daily living and adding to and supporting existing symptomatology. McCann and Pearlman (1990, p. 29) indicated that "Fragments of a traumatic memory may become intrusive or disruptive to the individual's psychological or interpersonal functioning."

To return to the concept we discussed before—how our brains are similar to how a computer operates and how our memory works—we bring the memory/trauma from the floppy disk (short-term memory) to the screen, experience it, work through it and defuse it, and then store it on the hard disk (long-term memory). The memory will always be there, but it will not have the reactionary strength in our subconscious that affects daily living. We will have access to the memory but it will be well integrated into our healing experience. Burgess et al. (1990, p. 8) indicated, "The task of treatment is to identify, neutralize, and unlink traumatic memory and cue traces, and to correct cognitive distortions and meanings set during the abusive experience." Burgess et al. (1990) indicated that the information processing occurs in phases and consists of Pre-Abuse Factors, Traumatic Event Phase, Disclosure Phase, and Post-Trauma Outcomes.

The following outline is Burgess's outline. I have added my own explanations of how this has reinforced the work at Bridgework and how this model works with our clients.

INFORMATION PROCESSING OF TRAUMA: A CONCEPTUAL MODEL*

Phase I: Pre-Abuse Factors
     1. Age, gender
     2. Personality development
     3. Family structure
     4. Prior trauma

Phase II: Traumatic Event Phase

     1. TRIADS and offender behavior
       ● access

---

*From A. W. Burgess, C. R. Hartman, and S. J. Kelley (1990). *Assessing Child Abuse: The TRIADS Checklist.* An instructional handout sheet from a Conference by Forensics Mental Health. Tampa, FL.

- secrecy
- control

2. Victim defenses/coping (through-put)
- denial
- dissociation
- self-fragmentation
- arousal disharmony
- repression
- splitting

3. Trauma learning (output)
- stored information: cognitive, sensory, visual, auditory, interpersonal

4. Trauma replay
- reenactment
- repetition
- displacement

Phase III: Disclosure Phase
1. Non-disclosure
- encapsulation of the trauma learning
2. Disclosure
- social responses: family, peers, school, work, hospital staff, treatment team, legal
- trauma learning
- reformulation of trauma learning

Phase IV: Post-Trauma Outcomes
1. Symptom response
2. Behavioral pattern

Phase I and the pre-abuse factors, also often referred to as person variables, are recognized because of their influence on the victims' reaction to trauma. These pre-abuse factors were listed as: age and gender, personality development, family structure, and prior trauma. These factors look at the age and gender of the victims to gauge their propensity for being abused and probable reactions to abuse based on age and gender; the age of onset of abuse; male versus female identity (ego integrity); personality development of victim including strengths, weaknesses, and any preexisting personality disorders and how these would be affected or enhanced by the abuse; family structure, including open and closed communication, alcohol and drug addictions, dysfunctional family issues, and any prior traumas for the victim; and whether the resolution of those issues has occurred, or whether this trauma will exacerbate the situation because of the lack of resolution of prior trauma. Courtois (1990) also added that these person variables consider traits, beliefs, values, abilities, cognitive structure, mood, coping style, defensive style, and genetic propensities of the victim, which are all personal and differ from victim to victim.

Trauma affects personality and changes how the victim reacts to trauma. This can be seen in distortions in thinking (Spitzer, 1990) and even possible chemicals that are released through posttraumatic stress disorder (PTSD) experiences. This chemical reaction can be a setup for future victimizations (van der Kolk, 1990). (See the Psychobiology of Posttraumatic Stress later on in this chapter.)

Phase II: Traumatic Event Phase (In-Put of Event: Alarm Response)
      1. TRIADS and offender behavior
- access
- secrecy
- control

This segment focuses on offender behavior and how it affects the victim. What type of access did the offender have to the victim (familial vs. nonfamilial), and how did the offender maintain secrecy (threats, coercion, deception, corruption, positive attention)? How did the offender maintain control of the victim; what kind of control did the abuser have over the victim's family? Was he a domineering head-of-household? Was he the family patriarch? Was he an unknown to the family?

      2. Victim defenses/coping (through-put)
- denial
- dissociation
- self-fragmentation
- arousal disharmony
- repression
- splitting

This segment defines victims' coping mechanisms during and following the abuse: denying that it happened, dissociating from their body during the abuse to protect the inner core of their psychological self, or fragmenting parts of themselves to handle different aspects of the abuse. Arousal disharmony is seen in the flight/fight syndrome, repression of thoughts, feelings, and memories when they try to come to the surface for resolution, and splitting the abuser into two persons, the one they love and the one who abuses. To the victims, offenders can't be the same person if they love them and need them, yet they hurt the victim. (This is applicable to trauma that occurs from a loved one, i.e., family violence such as child, spouse, and elder abuse, and sexual abuse).

  3. Trauma learning (output: encoding)
     ● stored information: cognitive, sensory, visual, auditory, interpersonal

Trauma learning is a definition of what occurs to the victim during the abuse. The victim learns about trauma firsthand through various avenues. Memories are stored in victims' minds cognitively (how they perceived the abuse), sensorily (taste, touch, i.e., the taste of semen, the way a penis felt, how blood tasted in the domestic violence victim's mouth after a beating), visually, (what they saw, i.e., the way the abuser was dressed, any equipment used during the abuse, the way the room looked when the abuse happened), auditorially (what they heard, i.e., what the abuser said, music playing in the background, or other background noises), and interpersonally (what they experienced in the context of the relationship with the abuser, i.e., did they identify themselves as victims or did they identify with the abuser, how did their relationship change with the abuser, was he always trying to get close emotionally and physically afterwards). This includes ways in which the victim was told either verbally or nonverbally to "keep the secret" of the abuse. These messages given to the victim could have been verbal, sensory, visual, auditory, or interpersonal.

This trauma learning was encoded in the limbic region of the brain. However, trauma disrupts the way in which information is stored in the brain. When this trauma and its symptoms were being encoded in the limbic system of the brain, it was being stored in disconnected ways. This faulty storage of information will dramatically affect how the victim can and will process the trauma information.

  4. Trauma replay
     ● reenactment
     ● repetition
     ● displacement

Trauma replay is the way the victim attempts to deal with the trauma subconsciously. When unresolved trauma is occurring on a subconscious level, the result is an attempt at resolution by playing the trauma over and over again in a physical manner. Freud believed that some clients had a tendency to repeat or reexperience the trauma in an attempt to master it. Trauma replay occurs with victims on both a conscious and subconscious level. We expect to see it in children who were abused as they play out their themes in their actual play or drawings (Burgess et al., 1990), yet I see the same types of replay in adult survivors.

Reenactment: Victims will often reenact aspects of their own abuse on themselves, others, or objects. This can be seen in a personal area in masturbation problems if part of the abuse involved sexual digital stimulation. Others who were penetrated by instrumentation may go on to abuse animals, self, or others by the same means. Reenacting the abuse is a subconscious way of trying to work out the psychological pain of the abuse. Reenactment can result in physical abuse as well.

Repetition: Victims will often continue to repeat the reenactments or will displace their abuse on others. Repeating the same types of abuse, either on self or others, is a similar dynamic seen in victims who continue to pick abusive partners. By repeating the incident of abuse (or a similar abusive event/relationship), victims conceive that they may gain the opportunity to change the traumatic outcome. This is often the cause of multigenerational cycles of abuse.

Displacement: Displacement is seen in long-term effects that turn victims into sexual offenders. Displacement is the placing of personal aggressive feelings regarding the abuse outward onto others and is a similar dynamic to the displacement of anger. The true and intense side effects of childhood trauma are seen in trauma replay. The victim recreates the original trauma and acts out the increasing levels of violence through murders, serial rapes, and other maladaptive ways.

Phase III: Disclosure Phase
  1. Non-disclosure
       • encapsulation of the trauma learning

The victim is trapped in the encoding of the trauma. When disclosure does not occur, the victim is left with the constant replaying of the trauma in the mind, trying to find resolution to this violence. This silence holds the entire trauma in a type of encapsulated, internalized cage. The victim does not move forward in resolution but rather is trapped by the undisclosed memory of the abuse.

  2. Disclosure
       • social responses: family, peers, school, work, hospital
         staff, treatment team, legal
       • trauma learning
       • reformulation of trauma learning

When disclosure does occur, however, the victim's disclosure and future disclosure of other victimizations or new memories of the same victimization will be determined greatly by the social responses of those who will come in contact with the victim. When disclosure is a positive experience, the trauma learning can be reformulated to surface and be expressed through cognitive reframing. Cognitive reframing is an exercise that allows the victim to look at a negative aspect of the abuse and "reframe" the experience to see it in a different, less threatening manner. This establishes a new, less disturbing meaning to cues that trigger emotional reactions. I have utilized reframing with cult survivors to change the emotional meaning attached to the image of blood. For them, the image is of violence, death, and pain. Yet, blood can be life-giving when utilized in blood transfusions to save people's lives. Altars and candles can be used for Satan, but they can also be a beautiful addition in weddings, baptisms, or other pleasant events.

Phase IV: Post-Trauma Outcomes
　　　　　1. Symptom response
　　　　　2. Behavioral pattern

Following the abuse and the victim's decision to disclose or not to disclose, symptomatic responses begin. These are followed by a behavioral pattern and issues of violence. If not corrected and worked through, a life-long problem of behavioral disorders may ensure. Nicholas Groth (1990) stated in a conference on sexual abuse that his clinical research has supported the association between sexually abused children and their abusive juvenile offender patterns. Additionally, in male adult survivors of childhood abuse who are now psychiatric patients, certain patterns link their aggressive or antisocial behaviors with their previous victimization (Carmen, Rieker, & Mills, 1984).

POSTTRAUMATIC STRESS DISORDER

Posttraumatic stress disorder (PTSD) is at the very heart of understanding and providing care for victims. Its symptoms are seen frequently in victims of violence because PTSD is a normal reaction to exposure to traumatic and abnormal life events (Niles, 1990). Of course the degree and level of PTSD will depend on the level of trauma the victim has experienced and the victim's own coping style. However, PTSD symptoms are common among almost all victims of violence. Therefore, when reading and working from the chapters on specialized victimizations, please refer back to this chapter for the *symptomatology*. McCann and Pearlman (1990) suggested that mental health professionals' approach to working with victims must not be based on the commonalities of PTSD or other clinical responses, but rather that clinical approaches must incorporate victims' experience as survivors and the uniqueness of their trauma experience.

The *Diagnostic and Statistical Manual of Mental Disorders* (DSM-III-R) (American Psychiatric Association, 1987) states:*

A. The person has experienced an event that is outside the range of usual human experience and that would be markedly distressing to almost anyone, e.g., serious threats of harm to one's children, spouse, or other close relatives and friends; sudden destruction of one's home or community; or seeing another person who has recently been or is being, seriously injured or killed as the result of an accident or physical violence.

Although this DSM-III-R classification seems to apply outwardly to those experiencing the event as a covictim, a relative of the victim, or a bystander witnessing the crime, it is also applicable to the actual victim. This classification of a disorder is readily seen in those who personally have suffered domestic violence or assault, child abuse, sexual abuse, robbery, and ritualistic torture or torture used in occult practices, as well as in those we would recognize as covictims, such as surviving family members of homicide and suicide.

B. The traumatic event/crime often reoccurs psychologically and emotionally for the victim in a number of ways. Again, according to the DSM-III-R, it is stated that it can cause the victim to relive the event through means such as:

1. Recurrent and intrusive distressing recollections of the event (in young children, repetitive play in which themes or aspects of the trauma are expressed).
2. Recurrent distressing dreams of the event.
3. Sudden acting or feeling as if the traumatic event were recurring (includes a sense of reliving the experience, illusions, hallucinations, and dissociative (flashbacks) episodes, even those that occur upon awakening or when intoxicated).
4. Intense psychological distress at exposure to events that symbolize or resemble an aspect of the traumatic event, including anniversaries of the trauma.

---

*Reprinted with permission from the *Diagnostic and Statistical Manual of Mental Disorders, Third Edition, Revised*. Copyright 1987 American Psychiatric Association.

C. The continuation of avoiding people, places, and things that remind the victim of the trauma or numbing of their general responses and affect (not present before the trauma) is indicated by at least three of the following:

1. Efforts to avoid thoughts or feelings of the trauma.
2. Efforts to avoid activities or situations that arouse recollection of the trauma.
3. Inability to recall an important aspect of the trauma (psychogenic amnesia).
4. Markedly diminished interest in significant activities (in young children, loss of recently acquired developmental skills such as toilet training or language skills).
5. Feelings of detachment or estrangement from others.
6. Restricted range of affect, e.g., unable to have loving feelings.
7. Sense of foreshortened future, e.g., doesn't expect to have a career, marriage, children, or a long life.

D. A persistent sense of arousal, not present before the trauma, can be seen by at least two of the following symptoms:

1. Difficulty falling or staying asleep.
2. Outbursts of anger or general irritability.
3. Difficulty concentrating.
4. Hypervigilance.
5. Exaggerated startle response.
6. Physiologic reactivity upon exposure to events that symbolize or resemble an aspect of the traumatic event (e.g., a woman who was raped in an elevator breaks out in sweats when entering any elevator).

E. Duration of the disturbance (symptoms in B, C, and D) of at least one month. Specify delayed onset if the onset of symptoms was at least six months after the trauma.

Other events in the life of the victim will engage the victim's reaction to the crime. This reaction will manifest itself by revealing a psychological response to an event that resembles part of the traumatic event for the victim and evokes the reaction that was prevalent or should have been prevalent at the time of the trauma. It seems that a never-ending cycle of reminders and events whirls a victim/survivor back into the midst of the trauma. Often these events or reminders are referred to as "trigger" events. These can be, but are not limited to, the following:

1. *Anniversary of the crime, abuse, or death.* As the anniversary draws near, the reaction may increase, even taking on the intensity of the reaction to the actual trauma. Victims have indicated that this seems

to be their "automatic internal time clock." Often they will begin responding to this internal time clock long before they associate their anxiety, tension, and fear to the anniversary date itself.

2. *Holidays and family events.* The holidays and other family event times such as births, deaths, weddings, and other family events elicit strong recurring emotional responses. Holidays in particular will often draw survivors closer to feelings of suicide than any other times of the year. This often is seen even when the survivor has been doing well for many months at a time. Seasons of "good will and peace on earth" remind victims of what they have endured and the violation of their safety and perception of a humane and kind world.

At Bridgework, even the survivors of sexual abuse struggle severely during the holidays because they are often reexposed to the abuser during family gatherings. The case is the same for adult, child, and elderly victims of domestic violence or ethnic/hate/gay violence. Most of our clients request that our groups continue through the holidays so they may have support and a focal point for their distress.

3. *Auditory and visual reminders.* Often victims will see or hear something that will remind them of their trauma. It is not unusual for this to expand to taste, touch, and smell as well, especially for victims of sexual abuse, some family violence, and ritualistic torture. (For more information on this see this chapter section on encoding of trauma.) When working with women, be cognizant of those who are trying to retrieve a memory. This is known as abreaction. Abreaction is the retrieval of memories or flooding of many memories and the reliving of the intense emotion attached to the traumatic event. Notice if they become very aware of certain smells or sounds. If they have been sexually abused, often their strong gagging reflex will be stimulated and will be a clue that they may be ready to abreact.

4. *Confrontations with the abuser.* Often the abuser or criminal is not incarcerated. Often the abuser comes and goes within the victim's life, especially if the victim has not disclosed, as in some forms of familial robbery, rape, incest, or physical abuse. Sometimes the abuser is on the run and has not been caught. The sheer agony of seeing or fearing seeing the abuser will often trigger traumatic emotions associated with the abuse. Physical reactions are not abnormal.

5. *The "system."* Whether it be the courts, police, the appellate system, mental health system, or another type of system, it continues to compel the victim to relive the events. Insensitive treatment and unfair laws or guidelines in bond reduction, parole, or sentencing all play a factor in a victim's ability to work through the grief process.

The victim may have to be a part of the system, unwillingly, for a number of years, especially if the abuser is trying to get free and the victim is striving to block the abuser's release. It may be necessary to speak at parole and other hearings to keep the abuser incarcerated. Although the victim would rather forget and get on with life, the victim may recognize the need to remain an active part of the victim advocacy system, even at the risk of retarding the healing process.

6. *Media.* All types of media events such as newspaper articles about their case or similar cases, news broadcasts, sensationalized talk shows, movies of the week, and those ghastly "Freddy-type" butcher movies play havoc with a recovering survivor. Victims are drawn to cases similar to their own. They are forever trying to process the reality of their loss and attach an appropriate reason for its occurrence.

After a recent airing of a show about a woman with a multiple personality disorder, Bridgework spent about a week of patching back together our sexually abused women clients who were drawn to the show. All felt they were MPD victims, or if they did not think they were, they were still severely traumatized by witnessing the TV portrayal of the woman's abuse. This is an example of a trigger reaction that sets off or brings to the surface consciousness the memory of victims' own abuse. These triggers can be events similar to their own, sights, sounds, or relationships that reconnect them in some way to their own victimization and cause abreactions to occur.

SECONDARY VICTIMIZATIONS

Victims soon recognize that the initial victimization is not where it all ends. The many "injustices" that occur to victims after the crime are often referred to as "secondary victimizations." Do not let the name and ranking of "second" fool you to think that these types of pain are not traumatic and do not evoke from the survivor similar PTSD reactions as did the original victimization.

Many victims/survivors have indicated that these secondary victimizations, were, in fact, more painful in many ways than the actual abuse because they were inflicted by others who were in caregiving roles, at a time in which others recognized the victims' vulnerability and abused them anyway, and by systems they thought were put in place to relieve pain, not enhance it.

The victims' pain must be raked up each time they have to go to court, and for some this goes on for a lifetime. A friend and fellow survivor, Susan, has been to our state capital area 14 times, at her own expense, to prevent the release of the two men who murdered her deaf-mute father.

Although her father has been dead 14 years now, she experiences the same PTSD reactions each time she must go before the Parole Board to plead for them not to release these murderers. Likewise, another friend and survivor, Wendy, had thought for the past 9 years that the fate of the man who murdered her 9-year-old daughter was sealed: death. However, to her shock, 9 years after the sentencing, his sentence was overturned and a new trial was ordered. Wendy must not only relive the murder, the facts, and the trial, but also face the possibility that this man may be released.

The notification process and how ineffectively it serves the victim is also a secondary victimization. In the past, many victims were never notified about parole hearings and their entitlement to speak against the release of their abusers. Many victims have also not been notified when parole was granted and their abusers were set free to stalk them should the abusers have decided to do so. The notification process has been a thorn in the flesh of many victims. Many state legislation efforts have been centered around a system that will notify victims of hearings or new court dates and appeals, where appropriate. Florida began a new service within the office of our governor to notify victims on the status of their cases and to inform them of hearings and other legal procedures which would be of interest to them or where they could participate in the legal process through attendance or by giving a written account of their opinions concerning their case.

Secondary victimizations are very painful for victims because these injuries are often inflicted by people they have decided to trust and with whom they may have developed a therapeutic or even an emotionally dependent relationship. The pain is often inflicted by others when they assume the victim "is over" the abuse, "should move on" with life, or has "overreacted " to the trauma. Pain is inflicted when careless statements are made or inferred, or when the victim's pain is overlooked, minimized, or even ignored. In fairness to those who inflict this pain, they are usually unaware of what it does to the victim. Symonds (1980) also wrote about the second injury, indicating that it results from unsupportive or blaming reactions from others. This has grown to be known as "victim blaming." These types of responses will also shape the victim's memory of the traumatic event. These responses actually become part of the memory associated with the trauma. A supportive or nonsupportive recovery environment has direct consequences on the impact of the trauma on the victim.

Secondary victimizations can be inflicted by:

- Family members, relatives and close friends;
- Teachers, school counselors, and school administrators;
- Employers and coworkers;
- Acquaintances and neighbors;
- Pastors, clergy, and other friends in their faith;
- Therapists, social workers, and counselors;
- Hospitals, doctors, and their personnel;
- The criminal justice system, police, and attorneys;
- The media: newspaper reporters, camera crews, and investigators;
- Impersonal sources such as "the newspaper at large"; and
- Even victim advocates, victim counselors, and those employed in victim systems, programs, and compensation.

The PTSD may be seen in victims for varying lengths of time. The length of time it may take one victim to process and work through grief may differ from that of another victim who has suffered the same type of victimization. Many different variables determine response to trauma. With these widely differing variables, it is impossible to assess accurately a victim's response to trauma. There can be, however, reasonable assumptions of time. Obviously the time it would take a robbery victim and the time it would take a homicide survivor to process and reorganize would differ greatly. Some victims require a 6-month's processing time, whereas homicide victims may need a 5-year time span to do their grief work.

Niles (1990, p. 10) remarked about PTSD:

Emerging PTSD research evidence reveals (1) higher levels of exposure to violence (combat/physical and abusive/psychological) are associated with higher levels of psychosocial problems; (2) higher levels of PTSD are associated with higher levels of substance abuse; (3) left untreated, PTSD becomes more severe with age; (4) age, race and gender factors influence severity of PTSD; and (5) PTSD or posttrauma stress reactions are a universal biopyschosocial process with unique individual reactive characteristics.

The major factors influencing the victim's posttrauma stress response and emerging research evidence require that mental health counselors are carefully trained in accurate diagnosis of PTSD and intervention strategies. Specifically,

PTSD can be missed in the diagnosis by the therapist if there are substance abuse and personality disorder factors masking the underlying problem.

THE PSYCHOBIOLOGY OF POSTTRAUMATIC STRESS

I do not pretend to be a doctor or chemist as I explain the psychobiology of PTSD. Yet, understanding this element has had an enormous impact for me and our work. Have you ever wondered why an adult survivor of incest or severe physical abuse is later jumped and assaulted, and then goes on to be the victim of two date rapes? Why is it that once you've been victimized that your chances of being a victim again are 10 times greater? Those victims who do not integrate their victimization experiences, as we have seen in trauma encodement, by moving the victimization experience to past memory, will manage to keep the trauma recurring. They display a compulsion to repeat the trauma. Not only are they unable to integrate their memories, but they have lost the ability to assimilate experiences. Their personality development stops and does not enlarge to add new elements and abilities of coping. They become attached to an unsurmountable obstacle.

They repeat the trauma behaviorally, emotionally, physiologically, and neuroendocronically (van der Kolk, 1990). We saw the behavioral dynamic previously with Burgess's explanation of repetition, reenactment, and displacement of the abusive experience. Victims repeat the trauma emotionally by aligning themselves with people who will continue to abuse them in some form—emotionally, physically, sexually, psychologically, and even spiritually. Victims continue the trauma physiologically by reexperiencing body memory of abuse that has been unresolved. Body memory may be the experiencing of the actual pain associated with prior abuse. Some women have vaginal pain as they experience a sexual abuse memory, or a specific area of the body may hurt when they remember being beaten. These unresolved abuses and memories come up again and again, causing actual physical pain or stress-related illnesses.

Victims recreate the trauma neuroendocronically in their systems when they constantly replay the traumatic event. This traumatic event can release chemicals in the brain that override the fight/flight system and alarm system, thus keeping victims vulnerable to further dangerous situations (van der Kolk, Greenberg, Boyd, & Krystal, 1985).

Victims live in a state of dependent learning. Because of the delay in their personality development, they do not learn ways of keeping themselves safe or dealing with stress. They reactivate past learning when they are stressed and revert back to their old ways of behaving and reacting even if those ways are uncomfortable or dangerous.

To understand what happens in our body from chronic trauma in a psychobiological stance, we have to understand what happens to the brain chemically during trauma. The body produces natural pain killers or analgesics called enkephalins, endorphins, and opiod peptides. These analgesics can affect both physical and emotional pain. When a painful input reaches your system, it triggers activity in your autonomic nervous system. Your body releases epinephrine, norepinephrine, and other chemicals that arouse you to action. But your body also protects you against pain by secreting endorphins and other related substances. The automatic release of endorphins during stress apparently reduces activity in the emotional centers in the brain. It also slows down activity in the autonomic nervous system. The victim can experience this reduced activity as a decrease in the "emotional significance" of the painful input (McConnell, 1986). A common response of a victim is, "I knew it was happening, I felt it, but it just didn't seem to matter."

During the trauma one of the above-mentioned analgesics activates hormones during PTSD, affecting stress levels and how the memory will be stored. The brain has two separate mechanisms for controlling emotional/physical pain. One mechanism seems to involve a release of endorphins while under stress. The other mechanism involves a "blocking" of painful input at the level of the spinal cord. The release of endorphins accounts for the pain-reducing effects. The second mechanism explains the analgesic effects of "cognitive strategies" and dissociation (McConnell, 1986).

The brain, during stress, reacts by decreasing the overall pain and hyperarousal the victim is feeling. This helps to calm the victim and interrupts memory storage (numbing and dissociation). There is also a disruption to a normal safety reaction called the "fight or flight syndrome," which enables us to react to unsafe conditions. This system is overridden by the biochemical reaction, and the victim does not respond to the internal safety message to flee.

Trauma also affects how the brain will organize the memory, store the memory, and retrieve the memory. This affects how the victim perceives the events leading up to, during, and after the trauma, whether the memory is stored in the same order or not, and how the victim must access the memories.

POSTTRAUMATIC STRESS AND
THE GRIEF PROCESS

The posttraumatic stress disorder is not diametrically opposed to the grief process we note in William Worden's book *Grief Counseling and Grief Therapy* (1983). There are direct similarities. While teaching about PTSD to therapists, I also teach the grief process. Often in working directly with victims and explaining their responses, it is much easier for them to understand the concept and vocabulary of grief or loss than it is for them to understand a psychological term like posttraumatic stress disorder.

The word "disorder" in and of itself is often distressful to the victim. In a recent article in *The Advocate* Niles (1990) stated that the word "disorder" as it pertains to posttraumatic stress should not be noted as a disorder. It should be noted as a "response." We have noticed clinically that this is *the* normal response to an abnormal event. A person who *did not* react with posttraumatic stress would have a disorder. Therefore, a victim experiencing some level of violence would have a posttraumatic stress *response*.

However, the acknowledgment of victims' grief and loss is much easier for them to understand and identify with than the concept of posttraumatic stress disorder. It is important that a therapist understand that grief and loss are not indicative of death alone. All victims must work through the grief process, whether the trauma has resulted from robbery, sexual abuse, homicide, suicide, or another event. Much is lost to the victim of robbery and rape, just as it is for a victim of a homicide or suicide. Therefore, we are going to take a look at the similarities and differences of grief versus PTSD.

William Worden in his book *Grief Counseling and Grief Therapy* (1983) indicated there are four tasks in mourning:*

1. To accept the reality of the loss (often referred to as the phase of shock and numbness);
2. To experience the grief (often referred to as the phase of searching and yearning);

---

*The four phases of grief and the acronym TEAR are from J. William Worden, *Grief Counseling and Grief Therapy*, © 1983, Springer Publishing Company, Inc., New York 10012. Used by permission.

3. To adjust to an environment in which the deceased (or their perceived loss) is missing (often referred to as the phase of disorganization);
4. To withdraw emotional energy and reinvest it in another relationship (often referred to as the phase of reorganization or recovery).

T—Testing of the Reality
E—Experiencing the Pain
A—Adjusting to the Environment
R—Recovery

The acronym "tear" adequately breaks down the grief process to an element we can all relate to well. The "T" in the acronym represents Testing of the Reality. This correlates to the first task in mourning as seen previously, and that is to accept the reality of the loss. Victims will often strive to accept the reality of the loss by testing it first. Did this really happen to me? Did I make this up? Why would I make this up? Have I really lost _____ (whatever the loss is, property, person, virginity, relationship, etc.)?

The "E" in the acronym represents Experiencing the Pain. This relates to the second task of mourning, which is to experience the grief. To accept the reality of our trauma, we must move into the task of experiencing the emotional pain associated with that trauma and to allow the grief to begin.

The "A" in the acronym represents Adjusting to the Environment and correlates with the third task of mourning, which is adjusting to the environment in which the perceived loss is missing. What is my life like without _____ (whatever the loss is)?

The "R" in the acronym represents Recovery and relates to the fourth and final task of mourning, which is to withdraw emotional energy and reinvest it in another relationship. After the victim has adequately tested the reality, felt the pain, and grieved and adjusted to the environment regarding the loss, the final phase is to reinvest energy and emotion in other objects, careers, persons, or causes.

In understanding grief, it is important to remember that grief is as individual as our fingerprints. No two people will grieve the same loss the same way. This often complicates a victim's recovery. In one case, two sisters and a brother all mourned the loss of their father, yet each reacted quite differently. One was open with mourning, another closed off, and still another repressed for months. These grieving reactions were judged by one another in a negative manner because all three assumed that each of them was grieving the "proper" way. Because they were all grieving for the same person, it was a problem to understand why there was such a vast difference in the display of emotion. This lead to friction in the family and began to close down communication in an already traumatized family system.

Grief also is not concrete; it is fluid, flowing. We move through grief like waves washing up on a shore. They roll in and they roll out. Our grief comes in waves; we progress for a while, then we regress for a while. There are no concrete stages that say I have experienced this emotion and therefore I can move on to the next stage. I prefer to think of grief in phases, not stages. Phases seem to indicate the need for flexible boundaries, two steps forward and one back, the ability to allow our grief to flow from one state to another and back again. Grief just can't be, or ever seems to be, cut-and-dry.

Normal Grief Reactions

Does normal grief exist? What we really refer to is uncomplicated grief, a reaction that is common after a loss or victimization. Worden (1982) broke down the grief manifestation reactions into the following categories: feelings, physical sensations, cognitions, and behaviors. Feelings include: sadness, anger, guilt, self-reproach, anxiety, loneliness, fatigue, helplessness, shock, yearning, emancipation, relief, and numbness. Certainly these are feelings that a victim would experience after trauma, whether it be a robbery or a rape.

Physical sensations include: hollowness in the stomach, tightness in chest or throat, oversensitivity to noise or startle response, sense of depersonalization, breathlessness, weakness in muscles, lack of energy, and dry mouth.

Often physical sensations and problems are those least recognized during trauma after the initial obvious physical problems are tended to. Many victims and counselors are surprised to find how many medical problems are later attributed to and connected to the trauma. Some medical problems are stress-related illnesses, whereas others are created by blunt trauma (physical beatings, etc.) or result from internal injuries from penetration.

Cognitions include: disbelief, confusion, preoccupation, sense of presence, and hallucinations both visual and auditory. Other serious cognitions could be added to certain categories of victimization such as incest and ritualistic torture. Please see chapters 8 and 10 on these traumas for more specifics.

Behaviors include: sleep and eating disturbances, absentminded behavior or dissociation, social withdrawal, dreams of the event, avoiding reminders of the event, searching or calling out, sighing, restless overactivity, crying, visiting places or carrying objects that are reminders of the person or event, treasuring objects that are reminders of the event, and remembering how one felt before the event or what one lost because of the event.

From looking at both PTSD and grief, we can see the wide range of similarities that exist. So where does grief end and PTSD start? Both grief and PTSD must be viewed on a continuum. There are varying degrees of severity in a normal and complicated grief reaction that lead up the continuum to a PTSD reaction. Likewise, PTSD can be seen in mild to chronic ranges.

Grief is a natural reaction to loss. PTSD is a natural reaction to an abnormal type of loss. Victims fall into both these categories: Their grief is a natural byproduct of their loss, and yet they may react to the abnormal life experience they had to endure.

```
l ------------------------------------------------------------------------------ l
   Grief              Complicated Grief              PTSD
```

It is not the act of the abuse we look to and measure, rather the victim's reaction to the trauma. The continuum of effect will often be related to extent, intensity, and duration of abuse as well as the victim's personal coping mechanism for emotional and physical pain.

RECOMMENDED READING

Hartman, C. R., & Burgess, A. W. (1988). *Journal of Interpersonal Violence, 3*(4).

McCann, I. L., & Pearlman, L. A. (1988). *Psychological trauma and the adult survivor—Theory, therapy and transformation.* New York: Brunner/Mazel.

Worden, W. J. (1983). *Grief counseling and grief therapy.* New York: Springer.

NATIONAL REFERRALS ON VICTIMIZATION

Bridgework Ministries, Inc. (author of this book)
1226 Turner Street, Suite C
Clearwater, FL 34616
813-443-0382

National Crime Prevention Council
1700 K Street, NW, 2nd Floor
Washington, DC 20006
202-466-NCPC

National Organization for Victim Assistance (NOVA)
717 D Street, NW
Washington, DC 20004
202-393-NOVA

National Self Help Clearinghouse
25 West 43rd Street, Room 620
New York, NY 10036
212-642-2944

National Victim Center
307 W. 7th St.
Fort Worth, TX 76102
817-877-3355

3

Effective Therapies for Trauma Victims

Traumatalogy, the understanding of emotional, physical, sexual, and spiritual trauma, sheds light on effective therapies for use with victims of violence. As I mentioned before, cognitive therapies are not always the most effective therapies in the victim's healing cycle. Therefore, we must be willing to explore various types of therapies, even those we may not have studied or known techniques for, in order to work most successfully with our client.

At Bridgework, prior to our work that focused on sexual/ritual abuse, our techniques centered mostly around cognitive therapies. As we moved further into sexual abuse counseling, we expanded our techniques by adding other types of therapies. As I traveled for training, I found myself drawn into workshops for various therapies. As we have incorporated them into our practice with our survivors, we have noticed an increase in expression, memory retrieval, and a propelled healing process.

Various types of therapies will be mentioned in this chapter. However, detailed techniques of these therapies will not be explained because that is beyond the scope of this book. There are books on all the therapies discussed here that provide clinical information on techniques.

ART

Among expressive therapies, art has always been effective in the healing process. It is a wonderful tool for noncognitive children to express sexual and physical abuse. We are fortunate to have trained and professional art therapists who can be used in a team approach when working with survivors. They are trained in various forms of art and its interpretation. Art therapy can be most helpful in child sexual abuse cases, especially during prosecution, in providing clarification and proof of the abuse. It also allows the child to express fear of the court proceedings. Through art, children can express fears that they may not be able to explain cognitively due to their age, ego strength, or psychological development. Art therapy allows early intervention that may not have been possible without information obtained through it. Burgess et al. (1990) indicated that the child will communicate the dominant memory. Art can be a tool for unlinking cognitive disturbances associated with dominant memory and intrusive thoughts.

Art also gives voice to adult survivors' damaged "inner child," which demands expression of its pain and torture. Some survivors' art is so intense and compelling that no words in the vocabulary could adequately describe the agony that the art conveys.

Group murals depicting a theme (healing, the "fantasy" of a healthy family, or even the abuse) can bring dramatic insight into the group's and individuals' progress. It can also be a source of unity, strengthening the group or the individuals. Painting, sketching, and drawing can be used with various victim populations. Expression, not accuracy or aesthetics, is the aim of these art forms.

CLAY MODELING AND SAND TRAYS

Clay modeling as a treatment component can allow adults and children to recreate themselves, as they view themselves either in the present, past, or future. Using sand trays is a new form of art therapy with trauma victims. Survivors are provided with large trays of sand along with miniature objects (people, animals, houses, cars, trees, etc.), which they arrange to create their inner world in the sand. This gives great insight into a child's perspective of his or her current or past inner environment or perceived home environment. This also works well with adult survivors who cannot express themselves cognitively because of their encodement of trauma, those who have been abused ritualistically, or those who have been subjected to mind-control techniques.

Recently, one of our art group activities took place at an "Inner Child Pajama Party" that we planned at Bridgework. While working on their deprived inner child, the women finger painted a group mural, made objects with play dough, and utilized other art therapies for expression.

MASKING

During one of our wilderness retreats, we scheduled time for masking. Masking is a powerful analogy of the mask abused women lived behind during the abuse. In this art process, strips of gauze covered in papier-mâché powder are dipped in water and placed over the entire face, leaving openings for the eyes, nostrils, and mouth. The women had completed 14 weeks of cognitive group therapy together, had taken 3 weeks off, and had come back for the next 14-week cycle of cognitive group therapy. It was during the second cycle that we arranged the retreat.

On the first night, we began the masking. The counselor assigned two women to work with each other. The counselor usually picked women who were having some difficulty with one another in the group. We avoided pairing those who had strongly bonded together in the group for this activity. We played classical music as a soothing backdrop.

In masking, one woman prepares the other's face with vaseline. This is also an activity in touch therapy. The strips are then dipped into water and placed so they outline the woman's face—forehead, sides of face, and jaw line. They are spread and secured by gently rubbing with the fingers. Then the interior of the face is filled in with the strips. A woman must sit about 10 minutes until the mask dries. Many women must wrestle with the issues of having been touched, and the restraining feeling of the hardening mask on their face.

When the mask is hardened, the "birthing" process of the mask begins. The woman bends over and squeezes her face rhythmically until the mask pulls free from her face and falls into her hands. She then turns it over and sees, for the first time, that which she feels "she has hidden behind her entire life." Many of our women cried or were so intensely moved that they were unable to vocalize their feelings.

We took the masks to a large bonfire and propped them on a table placed in front of the fire. We could see the flames flash from behind the openings of the eyes. It was very dramatic. All of us sat around the fire and processed the experience of being touched, restrained, giving birth to the mask, and seeing the painful expression or hollow emptiness of the expression on the masks. Many were moved because the masks so adequately expressed their fear and pain. Some threw the masks in the fire, not wanting to live behind them any longer. Others said they wanted to keep them and learn to love what was behind them.

MUSIC

Music can compel us to action, stir the raging waters within us, or soothe the savage beast in us. Music can be coupled with movement/ dance. Certain motions and movements are primitive and are attached to preverbal memories of abuse that occurred before we were verbal, usually under 2 years of age. Music can also be utilized to create certain moods during therapy that may be conducive to memory retrieval. Music can make us anxious, angry, sentimental, sad, happy, or touch something within our inner child that may be unexplainable. Just as there are trained art therapists, some specialize in music therapy. It is an excellent avenue in a team approach and can be coupled with art and other types of expressive therapies.

JOURNALING

Journaling is at the heart of the work we do with most trauma victims. It is probably used more than any other expressive therapy. Conveying feelings in writing is an excellent avenue of capturing fragments of memory and verbal expressions that the survivor is unable to give in person.

Journaling can be expanded to poetry, songs, plays, or other forms. Many survivors can allow a true outpouring of their souls in a journal that they cannot express in group or individual sessions. Surely we all recognize the intimacy of the writing of well-known authors such as Hemingway, Whitman, and Fitzgerald, who expressed their pain and suffering so well in their great literary works.

The following is part of a client's journal. Joie has a multiple personality disorder, having been sexually abused by many, including her dad, who then prepared her and trained her to please others sexually in what appears to have been a child sex ring.

THE OWNER'S REWARD

On the day of my birth
his name was placed there.
On the certificate
proof of ownership declared.
His right to have me
body, and soul
and for that time

I never told.
The certificate of proof
was all he would need
to claim his reward
he had in me.
His ownership gave him
the right to touch.
He just kept saying
how he loved me so much.
He took time to train me
almost everyday.

How to make men happy
in all the right ways.
From the day I was born
I was always adored,
because my owner knew
I was his reward.

One of Joie's personalities is a wonderful gospel musician and singer. Here are the words to a beautiful song she wrote and sang to me one day after counseling.

COME LITTLE CHILDREN

I say come little children
Come and follow me.
I will give you rest
In my company.
I say come little children
There's no need to fear
You're safe in my arms now
I'll wipe away your tears.

CHORUS

For He loves you and me
He loves us as we are.
He can be what we always
Wanted our Daddy's to be
For he loves you and me
Just trust in Him and you'll see

He says come little children
From your burdens, I've freed.

I say come little children
I know your trust is weak.
Look only for the Father
He is the one you seek.
I say come little children
For I know you're burdened down
I died on the cross for you
Your burdens were my crown.

Joie's journal is about 2 inches thick, the last I saw it, and represented only about 2 months' of writing. She has utilized journaling in her recovery well.

PLAY THERAPY

Play therapy has long been noted as a vital pathway to effect counseling with children; however, I find it equally necessary for adult survivors. When adult trauma victims decide to focus on their "inner child" work, the process often incorporates many of the play and expressive therapies previously mentioned. It is often difficult for adults readily to "play" or "finger paint." Most were never allowed to be children, and playing is foreign to them. An adult working on inner child work must be "taught" how to release in the present and reconnect with the child within. During one of our inner child parties, some women brought paper dolls to play with, some brought coloring books, and others brought their tea sets to share in "Show and Tell." It was a revealing evening that demonstrated to us how disconnected we have been from our inner child and just how void our childhood had been of appropriate child activities and development.

Play therapies with children can elicit a wealth of information about their family structure, their inner environment as well as home environment, their anger and aggression, and specifics on how the abuse was perpetrated. Many play therapists incorporate the use of art and music but also use dolls (anatomically correct and regular dolls), doll houses, and furniture with which the child can recreate the scene of the abuse or present home arrangements. They also use puppets, which allows verbal interplay, and sand trays with miniatures to allow family sculpting (who interacts with whom, family dynamics). In addition, drama, with kids and also with adults, can reveal actual reenactments that are being played out from the subconscious to the conscious.

WILDERNESS RETREATS

Wilderness retreats are becoming a readily acknowledged form of therapy. These retreats can serve numerous purposes. They create unity, as does any camping experience, especially when the survivors must get together and plan the activities and events. These retreats enable the group to spend longer amounts of time together, which brings any cognitive therapy to a deeper level. Spending so much time together forces the group to work out conflicts with one another. The time frame allows for art and music therapies as well as group outdoor recreational therapies, which build unity and cohesion.

One of the most effective forms of therapy used in a wilderness retreat is an ETR (Escape To Reality) or ropes course. These courses are developed in a wooded section utilizing low, medium, and high element maneuvers. These maneuvers can including walking on a log, a group standing on a log and rolling it with their feet, swinging from ropes, climbing rope bridges, swinging through a row of tire swings, and swinging from a wire and trapeze at the top of a 20-foot telephone pole. These activities, no doubt, induce great fear! Yet overcoming the fear is the therapy itself and serves to improve unity, group cohesion, trust in others who are spotting you for falls, self-esteem when you have completed an obstacle, and awareness of touching issues.

We have been fortunate to locate two camps in our state that have both excellent lodges and some ropes courses. There may be a number of hospitals in your area that have ropes courses available that you can rent for an afternoon. The rental covers the trained therapists who will work the ropes course with your survivors. However, we are partial to retreat camps that have both the "woodsy" feeling, the overnight experience, and an available ropes course.

Although ropes courses may not be available in your area, you may still want to utilize wilderness/camping experiences. If you are not aware of available camps, try arranging to use Girl and Boy Scout camps at off-season times, state parks that have cabins, or religious retreat camps.

RECREATIONAL THERAPY

Recreational therapy can be utilized apart from wilderness retreats. Recreational therapies can be designed for both indoor and outdoor use. We are fortunate to have a master's PE person on our team who frequently plans recreational outings with our women. These have included hiking, beaching, and biking.

Group recreational events can be created by utilizing simple instruments such as an unfolded parachute, bean bags, and toys. The goal is to develop unity and teamwork by victims' having to work together to establish a rhythm in the parachute game or set team goals in other games. The victims have to work together, hold hands, touch, support one another physically, and support each other emotionally through cheers and encouragement. Victims have to rely on one another and trust that their teammate will be there during a game or high/low element maneuver. In our wilderness retreat, we incorporated canoeing, parachute games, blindfold games, old-fashioned tugs-of-war, and other outdoor games.

Often groups will develop an unplanned recreational activity. We regularly recommend that the women get involved in some sort of recreational therapies, either our planned events or ones they plan themselves. One of our planned events for the fall is to go to a well-known river site and actually ride and feed a manatee!

GROUP THERAPY

One of the most well known and utilized therapies for victims of violence is group therapy. Group therapy helps to reduce feelings of isolation, provides a ''mirroring effect'' that shows victims that their responses to violation are similar to others', and offers support and education as well.

VICTIM-OFFENDER PROGRAMS

The sometimes controversial victim-offender programs originated in California and consisted of allowing some victims and some offenders to be together in a group format to express elements of their victimization and crime-related histories. The idea of this format was twofold. Both aspects seemed to be more victim-related than criminally focused. The first principle was that this format allowed the criminal to see the victim's pain firsthand. The criminal was able to see that there was actually a face behind the crime. The criminal heard what the victim lost emotionally, physically, socially, spiritually, and psychologically. The criminal heard of the victim's struggles and learned that many crimes cause irreversible losses for which there is no compensation. Victim-offender programs were used as a crime deterrent for recently released criminals.

The second principle was that this format allowed victims to feel they were helping to deter crime by venting their emotions and providing insight and awareness to criminals. This process served as a ventilator for victims. Taking taking care of victims was also good public relations for the governor's office.

Some programs took it a step further. Young juvenile offenders, whose main crime was breaking and entering or crimes against the elderly, were also mandated to restitution. This consisted of going to elderly crime victims' homes and installing dead-bolt locks, bars on the windows, and alarm systems!

Bridgework has just begun a two-way program with a halfway house for released prisoners. Our women have agreed to make a video to be released to the men who were sexual offenders. The film will show open displays of emotion, anger, crying, rage, isolation, and the women's stories of what their life has been like since the incest, adult rape, or assault. In return, the men will send a tape in which they talk about themselves, what they feel, what they've learned, and perhaps what they haven't learned.

There are, however, some rules. The men are not allowed to justify, minimize, or deny their actions. They must remain accountable. Once the tapes have been exchanged, it will be up to the women if they wish to experience a one-time group with the men. Remember, these are random victims and offenders. I, personally, would not ask a victim to meet with her particular offender. The women expressed some anxiety about the idea, but weighed the pros and cons and felt it worthy of their investment.

INNER HEALING

Inner healing is a widely overlooked area of immense value in trauma care. It has always amazed me that we, as clinicians, claim to work from a holistic approach (healing the entire person), yet consistently overlook and often purposely run past a person's need for spiritual healing. Most victims, understandably so, struggle with the questions of an omnipotent God who either overlooked their pain and did not respond and rescue them from it, or who might have been on a coffee break and did not see it at all. There is enormous conflict of hating

God/holding God responsible and the fear/guilt of hating someone so powerful. We are by nature spiritual beings with a need to be in touch with that element of ourselves. If we recognize that we are body, soul (emotions), and spirit and do not seek inner healing of that relationship with God, a third of our healing remains incomplete.

> There is a pain that goes beyond all others
> A pain that words cannot describe
> Pain from the soul that is rejected of God
> The soul that He abandoned
> He turned His back
> Shook the dust from His feet
> And walked away
> Leaving the soul in its sinful state
> Surely if this God is a loving God
> As they have all taught
> Then this soul must be very bad indeed
> Because there is a God
> All the beauty and wonder of creation sings of Him
> There are things beyond understanding
> Like child abuse and abortion
> Mankind has been allowed his way
> And children and the weak suffer
> As an adult I can understand
> But the child within my soul cries out
> The pain of feeling God doesn't care
> Doesn't love me for myself
> Because I'm not good enough. . .
> —*by Marie Yen, a sexual abuse survivor*

Inner healing incorporates God back into a person's life while integrating the experience of trauma into long-term memory. These processes are not exclusive of each other.

As with any of the expressive therapies (art, music, and play), a professional is utilized. With inner healing, it is imperative that the person be *trained* in inner healing. This is usually someone who has had specific training in inner healing, is a licensed religious counselor, and possibly also a licensed minister, rabbi, or a leader of another faith. According to Dr. Benjamin Keyes, a professional utilizing the techniques of inner healing, this healing is a psychological technique used to abreact to deep-seated and repressed feelings and memories of pain that affect present-day living.

Victims' memories include feelings, concepts, patterns, attitudes, and tendencies toward actions that accompany the pictures their mind holds as they see a past traumatic event and abreact to the memories. Stored memories of the traumatic event can influence them to exhibit behaviors and actions when they are not confronted and worked through, and these can later lead to dysfunction. The process of inner healing becomes a form of counseling that focuses on the healing power of God (in AA terms, God as you perceive Him; in Christian terms, God embodied in the Trinity: The Father, Son, and Holy Spirit) in specific areas of emotional and spiritual problems.

When emotion and memory have not been effectively addressed, feelings are repressed or compensated for in ways that allow a person to cope and to manage a problem situation. One avenue, especially in physical and sexual abuse cases, is dissociation or disconnecting from the actual feelings resulting from the violation in order to cope with the traumatic situation. Later because of the disconnection/dissociation, the child or adult may continue to idealize the perpetrator, especially if that perpetrator is a close family member, because the affective memory of the trauma has been effectively blocked. Our minds act as a protective defense mechanism in severe trauma situations—the fuse trips when it is overloaded. When the fuse trips, the denied problem goes underground or to the subconscious, and later often reappears as physical illnesses or unhappy marital situations that spiral in recurring cycles of defeat.

Inner healing can also be effective for painful emotional hurts, shameful situations, death of a family member, severe trauma, war trauma issues, child abuse, and other problems. The technique allows individuals clearly to see and recreate the experience of the submerged memory. Often the experience of reconnecting to a horrific situation causes a reexperiencing of an affective response, which then needs to be worked through and processed in a counseling situation. In these situations, victims have blamed themselves when the blame was not in any way theirs. In a religious context, issues with the victims' view of God, often from a distorted frame, must be confronted at this point because victims often feel that God did not protect them or rescue them from the situation. The healing process moves through the series of events to allow the adult self emotionally and spiritually to reach out to and rescue the "child within." From a religious context, because God is not a God of time, we allow God to travel with us back to the memory and work toward a healing of that memory to allow us to bring it back to our present awareness. In a very real sense we are allowing our adult self to minister and reach out to our inner child. To some victims, realizing that God was present during the violation and they were not alone, is of great comfort. They must, however, wrestle with their own theology about why God does not "rescue" during times of severe abuse.

Often the issue of forgiveness becomes a primary focus of the overall process. The real difficulty does not lie in victims' forgiving the abuser but of forgiving themselves. Forgiveness of self is essential. The final stage of the process is the reconnection, or, in Gestalt terms, the "parts becoming whole." Reconnection with the inner child and feeling the presence of God can bring closure.

This process can be effected, or at least begun, in the course of a therapeutic session (1 to 2 hours). It is more common for this entire process to evolve over a period of time, which for severe trauma may take several years. However, lesser issues of hurt, shame, and so forth can be worked out in a matter of weeks to months. For victims who claim to be "nonvisual," remember that memories incorporate much more than visual elements, as stated earlier and as shown in Burgess's work mentioned in chapter 2. The process of abreacting may occur through the use of any of the other senses (Keyes, 1990).

I have personally long believed that mental health counseling and religious counseling do not have to be at separate ends of the spectrum. When working with victims of violence, their healing will often come to the point of needing to work on their issues with and about God. All mental health counselors would be wise to have in their resource network a reputable religious counselor who understands issues of violence and is sensitive to the victims' need of working slowly and gently with their struggles with God.

At Bridgework, we incorporate a definite faith-stance in all our work. We readily recognize the victims' faith or lack of faith in their recovery process and allow them to confront their issues with God in a non-judgmental atmosphere. We address spiritual issues and questions in certain phases of all our groups. The spiritual element is not a haphazard topic that may or may not be dealt with, but an intricate part of our program development.

When I had been part of a homicide therapy group, the spiritual element of our pain of having lost someone to murder was "allowed to exist" but was neither confirmed nor challenged. Consequently, it remained in a stagnant position, not moving forward toward resolution nor incorporated into our healing process. Consequently, we had to deal with our spiritual issues outside of our therapy in the homicide group. This left a definite impression that the group was focused only on a psychological, not a holistic approach. Survivors' healing can be propelled rapidly by allowing and giving place to their faith in recovery.

> Thank you Lord for people who hurt
> And are open and honest enough to share
> To let us see their torn and bloodied souls
> That help us realize we are not alone in our pain
> People who have experienced the tragedies of life
> And have gone on to survive, broken but stronger
> Who have somehow hung on to their sanity
> And care enough to use God's gifts to help others
> To see the reality of life as it is
> To summon up the courage to lay their souls bare
> Admit that even as dedicated people of God
> There are unexplainable, unfathomable pains
> Utter despair and loss of hope and faith
> But they let us know by their sharing
> That there is survival—a continuing on
> For each of us the pains and hurts are different
> As is the path to take us to survival
> But the same loving Christ is by our side
> To lead us to the source of His strength
> When He faced His experience of terror
> Rejected, scorned, betrayed, abused, disbelieved
> True, He was a God, and we are not
> And His ordeal had a divine and eternal purpose
> To show us His Father's unlimited love
> But He took on a human body and became one of us
> And in that body, He felt it all, just as we do
> The only difference was that He had a choice
> And He, the Almighty God, chose us. . ..
> —*by Marie Yen, a survivor of sexual abuse*

RECOMMENDED READING

Allender, D. (1990). *The wounded heart*. Colorado Springs, CO: Navpress.

Bradshaw, J. (1987). *On the family*. New York: Health Communications.

Bradshaw, J. (1988). *Healing the shame that binds you*. New York: Health Communications.

Bradshaw, J. (1990). *Home coming—Reclaiming and championing your inner child*. New York: Bantam Books.

Corey, G., & Corey, M. (1987). *Group process and practice*. Pacific Grove, CA: Brooks/Cole.

Seamands, D. (1981). *Healing for damaged emotions*. Wheaton, IL: Victor Books.

Seamands, D. (1989). *Healing of memories*. Wheaton, IL: Victor Books.

4

Victims of Robbery

- One violent crime occurred every 20 seconds in 1988 (FBI, 1989).
- A fourth of the 92 million households in the United States were touched by a crime of violence or theft in 1988 (FBI, 1989).
- Forty-six percent of all robberies were committed in the presence or use of a weapon (FBI, 1989).

Household burglary ranks among the more serious felony crimes, not only because it involves the illegal entry of one's home, but also because a substantial proportion of the violent crimes that occur in the home take place during a burglary incident. Thus burglary is potentially a far more serious crime than its classification as a property offense indicates; for many victims, including those that avoid the trauma of personal confrontation, the invasion of their home on one or more occasions constitutes a violation that produces permanent emotional scars. (Schlesinger, 1985)

Burglary, robbery, or breaking and entering violates more than just a person's domain. And the propensity for face-to-face confrontation cannot be overlooked. Victims of robbery feel violated, much in the same way rape victims feel that the boundaries of safety have been violated. In robbery, victims may feel that their personal life has been laid bare, their personal possessions and papers ransacked, their prized possessions or heirlooms stolen, and a part of themselves, their history, or heritage wiped out in a single incident of violence.

Because many robbery victims feel a sense of impending danger and are unable to regain a sense of security, they choose to relocate to other housing. This, for many, is a violation of their heritage and their free choice to maintain a home in a place of their own choosing. With aged victims, leaving a home they have lived in for years can lead to premature death (Waller, 1985).

Face-to-face confronations, especially those involving a weapon, can invoke severe posttraumatic stress disorders. Debriefing and integration are often necessary for clerks or hotel personnel who have been held at gunpoint, locked in vaults, or tied up and abandoned.

In the face of the recent crime wave in the United States, there is a tendency to downplay robbery, which seems less severe than rapes, abductions, and murders plaguing our country. The trauma of robbery is one of the most frequent and yet neglected traumas (Waller, 1985). Robbery can and often does lead to serious physical injury and almost always leads to an emotional injury of violation and threat to security.

Three types of burglaries exist:

- *Forcible entry:* Force is used to gain entry (breaking a window, breaking a lock on the door, etc.);
- *Attempted forcible entry:* Force is used as an attempt to gain entry; and
- *Unlawful entry:* Someone without legal right to be on the property gains entry even though force is not used. (U.S. Dept. of Justice, Bureau of Justice Statistics, 1985).

In the three catagories of burglaries, over 75% of the homes burglarized reported $1,000 worth or more of property taken (U.S. Dept. of Justice, Bureau of Justice Statistics, 1985).

According to the U.S. Dept. of Justice, Bureau of Justice Statistics (1985, January), the probability that a burglary will be reported to the police is related to various aspects of the burglary: the kind of intrusion, who committed it, whether a household member was present, whether a violent crime was committed during the robbery, whether anything was stolen, and if stolen, the value of the property. Forcible entries were reported almost twice as often as nonforcible entries. Robberies committed by relatives (including spouses and ex-spouses) were reported to police more frequently than those committed by strangers. However, not all victims felt that robbery of a home by a relative constituted a crime. Robberies in which violent crime was involved were reported in higher numbers than those where no violent victimization occurred.

CRISIS INTERVENTION

The emotional trauma or "invisible wound" is the least evident but often the most brutal effect of the crime. According to Waller (1985) there are six ways victims suffer from crime.

1. Loss of property and money;
2. Personal injury;
3. Feelings and behaviors that occur because of PTSD;
4. Effects of the crime on family and friends of the victim;
5. Variety of inconveniences caused by the state's action of trying to identify, convict, and hold an offender accountable; and
6. Lack of access to specialized services for victims.

To victims, either being there during a robbery or coming home and finding that their home has been robbed is a terrifying experience. Most victims react with shock and then fear, not knowing if the criminal has left the premises. They may remain shocked or numb, appear disoriented, and have trouble relaying information to the police.

During the crisis, victims may find it difficult to notice everything that has been stolen, or they may have a desire not to relay that information to the police, choosing to focus on an element that is more important to them, yet not important to the investigation, such as an heirloom or item of sentimental value that was taken.

A study by Bourque, Brumback, Krug, and Richardson (1978) showed that more than 70% of the victims displayed crying, shaking, and fear, 20% maifested physical upset and memory loss, and 5% recorded long-term rcsidual effects.

Following the loss of items of sentimental value or heirlooms, the victim will need to engage in a grieving process. Some clinicians do not realize that victims recognize the loss of heirlooms or property as a loss. The process of grieving must accompany any loss if the victim is to work through successfully the feelings associated with that loss (see the section in chapter 2 on the grief process). Of course, the length of time it takes to grieve the loss of material property is normally less than grieving the loss of a person. However, the robbery victim's grief in response to the loss of heirlooms or other attachments to his or her heritage or roots must not be overlooked. Sentimental possessions mean much more to a victim than the equivalent cash. A photo of a deceased loved one or a wedding ring are noncompensatory losses.

If the victim's home was also senselessly destroyed by breaking and rampaging, the victim may feel a heightened degree of fear, sensing the level of violence of the person who was involved in destroying his or her possessions and home. Visible signs of violence, such as cushions slit with a knife or bullet holes in the wall, enstill a vivid picture of the act of violence in the victim's mind. Such acts of violence can be especially disturbing to the elderly or to single women living alone (Waller, 1985).

It is important for counselors to encourage the victim to notify law enforcement officials. The possibility of recovering stolen possesions without law enforcement efforts is remote. However, the victim's right to decline to report must be respected. Victims may decide to report as they begin to deal with the crime more cognitively.

After a robbery, victims' sense of personal boundary violation and fear will be heightened. They will probably want someone to stay with them, or stay with friends or family until the police indicate it is safe for them to return. However, one must be aware of the possibility of secondary injury to the victim by inept caregivers. A study by Friedman, Bischoof, Davis, and Person (1982) reported that 80% of supporters of victims suffered some form of discomfort from helping the victim, including fear or suspicion, insecurity, and vulnerability.

Locks may need to be changed, windows replaced, security devices installed, security inspections ordered, or neighborhood watches organized. Some choose to purchase a guard dog for their homes. All these actions assist the victim in trying to reestablish a security and safety schema.

The victim who may be suffering from posttraumatic stress might be unable to accomplish all the necessary tasks involved in recuperating from a robbery. Either a counselor, a family member, or a victim advocate associated with the police department may need to assist the victim with all these matters.

Client Concerns

- Return of stolen possessions;
- Inventory of what was stolen;
- Is criminal off the property?
- Will the criminal return?
- Will insurance cover the stolen articles?
- Is there anything that could have been done to prevent the robbery?

- Installing security devices;
- Personal safety; and
- Fear of repeat robberies or revenge robberies for reporting.

Secondary Victimizations

- Replacement cost of articles stolen;
- Loss of articles of sentimental value;
- Cost of security devices;
- Cost of a gun or other weapon purchased for protection;
- Missed time at work;
- Insensitive law enforcement, family, and friends;
- Loss of a sense of safety;
- Cost of relocating; and
- Change in life-style.

Social Services Needed

- Crime investigator;
- Victim advocate;
- Crime Compensation Bureau;
- Inspection of safety and status of house and assessment of reentry possibilities;
- Crisis intervention counseling; and
- Medical treatment if injured during break-in.

SHORT-TERM COUNSELING

Issues to be addressed in counseling during this time will most likely continue to focus on elements of safety. Victims will want to replay the crime over and over in their minds, incorporating new elements such as how different safety devices might have been a deterrent, how they may have interacted with the robber, and what they would do should future victimizations occur.

As the shock and numbness of the event begin to subside, victims' anger will begin to mount. Their anger may be directed at the criminal for the articles stolen, at the criminal justice system for not apprehending the criminal, at a family member for not securing the house or property, or at friends for inappropriate responses or lack of support.

Directing anger to positive constructs for change can be an asset to the victim. The victim's anger may be the motivation for neighborhood watches, the organization of a program where property is engraved for indentification, or other preventive programs. Anger channeled to positive contructs is preventive medicine to irrational and dangerous retaliation.

A general sense of not being safe, not having control over one's domain, uncertainty about the future, and fear of possible additional victimizations are all normal reactions. Children who are involved may suffer from an increased feeling of not being safe and may be fearful of being left alone at night or entering the room that was robbed.

The victim may harbor some harsh feelings about comments made by law enforcement officials or family regarding "what they could or should have done to prevent the robbery." Case studies show that this exacerbates the difficulties a victim is already suffering (Waller, 1985). Such reactions of others may trigger victims' guilt, especially in cases where face-to-face confrontation may have occurred and where children were present.

If victims are involved in a hearing, they may be unfamiliar with court procedures and may need the assistance of a victim advocate to help them through this process. They may be concerned about retaliation by the criminal and future safety after the criminal is released. Often if the property is retrieved, it is not returned to the victim immediately. It is held for trial, which means waiting several months or longer.

Client Concerns

- Safety;
- Retaliation;
- Victimization by another criminal;
- Learning how the criminal justice system operates; and
- Return of property.

Secondary Victimizations

- Dealing with the criminal justice system;
- Lack of support from family and friends over an extended period of time;
- Increased insurance premiums;

- Unreturned property; and
- Missed time from work for court appearances or court-related business.

Social Services Needed

- Victim advocate;
- Short-term counseling/support programs;
- Crime Compensation Bureau;
- Neigborly services for safety equipment installation;
- Insurance company contact; and
- Assistance with moving (if appropriate).

LONG-TERM COUNSELING

Victims of robbery are usually not seen over a long period, unless additional crimes such as murder, rape, or assault were also involved in the crime. Additional reasons that robbery victims are not seen in long-term counseling are that society minimizes the effect of robbery (as compared with more serious crimes), and many victims are not willing to continue to express distress past the point of social support. Second, there are no major support groups geared toward robbery victims. However, in areas of the country where robbery is prevalent, these groups are growing in number. Third, because of a lack of specific robbery support groups, victims have had to be mixed with other types of victims, often rape and assault victims. Unfortunately, robbery victims will often feel invalidated in their victimization when having to face and hear of other more violent types of crime. However, serious trauma will occur in one in 20 cases that will cause sleeplessness, nausea, and a long-term fear of entering rooms of the residence (Maguire, 1980; Waller & Okihiro, 1978; Bourque et al., 1978).

In the event that the victim was held at gunpoint, or someone was murdered during the robbery, long-term counseling interventions would be necessary. Placing a victim in a homicide survivors' support group is often helpful to those having experienced murder, or in a rape support program if they were raped during the course of a robbery. During these specialized support programs, the victim can work not only on violence issues (such as rape or murder) but the issues surrounding the robbery itself. (See chapters on assault, sexual trauma, and murder.)

RECOMMENDED READING

Clarke, R.V.G., & Hope, T. (Eds.). (1984). *Coping with burglary.*
  Boston: Kluwer-Nijhoff.
Maguire, M. (1982). *Burglary in a dwelling.* London: Heinemann
  Educational Books.
Waller, I., & Okihiro, N. (1978). *Burglary: The victim and the public.*
  Toronto: University of Toronto Press.

REFERRALS

See chapter 2 for a listing of referrals for victimization.

 **Overview of Robbery**

Crisis Intervention Issues:	Shock, numbness, disorientation, heightened sense of fear, beginning of the grieving process, notification of law enforcement agencies and insurance companies, boundary violation, changing locks, installing safety devices, general safety issues.
Short-Term Counseling:	Safety issues, replaying of event, cognitive reframing of event, anger at systems, self, and criminal, revenge, lack of support from friends.
Long-Term Counseling:	Most victims do not engage in long-term counseling.
Secondary Victimizations:	Cost of replacing stolen articles, articles of sentimental value not replaceable, cost of safety devices, increase in insurance premiums, lost wages, insensitive law enforcement or criminal justice system.
Social Services Needed:	Crime investigator, insurance adjustor, victim advocate, Crime Compensation Bureau, safety inspection services, crisis intervention counseling, short-term counseling.

5

Assault

- An estimated 2.2 million victims of crime were physically injured every year from 1979 through 1986 (FBI, 1989).
- Approximately 31% of all assaults involve the presence or use of a weapon (FBI, 1989).

Assault is defined as "an intentional unlawful threat by word or act to do violence to a person of another coupled with an apparent ability to do so and doing some act which creates a well-founded fear in such other person that such violence is imminent" (Metro Dade Police Department, 1990).

Basically, assault is the actual doing of harm or a threat to do harm so that the victim believes that harm can or will be done. Assault is a broad category and is primarily a legal term. When we are talking about victims whose lives have been touched by "assault," we are talking about many different types of violence that can be perpetrated in many different ways.

Assault can be directed, such as attacks against certain populations as demonstrated by the Klu Klux Klan, or premeditated, such as robberies. Assault can be random, such as crimes influenced by gang emotionalism, or muggings, rapes, robberies, or serial events. Campus assault is any criminal violence that is targeted at campus populations, based either on selected targets living on campus or a wide array of victims who make easy targets because they live in a concentrated area in a mostly unprotected environment.

Assault can be perpetrated by strangers, as in muggings, for example. It also can be familial such as in spouse abuse, child abuse, or elder abuse. It can be person-directed, such as gay, hate, or ethnic assault. It can begin physically in the course of a robbery or a mugging and can escalate to rape, physical injury or death, or even murder. Assault also can be verbal, where language and meaning are the weapons.

Assault, then, can take many forms and be directed at many different populations. The end result is always the same—violence and devastation—physical, emotional, social, and spiritual.

Because assault comprises such a broad category of victimization, clinical assistance is geared to the type of assault, the strength of the victim, and any specialized attention necessary based on the type of victimization. Each category of victimization is different, therefore treatment approaches will differ. The needs of an elder abuse victim will differ greatly from the needs of a hate/gay violence victim. Therefore, the categories of assault victimization have been broken down to better meet your needs in assisting these victim populations clinically.

ELDER ABUSE

- Strangers are more likely to attack the elderly than younger victims (FBI, 1989).
- Forty percent of nursing home residents are the victims of verbal abuse and 15% may be the victims of physical or sexual abuse.
- Only one in six cases of elder abuse is reported (Select Committee on Aging, 1981).
- By the year 2000, more than 50% of our population will be over the age of 50 (Butler & Lewis, 1983).

OVERVIEW OF ELDER ABUSE

With the onslaught of various types of domestic violence, we have clearly seen an increase in the recognition of elder abuse. Until recent years, we assumed that the elderly grew old safely and were loved. Yet we have come to realize that they are highly targeted victims for robbery, scam artists, and assault, and are frequently abused in their own homes by family members. People are increasingly aware of the horror stories of neglect and abuse prevailing in convalescent care facilities and state mental hospitals. Some studies have indicated that only 1 out of 14 cases of elder abuse comes to the attention of authorities. It is estimated that in 1988 about 2 million elderly were abused, although only a fraction of the abuse was reported. In a recent study, it was stated that by the year 2000, 50% of our society will be elderly (over 50 years of age). If this comes to pass, we can expect to watch the incidence of abuse rise. It is amazing that the frequency of elder abuse is only slightly lower than that of child abuse, but it is much less frequently reported than child abuse.

Three factors seem to limit access to accurate information about elder abuse: unclear and differing definitions used by researchers; lack of awareness of the problem; and reluctance by victims to report abuse for fear of retaliation in the form of further abuse, abandonment, or institutionalization. When victims do complain of abuse, their reports often are dismissed as symptoms of senility.

Like other forms of family violence, elder abuse is rarely an isolated incident and usually follows a cyclic pattern. Because of the frailty of its victims, elder abuse is always serious and can be fatal. And also like other forms of family violence, it is seen at all socioeconomic levels. Most victims tend to be White women over the age of 75 who have some physical or mental impairment and are being cared for by a family member. According to Steinmetz (1986), sons were responsible for two thirds of the physical abuse and almost 30% of the emotional abuse, whereas daughters were most likely to be involved in emotional neglect.

Abuse can been seen in the following areas:

Neglect (Active, Passive, or Self-Neglect)

Acts of omission or commission by an elderly person or the caretaker can result in inadequate care to maintain physical and mental health. This can include malnutrition as well as bedsores and cause serious physical problems. Elder abuse has also been defined as the mismanagement of the physical and emotional well-being of an older adult (Myers & Shelton, 1987).

Physical Abuse

Acts committed by a relative or caregiver may result in physical injuries. Unreasonable confinement and oversedation are examples. Most commonly seen is physical abuse resulting in broken limbs or other bones, bruises, cuts, sprains, lacerations, welts, dislocations, and abrasions.

Sexual Abuse

Sexual abuse is any type of sexual manipulation to which an elderly person does not consent. Both physical contact or nonphysical/verbal abuse could be involved.

Financial Exploitation

Financial exploitation is the caretaker's improper use or mismanagement of elderly persons' funds or property. As a result, the elderly are deprived of the use of their own resources that they have accumulated for basic retirement needs. This can be done through theft, misuse, force, or misrepresentation.

Psychological or Emotional Abuse

A caretaker's actions or verbalizations that are designed to humiliate, provoke, confuse, or frighten the elderly person constitute psychological abuse. It has also been described as active attempts to intimidate or diminish the mental well-being of the individual (Myers & Shelton, 1987). This can be done through threats, condemnation, insults, verbal hostility or assault, or invoking fear.

Violation of Rights

The violation of the elderly's rights can include locking them in or out of their home, placing them into a nursing care facility against their will, coercion, unreasonable confinement, opening or censoring mail, refusing access to a telephone or visitors, or any other breach of rights that citizens have under state, federal, or constitutional law, including state and federal statutes (Martin, 1987).

There are several causal theories surrounding elder abuse, and it is likely that several of these are mixed together to produce the actual abusive circumstance. Factors that contribute to the abuse of the elderly have similarities to factors associated with family violence. According to Henton, Cate, and Emery (1984), four categories involved in contributing to elder abuse are:

a. Personal characteristics of the abuser and of the abused;
b. Interpersonal characteristics of the relationship between the abuser and the abused;
c. Situational factors that increase the likelihood of abuse; and
d. Sociocultural factors that impinge on the use of violence.

Myers and Shelton (1987) also indicated the following factors contribute.

Personal Factors

Personal stress factors such as a lack of family support or relief support, lack of elderly social services, poverty, and isolation from others who are performing home health care contribute to the mounting tension that explodes into abuse.

Personality disorders or personality traits of the abusers/caregivers may add to their abusive nature. Some are alcohol or drug addicted, mentally or emotionally ill, incapable of providing adequate care, or may be experiencing marital or financial difficulties.

Because violence is a learned behavior, those caregivers who were abused run a significantly higher chance of abusing those in their care. Some cases of elder abuse occur in homes with a lifelong pattern of violent relationships as seen in previous spouse or child abuse situations. If the caregiver was specifically abused as a child by the elder who is in his or her care, retribution and revenge may motivate the caregiver.

Interpersonal Factors

Serious physical and mental illnesses that are common among the elderly lead to dependence upon family who may not be in a position financially or emotionally to meet these intense long-term caregiving needs. Because of the stringent amount of work that home caregiving requires, the family members become resentful, exhausted, and burned out, which leads to guilt. These emotions are released in the form of abusive behaviors.

In addition, interpersonal factors may include unresolved previous conflicts. Power struggles may punctuate the relationship and add to existing stress and conflict in the relationship. Caregivers may feel they are not receiving enough gratification for their caregiving.

Situational Factors

Situational factors relate to any increased stress by the addition of another family member and the added responsibility of caring for someone physically and financially. This can create a "sandwich" position for caregivers, who have to provide both for their own children and also for their parents. Additional factors could be financial, material, and employment problems related to caring for the elder.

Sociocultural Factors

Social attitudes against aging devalue the worth of the elderly and make them vulnerable to abuse and neglect. Elder abuse parallels child abuse in a number of ways. According to the manual *Advocacy in Action* put out by the National Victim Center (1990), the similarities include:

- Both are usually perpetrated by a family member;
- Both involve the abuse of a dependent person by a caregiver;
- Both situations involve stress on the caregiver, and the pressures may be the same;
- The abusers in both situations may have been the subjects of violence and abuse themselves; and
- Society stigmatizes the abusers in both situations, and they may be reluctant to seek help.

Elder abuse also holds many of its own stigmas, including age discrimination. The elderly are seen as incapable of leading productive lives, which can result in the violation of their civil rights. Social attitudes toward the elderly may contribute to their neglect, abuse, and exploitation. These attitudes include: negative attitudes toward aging, stereotyping the elderly as nonproductive, setting a low priority to their needs, the lack of options and social services for the elderly, and inequality in salaries and job opportunities for this population.

CRISIS INTERVENTION

When working with the elderly it is important to note certain barriers that may hamper effective intervention and treatment. These can include:

- Lack of eyewitnesses of the abuse;
- Fear of retaliation;
- Fear of relocation;
- Embarrassment;
- Fear of having to go to court;
- Feeling that ''It won't do any good to tell'';
- Religious justification—purpose will be revealed in time;
- Nonassertive personality;
- Learned helplessness; and
- Inability to realize one is being abused (too impaired mentally or physically).

These barriers may affect counseling at different levels and stages of the counseling process. Some barriers may be evident immediately during the crisis intervention stage (lack of eyewitnesses, inability to realize one is being abused, etc.), whereas others will be seen during short- and long-term counseling.

Elder abuse is most likely to occur when the needs of the elder are extensive and the ability and coping mechanisms of the caregiver to meet those needs are inadequate (Martin, 1987).

It is important to realize that psychological abuse can be profound and usually is an integral part of other aspects of abuse. The elderly are often threatened with being placed in a nursing home if they reveal physical/sexual/financial abuse. Living with constant threats of being placed outside the home, threats of increased physical abuse, or having medicine withheld is extremely debilitating. If the elderly are physically impaired, they soon realize their dependence on the abusing caregiver.

The reactions of the elderly to abuse are not unlike those of other victims. Their reactions can range from becoming very passive to severe anxiety resulting in suicide. Their abuse can produce increased confusion and disorientation, verbal withdrawal and referral of all questions to the abusing caregiver, cowering in the presence of the caregiver, and fearfulness.

If the elderly are suffering from an organic brain dysfunction (such as Alzheimer's disease), their abuse may go undetected. The inability to communicate or disconnected and disoriented communication makes it difficult for others to observe the abuse. Often because of organic brain dysfunction of the elderly, we are seeing increased levels of geriatricide/euthanasia. Society has reduced the usefulness of the elderly by measuring it to output.

Crisis intervention can be difficult with the elderly victim because of the situations listed above. Obviously if the victim is in physical danger, removal and reporting is mandatory. It may be difficult to find another placement for an elderly person. If the elderly have extensive medical problems, their options may be limited to medical or nursing home placement, depending on their insurance or ability to pay. If they are medically disabled, the use of domestic violence shelters may not be an option. Requesting help from family members or friends may become necessary as well. In recent years, community elder day care facilities have been established. The overall emphasis in the advocacy for the elderly has been a push away from permanent and long-term institutionalization.

Intervention needs to be looked at in preventive, not in crisis-oriented terms (Block & Sinnott, 1979; Steinmetz & Amsden, 1983). Intervention can be seen in terms of educational efforts for the caregiver and family to help them learn about the developmental characteristics of aging and helping them to assess the limits of their ability to provide care.

The Flint, Michigan, Task Force on Elder Abuse (Cherry & Allen, 1983) identified four problems in caring for the elderly:

a. A general lack of knowledge and understanding about the aging process;
b. A lack of awareness of the dynamics of elder abuse among both professionals and caregivers;
c. A lack of knowledge of ways to assist families with cases of abuse and to mobilize support networks for assisting families in crisis, and
d. A lack of family awareness of how to care for older persons who are dependent on them.

Therefore, during crisis intervention with the victim, it is imperative to work with the family and caregivers of the victim. Crisis intervention becomes multiperson-oriented in that intervention must be provided to both the victim and caregiver, jointly. The focus becomes not only the protection of the victim but an improvement in the quality of life for both the victim and the caregiver as well as improved coping skills for both.

Formal crisis intervention can focus on:

- Providing support to the families through the use of various local programs and services available to the elderly and caregivers of the elderly;

- Helping the caregiver locate programs such as Meals on Wheels, respite care, hospice, or other community services to relieve the stress of caregiving, as well as services directly related to the caregiver such as support groups for caregivers, which assist in relieving and validating stress;
- Teaching techniques for enhancing positive interactions and dealing with stress in support group settings or in individual counseling;
- Taking advantage of assertiveness training for both older persons and caregivers to ensure that needs are being vocalized and met;
- Investigating the option of protective placements (removing the victim from the care of the abuser by placing the victim in a nursing home, for example), taking into consideration the physical condition of the victim;
- Treating the family unit by using family systems therapy approaches; and
- Invoking legal action such as obtaining restraining orders or bringing criminal charges against the abuser (although with most elderly victims, these are seldom implemented). The elderly fear reprisal, loss of home, institutionalization, and embarrassment.

Other crisis intervention issues with victims may include their wish to protect the abuser, especially if it is their child. Because of ethical concerns, it is difficult for a counselor to report abuse without the willingness of the victim. Check the state laws in your area.

Helping victims come to terms with their fear of institutionalization and the lack of mobility and independence that accompany it may be an important factor in treatment. Elder abuse victims may see reporting abuse more as a punishment to themselves than as a solution to their problems, especially if reporting might result in their removal to institutionalized care.

Abuse within medical or institutionalized care is also difficult for the elderly victim to report. Most forms of abuse in this setting are geared toward overmedication or improper medication and neglect. This abuse tends to be both active (improper medication or overmedication) and passive (neglect or lack of stimulation). You may need to work with the family to help them make the necessary reporting and removal of the victim.

In crisis situations, it may be difficult to ascertain what is abuse and what isn't, especially if victims do not consider their situation to be abusive. Obviously, the question of client safety and their becoming a danger to themselves (suicide) is paramount. But what about less overt behaviors? Does neglect include failure to make an older adult follow a diet specialized for a given health condition? Or when does the use of body restraints because of senility cross the line and become abusive? What is necessary and what is abusive? Many normal age-related changes may lead the elderly to form dependent relationships, which, when added to other role losses, depression, and physical ill-ness, may lead to self-abuse, including suicide or the tendency to tolerate abuse.

Knowing when to intervene is a difficult problem. Some guidelines do exist and are listed in the Bicentennial Charter for Older Americans (Federal Council on Aging, 1976). These rights include the right to die with dignity.

Many steps that you may take in providing crisis intervention may spread over into short- or long-term counseling. The educational as-pects of your intervention may bypass the immediate crisis state and become part of your focus in short- and long-term counseling. Like-wise, any family systems work initiated in crisis intervention will be followed through in short- and long-term counseling.

The Ferguson-Beck H.A.L.F. is a valuable assessment tool (Fer-guson & Beck, 1983). It can assist you with observing and intervening in dangerous elder abuse environments. This tool helps you focus on issues such as elders' health, aged adult abuse dynamics, adult child caregiver risk dynamics, adult child caregiver abuse dynamics, living arrangements, and finances.

Client Concerns

- Fear of retaliation (applies to abuse both by a relative or by an institution);
- Fear of relocation;
- Embarrassment by being abused by relative/child;
- Fear of having to go to court;
- Fear of institutionalization;
- Fear of further abuse/death; and
- Fear of having food or medication withheld.

Secondary Victimizations

- Feeling of punishment because of relocation to another caregiver;
- Cost of institutionalized care if moved from a home to a medical care facility;
- Loss of relationship with caregiver;
- Loss of health or will to live after being relocated;
- Overmedication or insufficient medication;
- Neglect, confinement, lack of mental stimulation;
- Lack of local community services; and
- Lack of elder advocacy.

Social Services Needed

- Elderly advocate;
- Community services such as Meals on Wheels, Community Day;
- Care center, hospice, or respite care;
- Support groups for caregivers;
- Family systems therapy for family caregivers;
- Stress reduction education for both victim and caregiver; and
- Educational groups for caregivers.

SHORT-TERM COUNSELING

Issues in short-term counseling usually focus both on prevention and on helping the victim deal with previous abuse. More so in elder abuse than in any other type of abuse, it is difficult to remove the victim from the abusive environment. It is problematic to find replacement care for the elderly. Services are few and expensive, and often both the victim and the caregiver recognize this fact. Perhaps this is why so much effort seems to be invested in working with the abusive family member in hopes of creating a suitable environment through counseling and support services.

Because of the lack of available financial services, counselors are more likely to be in a position of working with both offenders and victims in elder abuse cases than with any other population of victims. Therefore, short-term counseling may focus on empowering victims through assertiveness training to help them meet their needs (if they are cognitively able to benefit from counseling) and on educating the caregiving family how to divide work loads, handle stress, utilize available community services to alleviate personal stress, and to become familiar with the aging and developmental processes of the elderly.

In some situations counselors feel they are not dealing with both victims and offenders but with two separate categories of victimization. Abusive family members are often viewed as victims of circumstance and as being in a "sandwich position" of caring for both their own children and their aging parent(s). The resulting amount of stress and perhaps the reduced mental ability of the aging parent(s) present an abusive experience for the caregiver. Some aging parents who are senile have hit, slapped, and verbally abused their caregivers. The line between who is the victim and who is the offender becomes blurred. In some cases, both parties are victims and both are offenders. This presents a unique counseling experience for the counselor! Client concerns and the need of both parties need to be considered and addressed.

For those elderly being abused in institutionalized care (nursing homes, hospitals, or home health care), counselors' efforts are aimed at assisting either elderly victims or their families in gathering resources to report the abuse. The reporting may be directed to state protective services or state regulatory commissions for medical care professions. Help in finding replacement care will also be necessary. Contacting local community services for a referral or calling state agencies for a recommendation might have to be considered.

Client Concerns

Elderly Client Concerns:

- Inability to report abuse effectively;
- Inability to recognize being abused;
- Fear of retaliation;
- Fear of relocation;
- Lack of knowledge of available support services and community services;
- Fear of having to go to court;
- Loss of relationship with the caregiver and the rest of the family;
- Fear of institutionalization; and
- Fear of increased abuse.

Caregiver Client Concerns:

- Lack of knowledge of available support services and community services;
- Fear of removal of elderly parent;
- Fear of judgment of family for removal of parent;
- Continued physical or verbal abuse by elderly parent;
- Guilt and shame;
- Lack of knowledge concerning aging and developmental processes of elderly parent;
- Increased stress of caregiving;
- Loss of relationship with other family members because of increase in caregiving;
- Increased financial responsibilities; and
- Lack of personal time alone.

Secondary Victimizations

- Cost of care to both the victim and caregiver;
- Fear of loss of relationship with caregiver and family;
- Loss of health and will to live if relocated;
- Loss of adequate care if abuse is reported; and
- Cost of medical care if abuse is perpetrated by family caregiver and the elderly are moved to a medical facility.

Social Services Needed

- Protection services if family cannot help;
- Hospice care;
- Respite care;
- Community services such as Meals on Wheels, Neighborly Senior Services, etc.;
- In-home medical or nursing care (home health care);
- Support groups for elderly;
- Support groups for caregivers and family;
- Community financial aid;
- Senior day care centers; and
- Nursing home/medical residential care.

LONG-TERM COUNSELING

Issues focusing on long-term counseling may be viewed as adaptive, especially for the elderly who will be staying with the abusive/also victimized caregiver. Helping both parties adapt to this new life-style and helping both face new limitations and new reductions in independence will help in their long-term ability to stay together.

The primary caregiver is not the only one who needs assistance with adjusting. The "breadwinner" who feels the added financial responsibility and the children who must "share" the attention of the caregiver are also in need of adaptive skills. Again, focusing on extended families and family systems therapy will be of assistance and will encourage all family members to join support groups that validate what they have lost through the caregiving of an elderly person in their home. Groups such as these also help caregivers see what they have gained through the addition of the elderly person. The elderly give unique gifts of retrospection, insight, and wisdom. They can add security and stability and provide friendship and camaraderie for other family members. Long-term counseling can aid in viewing the positives of the addition of the elderly to the family unit, not only the burdens.

Client Concerns

Elderly Client Concerns:

- Fear of becoming a burden;
- Financial aspects of long-term care;
- Fear of senility;
- Fear of death;
- Fear of institutionalization; and
- Fear of relocation.

Caregiver Client Concerns:

- Unsure of ability to provide long-term care;
- Financial aspects of long-term care;
- Fear of senility of the elder;
- Fear of death of the elder; and
- Cost of personal time for other family members.

Secondary Victimizations

- Emotional toll on both victim and caregiver of long-term caregiving;
- Financial concerns of both victim and caregiver of long-term caregiving; and
- Lack of knowledge of community services.

Social Services Needed

- Protective services if family cannot help;
- Community services;
- Hospice and respite care;
- Financial assistance;
- Medical care facilities;
- Support group for caregiver and family;
- Support group/counseling for victim;
- Education for both victim and family;
- Legal intervention, if necessary;
- Senior day care center; and
- Elderly advocate.

CONCLUSION

In recent years, legislation has been and is being passed to help develop unique and innovative programs designed to combat elder abuse and neglect effectively. Check to see what laws are on the books in your state.

RECOMMENDED READING

Cheatham, J. S. (1983, Spring). Physical abuse of the elderly. *Psychiatric Hospital*, pp. 102–103.

Ferguson, D., & Beck, C. (1983, Sept.-Oct.). Assessment tool: H.A.L.F.—A tool to assess elder abuse within the family. *Geriatric Nurse*, pp. 301–304.

Hickey, T., & Douglass, R. L. (1981). Neglect and abuse of the older family members: Professionals' perspectives and case experiences. *Gerontologist, 21,* 171–176.

O'Malley, T. A., Everitt, D. E., O'Malley, H. C., & Campion, E. W. (1983). Identifying and preventing family-mediated abuse and neglect of elderly persons. *Annals of Internal Medicine*, *98*, 998–1005.

Steuer, A., & Austin, B. (1980). Family abuse of the elderly. *Journal of the American Geriatric Society*, *28*, 190.

NATIONAL REFERRALS FOR ELDER ABUSE

American Association for Retired Persons
601 E St., NW
Washington, DC 20049
202-434-6270

Clearinghouse on Abuse and Neglect of the Elderly
College of Resources
University of Delaware
Newark, DE 19716

National Aging Resource Center on Elder Abuse
c/o APWA
810 2nd Street NE, Suite 500
Washington, DC 20002-4205
202-682-0100

National Committee for the Prevention of Elder Abuse
University Center on Aging
University of Massachusetts
Medical Center
55 Lake Ave.
North Worcester, MA 01655
508-856-2153

Overview of Elder Abuse

Crisis Intervention Issues:	Safety, working with caregivers, removal, institutionalization. Intervention needs to focus on educating caregiver and is preventive.
Short-Term Counseling:	Working with abusive caregiver, finding community and support services, assertiveness training for elderly victim, cognitive reframing of event for victim. Some may not realize they've been abused.
Long-Term Counseling:	Adaptation to new life-style of being cared for, finding long-term support and resources, helping victims adjust to any loss of health or physical problems from abuse.
Secondary Victimizations:	Cost of institutionalized care, over/under-medication, lack of community services, loss of relationship with abuser/caregiver.
Social Services Needed:	Elderly advocate, protective services, stress reduction education for caregiver, Meals-on-Wheels, respite care, support groups for victim and caregiver, financial aid, senior day care program.

ETHNIC VIOLENCE

- On January 16, 1989, a lone gunman killed five Southeast Asian children and wounded 30 others when he opened fire on a Stockton, California, schoolyard.
- In Raleigh, NC, a 24-year-old Chinese student was beaten to death outside a pool hall by White men who said they resent all Vietnamese because of the war.
- In LaVerne, California, four racist skinheads were arrested for a May 1989 attack of a family they thought were Jewish.

OVERVIEW OF ETHNIC VIOLENCE

Daniel O'Connell, a 19th-century Irish statesman, best defined bigotry when he said, "Bigotry has no head and cannot think; no heart and cannot feel. Her god is a demon, her decalogue is written in the blood of her victims" (As quoted in National Victim Center Newsletter, 1990).

Bigotry now has a new name—it's called enthnoviolence. Racial violence has long been a part of American history, sad to say. Arson, bombings, threats, assaults, acts of vandalism, and even murder have been part of our history. All of these continue to disrupt the lives of victims and the stability and unity of communities. Despite the long history of ethnic and racial violence, there have been few comprehensive efforts to develop prevention programs for victims of this type of violence.

Ethnic violence victims are those who have been persecuted because of their nationality, ethnicity, or religion. Ethnic violence includes criminal acts toward people based on their age, gender, race, ethnicity, religion, or political beliefs. Blacks and Jews were long the targets for most ethnic/racial violence; however, we now see surges in other areas of violence. Groups such as the Klu Klux Klan and the skinheads (neo-Nazi groups) blatantly display their hatred for selected groups of society. In addition, highly targeted populations today include the Hispanics, Cambodians, Laotians, Koreans, the Chinese, Vietnamese, Iranians, and groups with Buddhist, Islamic, and other religious affiliations.

Often the line between ethnoviolence and hate violence becomes blurred. Ethnic violence is hate violence and often the two are blended.

Hate is directed toward certain groups not only for their ethnicity, but also for their political beliefs, religion, or sexual orientation.

Some ethnic violence is fueled by attempts to gain control and power, and threats evoke a violent response as seen in:

a. Violation of territory/property ("us and them beliefs");
b. Violation of the sacred (values, beliefs, customs); and
c. Violation of status (perceived normalcy). (Ehrlich, 1990)

It seems that the motivation for hatred toward those ethnically different is fueled by the availability of telephone numbers that can be called to hear recorded messages that encourage prejudices, certain cable television programs that carry messages of an "us against them" mentality, and other verbal assaults by groups that attack others because they look, act, or feel different (National Victim Center, 1990).

Does it horrify us to know that most Americans believe that it is socially acceptable to use violence to achieve certain goals or to respond to insult? The use of violence for social control is seen as acceptable, whereas violence used to achieve social change is not considered acceptable (National Institute Against Prejudice and Violence, 1988).

It is interesting that ethnic/hate violence shows some contrasts to other types of crime. In hate-motivated crime, most abusers are strangers, more so than in non-hate motivated crimes. As opposed to other types of crime, hate-motivated crimes usually involve more than one perpetrator. Other assaults usually involve one victim and one perpetrator. In most non-hate motivated crimes many victims know their perpetrator, whereas in hate crimes most victims do not know the perpetrator. In non-hate crimes, such as a property crime, something of value is taken, but in hate-motivated crimes, something of value is damaged or destroyed (Berk, 1990). Victims of ethnoviolence report an average of almost two and one half times more symptoms than do victims of other types of violence and crime (Ehrlich, 1990).

Why is hate violence different from other types of crime? Can these differences influence our counseling approaches? Do they imply a need for more empirical research in this interesting analogy?

CRISIS INTERVENTION

It is not the purpose of this segment to duplicate information already given in other chapters. Ethnic violence is not treated here as a category of victimization but rather in terms of the population of victims. Therefore, it will be necessary for you to cross reference to the chapter that covers the *type* of victimization perpetrated against the victim (such as assault, rape, domestic violence, etc.). This chapter will cover issues that are *different* for this type of victim that you will want to consider in the three stages of counseling (crisis, short-term, and long-term). If your client was raped, or is a homicide survivor, for example, please refer to the particular chapter covering that subject in addition to what is listed here. That will give you the basics for handling that type of victimization. This section deals with idiosyncrasies of the victim of ethnic violence.

Ethnoviolence is widespread in America today, and only a small portion of this type of violence is ever reported. As a result, the prevalence of this type of violence is ignored or unknown. A study by the National Institute Against Prejudice and Violence (1986) indicated that 65% of their study group experienced multiple interconnected attacks. Physical attacks were the predominant form of violence. Victims of this type of abuse, of course, suffer various damaging effects.

The "survivor syndrome" of the Nazi Holocaust, for example, included severe affective, behavioral, and cognitive constriction. Depressed mood, survivor guilt, anxiety, and personality constriction also were common (Niederland, 1968). Yet the good news is that more recent studies of aging survivors indicate that they were found to have "remarkable resilience and psychological well-being" (Kahana, Harel, & Kahana, 1988). The study by Kahana et al. further indicated that the positive outcome was due to the fact that many survivors were able to draw a positive meaning from their experience in later stages of adult development.

Whereas some Holocaust victims seem to have adjusted well in later life, studies of Southeast Asian populations reveal a high incidence of posttraumatic stress disorder (PTSD) and major affective disorders among Cambodian refugees who experienced deprivation, physical injury or torture, sexual assault, incarceration in reeducation camps, and having to witness killing or torture (Kinzie, Fredrickson, Ben, Rleck, & Karis, 1984; Mollica, Wyshak, & Lavelle, 1987).

This information may have serious implications for our views in crisis intervention and the course of therapy itself. It is easy to see that both Holocaust survivors and the Cambodians were subjected to the same types of victimization. Both experienced deprivation, physical injury and torture, sexual assault, incarceration in camps, and the witnessing of killing or torture.

Why the differences between ethnic populations in terms of coping style and recovery? Is it simply because we have yet to interview an aging Cambodian population to see if the victimization experiences have been integrated in a positive manner into their present life-style? Or are there some other implications for counseling here? Are there implications for specific counseling techniques in the crisis intervention phase? McCann and Pearlman (1990) indicated their belief that the Cambodians had more recently experienced the devastation to self and to their social world. This included the obvious physical destruction of their country, the genocide of their people, the destruction of their cultural values, and the relocation to a culture very different from their own.

As opposed to the Holocaust survivors, Cambodian survivors, according to some reports, show an ongoing pattern of avoidance that lasts for many years, and intrusive symptoms that worsen with exposure to new life stressors (Kinzie, 1988). The long-term effects have been seen in psychosomatic blindness among Camodian women who witnessed atrocities committed against their loved ones (Smith, 1989, reporting the research of Gretchen Van Boemel).

These studies reveal that PTSD bypasses cultural boundaries and is a normative reaction to abnormal events. They reveal that counseling the ethnically different client may be similar in terms of PTSD reactions but very different in terms of social systems support and other cultural aspects that influence recovery.

For instance, ethnic groups face a number of problems in reporting abuse and obtaining services. For some, their communication in English is so poor that they are unable to make their needs known to authorities or counselors. This is particularly crucial in crisis intervention, in which victims may be hysterical or in shock. Without an interpreter, they may be unable to receive services or may receive inadequate services because of the communication deficit.

Crisis intervention must still focus on stabilization, which may be difficult at best if communication is poor. Educating victims about available services is important, especially among ethnic populations who may feel misplaced or feel that the United States couldn't possibly be concerned with their victimization. Many may be afraid to report because of illegal immigration status. Showing acceptance of the victims as persons, and conveying to them their right to proper treatment and services will help them to reach out and accept services that are available.

Additionally, all phases of counseling will need to address an area of fear for ethnic victims—that they were targeted because they are different. They were not random victims of crime. People can face more easily the fact that they have been victims of a random crime, but find it difficult to face the knowledge that they were selected as targets because they are from the culture that the perpetrator hates.

Client Concerns

- Being deported, if here illegally;
- Lack of ability to communicate effectively;
- Fear or retaliation to themselves or their families;
- Fear of lack of concern or fear of not being believed;
- Not understanding our laws, systems, or services; and
- Having to accept laws, systems, or services that are contrary to their cultural/religious beliefs.

Secondary Victimizations

- Prejudices of system caregivers;
- Communication problems based on language skills;
- Loss of income because of victimization;
- Loss of income to send to family members in other countries;
- Retaliation, sometimes by their own family, for reporting;
- Shame over their culture or their country; and
- Feeling "second class."

Social Services Needed

The social services utilized for any other type of victimization can be utilized with ethnic victims. In addition, however, you may need an interpreter and may need to structure group therapy around ethnic values, keeping in mind services that may violate victims' belief systems.

SHORT-TERM COUNSELING

For a counselor to work effectively with a client from an ethnic minority, it is important that the counselor have specific didactic and experiential knowledge of the client's culture, and an awareness of the ways in which the client's cultural patterns have interacted with the majority culture (Sue, Akutusu, & Higashi, 1987). This is particularly important when counseling is going to extend past crisis intervention into short- and long-term counseling. This may well call for the counselor to do research in the area of the ethnic culture focusing on values, belief systems, rituals, ceremonies, superstitions, how family systems are developed and maintained, and other important information. Without this, the counselor may well advance into areas that clients might deem to be a violation of their customs or beliefs.

A major problem in beginning the counseling process with ethnic minority clients is that cultural differences are still so confusing to them and they may not understand our programs, theories, or therapies. Likewise, counselors are often unaware of clients' cultural family dynamics or strong sexist beliefs or roles. Beliefs, value systems, family structure and dynamics, rituals, and religions also play a significant part in relating, and familiarity with these areas allows us to enter the world of those affected by ethnic violence.

Also crucial to working with many different ethnic populations is the understanding of what is called "chain migration." Extended family members pool their limited financial resources in order to send to the United States the family member considered most likely to find a job. That person then sends money to relatives back in their native country to support them and to enable certain others to migrate to the United States (Buchanan, 1979; Laguerre, 1984; Seligman, 1977). The new arrivals often share quarters with their benefactors until they can locate their own housing. Moving away is particularly important to a child who is being abused by an extended family member who has supported the child's caregiver to get here to the United States. Likewise, this information about "chain migration" could be important if a woman is involved in domestic violence, or if a family member has been a victim of a crime that was nonfamilial, yet the crime cost the family financially, and that outlay of money (because of the crime) was the money that was usually sent back to their native country for survival.

Most ethnic minorities are so disillusioned by the continuation of violence once they have reached the "promised land" of the United States that they do not reach out. Many have undergone violence and persecution in their own countries only to find it also here. Some who do reach out meet with prejudices within our "systems" of criminal justice, law enforcement, and mental health. Many are here illegally and fear they will be turned in to immigration, therefore they are reluctant to receive services or even to report a crime. Some do not recognize the victimization as a crime, especially in some cases of spouse abuse or elder or child abuse, which are not considered to be violations in their culture. In some cultures, any reporting of domestic violence is seen as the ultimate betrayal and an attempt to strip a male head of household of his power and authority.

Many prejudices exist toward ethnic groups. Most group members are well aware of the stereotypes and negative images associated with their culture. Because of these prejudices, many do not reach out for help following a victimization. This could be significant, for instance, for members of the Haitian culture because many Americans associate their influx into our country with the AIDS epidemic. A young Haitian woman who has been raped or assaulted and is bleeding may fear asking for help based on her knowledge of the existing AIDS phobia associated with her nationality. Given the AIDS phobia and the severe hatred toward Haitians because Americans feel they have brought the virus to this country, many Haitians and other ethnic populations may be forced to deny their own heritage. Some are ashamed to be associated with their native country and culture.

Finally, the lack of skills in the English language may prevent any real formal counseling sessions. It may also inhibit the use of group therapy, or other types of therapy normally used with victims of violent crime.

Client Concerns

- Language barrier that prevents ongoing counseling;
- Language barrier that may prevent participation in group or other treatment programs;
- Culture does not accept the concept of counseling;
- Financial loss;
- Prejudices from system caregivers;
- Fear of retaliation against self or family;
- Fear that relatives in their native country may insist they come home because of their victimization here;
- Shame for their culture or their country; and
- Not understanding the laws, systems, or services here.

Secondary Victimizations

- Language barrier;
- Lack of insurance or ability to provide for self while recuperating;
- Financial loss;
- Loss of trust in the United States and the "American dream";
- Being reprimanded by family for reporting; and
- Not understanding laws, systems, or services here.

Social Services Needed

The social services utilized for any other type of victimization can be utilized with ethnic victims. In addition, however, you may need an interpreter and may need to structure group therapy around ethnic values, keeping in mind services that may violate victims' belief systems. Whether or not family systems therapy would work may well be based on the culture and belief systems of your clients and their families.

LONG-TERM COUNSELING

Understanding the culture of your client will be important in ascertaining the possibility of long-term counseling. The concept of counseling itself may be novel for certain populations and may be interpreted as a sign of "weakness," an affront to "maleness," or lack of ability to act as "head of the household." Therefore, long-term counseling may not be a realistic option for clients from certain cultures. Perhaps group counseling for ethnic minority clients from similar cultures and similar victimizations may prove successful for you and your clients.

Again, the barrier of the English language may be an obstacle for formal counseling sessions or the inclusion of group sessions. Exploring the utilization of a counselor who is from the same ethnic background to run a group for those victimized in a similar way may be effective. Lacking that, the roadblocks of language, transportation, and cultural acceptance of the counseling process may rupture the counseling relationship.

An important aspect to consider in long-term counseling is the possibility of building a solid relationship not only with the victim but with the family as well, especially if the culture is one in which the entire family is seen as a "unit." The separateness of identity is not considered as important in many cultures as it is in American culture. What we may term "enmeshment" may well be the stable condition of the family unit in another culture.

Educating ethnic minority victims and family about how our culture's laws work in terms of helping the victim, how our systems are geared toward catching the perpetrator, and how our services are here to equip the victim with the necessary tools for healing will go a long ways toward "opening up" our culture to them.

Informing ethnic minority victims of their rights not only as victims but as persons living in the United States; teaching them positive coping mechanisms; training them in preventing further victimization; suggesting counseling and other community services available to them; role modeling accepting, nonprejudicial behaviors toward their culture and customs; promoting ways of healthy resolution and adaptation to our culture; and respecting the integrity of their belief systems, cultural values, and religious affiliations are all integral parts of the counseling experience, both for you and for them!

Counseling, advocating for, and working with culturally different clients is an affirmative way of getting to know the world around us! Helping these clients through the pain of victimization in their new land is a kind hand extended.

Client Concerns

- Language barrier that prevents ongoing counseling or group counseling;
- Culture does not accept the concept of counseling;
- Loss of "maleness" or loss of feeling as "head of household" if a male victim accepts counseling;
- Prejudices from system caregivers and criminal justice system;
- Financial losses both to the family here and the family in their native country to whom they were sending money;
- Fear or retaliation for self or family;
- Not understanding laws, systems, or services here; and
- Lack of transportation to stay involved in long-term counseling.

Secondary Victimizations

- Language barrier;
- Lack of insurance or ability to provide for self while recuperating;
- Financial loss;
- Loss of "maleness" or perceived "head of household" status of male victims;
- Loss of trust in the United States and the "American dream";
- Being reprimanded by family for reporting; and
- Time off work and additional financial loss for counseling sessions and court appearances.

Social Services Needed

The social services utilized for any other type of victimization can be utilized with ethnic victims. In addition, however, you may need an interpreter and may need to structure group therapy around ethnic values, keeping in mind services that may violate victims' belief systems. Whether or not family systems therapy would work may well be based on the culture and belief systems of your clients and their families.

CONCLUSION

Within recent years, counseling professionals have shown increasing interest in understanding and counseling victims from different cultures. Until recently, those in the mental health occupations may have inflamed multicultural problems by not understanding cultural differences inherent in working with victims of ethnic violence.

AACD has organizations formed to work with culturally different populations. Contact AACD for more information.

RECOMMENDED READING

Allport, G. (1954). *The nature of prejudice*. Reading, MA: Addison-Wesley.

Grimshaw, A. (1969). *Racial violence in the United States*. Chicago: Aldine.

Ogawa, B. (1990). *Color of justice*. Sacramento: State of California.
Racially motivated violence. (1983). Hearings before the Subcommit-
    tee on Criminal Justice, U.S. Congress, House Committee on the
    Judiciary, 97th Congress, March 4, June 3, and November 12, 1981.
    Serial No. 135, 1983.
Wright, F., & Wright, P. (1982, Summer). *Violent groups, Group 6*.

REFERRALS

National Hate Crime Hotline
1-800-347-HATE

National Institute Against Prejudice and Violence
525 West Redwood Street
Baltimore, MD 21201
301-528-5170

 Overview of Ethnic Violence	
Crisis Intervention Issues:	Affective, cognitive, and behavioral constriction; having witnessed their own country destroyed; genocide of their people; relocation to different culture; difficulty in reporting crime because of language; afraid of deportation.
Short-Term Counseling:	May be disillusioned in America because of crime; feeling targeted because they are different; don't understand our laws, systems, and services; adapting coping mechanisms to cultural belief system.
Long-Term Counseling:	May not engage in long-term counseling because of cultural beliefs; bridging relationship of counselor with extended family members; education on law, services.
Secondary Victimizations:	Abuse ignored because they are not American; limited community resources geared to their language, prejudices by resource providers and systems; financial losses because of lost work time.
Social Services Needed:	The social services that would apply to anyone suffering particular types of victimization. See charts for robbery, sexual abuse, homicide, etc. Additionally, an interpreter and group counseling geared toward a particular ethnic population might be needed.

HATE/GAY VIOLENCE

- One in 5 gay men and 1 in 10 lesbian women have been victimized through physical assaults because of their sexual orientation (National Gay and Lesbian Task Force, 1984).
- Thirty-four percent of gays have been verbally abused (National Gay and Lesbian Task Force, 1984).
- Violence to gays more than doubled from 1985 to 1986, and is still rising (National Gay and Lesbian Task Force, 1987).
- A 1984 study by the National Gay and Lesbian Task Force indicated that 94% of the study population had experienced some type of victimization (including verbal abuse, physical assault, police abuse, weapon assault, vandalism, or being spat upon, chased or followed, or pelted with objects).

OVERVIEW OF HATE/GAY VIOLENCE

Hate violence is directed toward various segments of the population, predominantly the gay population, but it is not limited to that population. Hate violence is seen in ethnic victimization as well as victimization targeted at people because of their gender, race, religion, political beliefs, age, physical condition, and sexual orientation. Because so much hate violence is directed at the gay population, we have chosen to link hate violence with that population (both homosexual men and lesbian women). However, be aware as a counselor that many other populations can be targeted as well.

Moreover, hate/gay violence is not a category of victimization but rather a population of victims. Therefore, it will be necessary for you to consult the chapter that covers the *type* of victimization perpetrated against a gay victim (such as assault, rape, domestic violence, etc.). This chapter will cover issues that are unique for this type of victim that you will want to consider in the three stages of counseling (crisis intervention, short-term, and long-term). The idiosyncrasies of this type of victim are covered here.

With the panic epidemic surrounding AIDS and ARC (AIDS-related complex), it is being debated whether there is truly an increase in hate and gay violence or whether it is just becoming more focused. "AIDS is probably less a cause of anti-gay sentiment than it is a new focus

and justification for expressions of preexisting anti-gay prejudice"
(Herek & Glunt, 1988). Gays and lesbians have become more visible
through the AIDS epidemic, both politically and through media attention surrounding political issues and AIDS deaths. Although this attention may lead to better understanding of gay issues, it has triggered
hostility toward lesbians and gays and made them more identifiable
targets for potential victimizers (Berrill, 1990). Hate groups have identified gays as targets similarly to Blacks and Jews (Segrest & Zeskind,
1989).

What has increased through the AIDS epidemic is societal homophobia. This has lead to a moral neutralization and a "denial of the
victim" (Sykes & Matza, 1957). This denial strips the victims of moral
worth as human beings and proves they are worthy of punishment for
violating gender norms. The offender can not only be excused from
any blame but can be seen as performing some type of gender justice
and helping to protect the natural order of gender-appropriate behavior
(Harry, 1990). Societal homophobia has increased stigmatization. Our
society is predominantly heterosexual. The gay population is stigma-
tized by: (a) what society views as a violation of gender norms, (b)
what society views as deviating from masculine or feminine characteristics, and (c) societal condemnation for those who do not conform
to gender roles regardless of their actual sexual orientation (Herek,
1990).

Our society values heterosexuality, which is an "ideological system
that denies, denigrates, and stigmatizes any nonheterosexual form of
behavior, identity, relationship, or community" (Herek, 1990). This
becomes the preliminary set-up for gay abuse. Because we think of
America as being primarily heterosexual, anything that runs against
the norm is attacked through violent means.

Somehow people in the mainstream society think that hatred and
violence toward those of different nationalities, religions, or sexual
orientation will protect them from the exact stigma that society hates
in the victims. Additionally, this hate violence may actually serve a
"value expressive" function to abusers by helping them express their
own personal values (Herek, 1990). It can also serve "social-expres-
sive" functions by assisting those involved in this violence to win
approval from others (family, peers and neighbors, or gang members
involved in the violence), thus increasing the abusers' own sense of
self-esteem (Herek) or demonstrating loyalty (Weissman, 1978). It can
serve a "defensive" function by helping abusers resolve psychological
conflicts surrounding their own sexuality or gender. Some suggest that

those involved in gay violence are symbolizing unacceptable aspects of their own personalities or their own latent homosexuality (Herek). Some abusers involved in male-male sexual assaults wish to punish the victim as a means of coping with previously unaddressed conflicts surrounding their sexual interests (Groth & Burgess, 1980). Thus, engaging in gay violence can become a means in which the abuser diverts personal internalized conflict by directing it outward to a symbol that is then violently attacked.

But violence toward gays has also been seen as recreational violence for youth who are struggling to establish their own status with their peers (Harry, 1990). It provides little risk of injury, immediate status in the eyes of peers, direct and corroborative evidence of their virility, minimal risk of being arrested because most gays do not report, and validation of their maleness. We as mental health counselors recognize that hate violence toward others does not change them to what the abuser wants the victims to be, but only represses them.

Gays have historically been a target for abuse. Gays were often singled out by the Nazis for persecution and murder. In the concentration camps, homosexuals were often assigned the most hideous work details and were subjected to medical experiments that included castration, hormone injections, mutilation, and exposure (Adam, 1987; Plant, 1986).

Here in the United States, the treatment of gays has not been much better. They have been abused in every conceivable manner and this abuse is notably widespread. However, little is known about how widespread the homicide rate is for gays/lesbians. The NGLTF (National Gay and Lesbian Task Force, 1989) has its own estimates, but states that these probably underestimate sharply the magnitude of the problem. If the police are unaware if the homicide victim was gay, the records would not indicate a gay death. Documentation in this area is difficult and is currently weak. Attacks are usually extremely brutal. A study indicated that seldom is a homosexual simply shot, but is more apt to be stabbed a dozen or more times, mutilated, and strangled (Miller & Humphreys, 1980). There is a gruesome viciousness to the crimes involving gay killings.

In the study, the task force found gender differences regarding the rates of victimization. Men experienced greater levels of verbal harassment (by nonfamilial members), threats, victimization in school and by police, and most types of physical violence and intimidation. Lesbians experienced higher rates of verbal harassment by family members and greater fear of anti-gay violence (NGLTF, 1984). They experienced higher levels of discrimination than did men (Aurand, Gross, & Adessa, 1985; Gross, Aurand, & Adessa, 1988). Both homosexuals and lesbians suffered comparable rates of familial physical abuse, men being abused in gay settings and women in non-gay settings. Black or Hispanic gays were more likely to experience threats and violence than their White counterparts, producing a "double jeopardy" of living in a society in which both racial and anti-gay prejudice are widespread.

Hate/gay crime offenders have been linked to organizations such as neo-Nazi groups known as The Order, the White Patriot Party, Aryan Nation, and skinheads—which were by far the most numerous and brutal of all the hate groups (NGLTF, 1989). "Gay bashers" tend to be White young men aged 21 or younger acting together with others in a small group.

Hate-motivated violence tends to perpetrated by strangers. It is speculated that this is so because it is during interactions (violence) with strangers that stereotypes can dominate abusers' perceptions, and the abuser may be in a better position to experience emotional distancing from the victim so that feelings of hostility can be physically acted upon and acted out (Berk, 1990).

Hate/gay violence is not limited to gay neighborhoods, although it is seen in great numbers in those areas. It also has been tracked to colleges, and seems to be widespread at the high school and junior high school levels. The consequences at the school level are seen in truancy and dropping out (Hunter & Schaecher, 1990). Violence toward youth also is believed to be associated with violence toward self, as manifested in suicidal behavior (Gibson, 1989; Hunter & Schaecher). Equally dangerous is the home setting in which verbal insults, intimidation, and physical violence occur. But nowhere is gay abuse as minimized or as inescapable as in jails, prisons, and correction facilities. Homosexuals are disproportionately raped in these settings compared to other men (Wooden & Parker, 1982). Attacks are often ignored and sometimes encouraged by prison officials.

A few years ago when I attended a National Organization for Victim Assistance (NOVA) conference, I listened in horror as a gay man told his story of incredible violence perpetrated against him. Two "straight" men followed him as he left a gay hangout and jumped him midway home. They dragged him into a nearby park, where they beat him nearly unconscious with a baseball bat, called him "fag and queer," and told him this would change his sexual preference. They raped him through instrumentation by rectally inserting the baseball bat and beat his testicles and penis with the baseball bat until they were 10 times their normal size. The injury was nearly fatal. They removed and stole his clothes, beating him further and leaving him for dead.

He regained consciousness and was forced to wander the streets nude, bleeding from the rectum, with a face so swollen he didn't even look human. He went from door to door trying to get someone to help him. Many shut the door and refused to help. One lady finally gave him a sheet, asked him not to bleed on her floor, and phoned the police. When the police arrived, their attitude was "this is another fag beating." He was treated as a second-class citizen and was further humiliated when he reached the hospital. He remained in the hospital for 6 weeks. His offenders were picked up and released on bail. They followed him, phoned him, and terrorized him further. When his case finally went to court, the offenders were released on probation. The jury was not as sympathetic as they might have been toward a heterosexual.

CRISIS INTERVENTION

Gays are often blamed for their own physical and sexual victimization. When they are raped, they are not taken as seriously as heterosexual victims. As gay victims struggle with normal feelings following a victimization such as the need to feel the world is a just and safe place, they also may feel they have been justifiably punished for being gay (Bard & Sangrey, 1979; Lerner, 1970). Self-blame (I am gay, they chose me to victimize because I am gay) can lead to feelings of depression and helplessness (Janoff-Bulman, 1979).

There are significant issues surrounding "coming out" (self-identification as being gay) for gays/lesbians. Being victims of a crime may force them into a position of coming out sooner than they would have been ready, or may put them in a vulnerable position once disclosure of their gayness has been made. If the coming out was forced because of the need to report a gay violence incident, they may not be in a position of having requisite social support from the gay community that could assist with their psychological resilience and coping skills (Miranda & Storms, 1989). Therefore, many gays minimize and deny the painful impact of the victimization. This tactic leads either to intensification or a delay in the appearance of psychological problems (Anderson, 1982; Koss & Burkhart, 1989; Myers, 1989) and may even delay any type of medical or physical treatment.

Gay victims are often "double" victims. They closet not only their gay life-style, but also their victimization. Add to that the problem of

AIDS (if it exists) and victims have closeted most of the significant struggles of their life: their gay life-style, their victimization, and AIDS.

During sexual assaults, lesbians may be targeted directly for abuse because they are lesbians. They also may be raped "opportunistically" when the abuser inadvertently discovers during another type of crime that a woman is lesbian and feels she is an open target because she is not under the protection of a man (heterosexual relationship) (Garnets, Herek, & Levy, 1990). In a gay male rape, some specifics can affect counseling. Even among gays, there is a general premise that sexual assault of a man is impossible without consent. Gays may struggle not only with accepting that the rape was real but that it happened at all. If they did not fight or struggle, they may question their own willing participation or compliance with the violence. If the victim ejaculated during the course of the sexual assault, further complications are added (Groth & Burgess, 1980) because the victim feels his own physiological response was evidence of personal involvement or consent to the sexual assault. Gays may perceive rape to be punishment for their gay life-style.

Gay persons' "significant others" are not treated as a covictims or affected family members because of their "illicit and illegal relationship." Unlike immediate family, they may be denied visitation in the emergency or hospital room, or may not be recognized for family treatment or therapy by counselors, social workers, or victim assistance agencies.

Legal protection and legal recognition do not exist for the gay population. Areas that often are unprotected and overlooked are housing, employment, and other services, largely because gay relationships do not hold a legal status. Many gay and lesbian parents lose custody of their children after disclosure of their sexual orientation, which can also happen after a crime (Falk, 1989).

Gays often have to struggle more after a victimization because they have fewer social supports than do other types of victims. Being blamed for their own victimization isolates them from social services, community support, pastoral counseling, and other types of services. This lack of support often adds to their own feelings of guilt and self-blame. They often suffer alone in fear of exposure and further victimization, or they may not be willing to tell authorities all pertinent information because they do not want to reveal their sexual orientation. In addition, some gays have encountered resistance and resentment for coming out during an incident of violence, which adds to the dilemmas of the already attacked gay community and gay rights movement. This can happen in the gay community just as it happens in society at large— when people feel the need to reduce their own feelings of vulnerability, they blame victims. Gay victims may be blamed for being "obvious" in their dress, behavior, or gestures (Garnets et al., 1990). In situations such as this, the gay community becomes an abuser not an advocate, thus imparting a secondary victimization.

As a counselor, you will need to examine your own feelings about homosexuality and lesbianism and any prejudices you may have about these issues. If you are not comfortable with same-gender relationships, refer your clients elsewhere. The potential of damaging the victim further by slips of the tongue or transferred attitudes and prejudices is always present. Keeping up with current information on gay identity and mental health issues is important. Also, the issue of confidentiality is especially important with gay clients because of the many ramifications that disclosure of their sexual orientation may bring (loss of job, home, children, legal prosecution, etc.). The victim has already been victimized once. Don't be the cause of a secondary victimization.

Client Concerns

- Disclosure of their sexual orientation;
- More abuse after disclosure of sexual orientation;
- For male sexual abuse victims, concern about not preventing or fighting off offender;
- For female sexual abuse victims, being raped by opportunist based on their lesbianism; and
- Fear of disclosing victimization and how disclosure will affect gay community.

Secondary Victimizations

- "Double victim"—being victimized because of sexual orientation as well as by crime;
- Exclusion of "significant others" from counseling, legal proceedings, or emergency medical treatment;
- Victimization following forced "coming out" and revealing sexual orientation because of the crime;
- Lack of adequate social services available to gays;
- Prejudiced social service providers;

- Prejudiced criminal justice system;
- Victim blaming by systems designed to help;
- Removal of natural children from custody after forced "coming out";
- Committing suicide after being victimized for being gay; and
- Lack of support from family because of sexual preference.

Social Services Needed

The social services utilized for any other type of victimization can be utilized for gay victims. However, in addition, you may need to check services such as counseling, and group and family therapy that may be offered through the gay community. Beware of counselors' prejudices that could further injure the victim.

SHORT-TERM COUNSELING

Issues during short-term counseling will need to encompass victims' feelings of their "symbolic status" that leads to hate-motivated violence (Grimshaw, 1969; Sterba, 1969; Nieburg, 1972) and their being targeted primarily because of their membership in a social category (Grimshaw, 1969). In addition, if this "symbolic status" violence served as a "message catalyst" for members of the victim's social or actuarial category, other prospective assailants, public officials, and the public at large (Berk, 1972; Nieburg, 1972), the victim may struggle with additional guilt regarding the possibility of additional violence to others.

Those targeted for gay violence often feel "exposed" when their sexual orientation is revealed, so they limit contact with the rest of the world, which increases their feelings of isolation. Some men are stereotyped as powerless and are called "sissies" or "pansies," and the women may be stereotyped as powerful and called "dykes." Those that struggle with the feelings of being too weak or too strong may have a difficult time dealing with the aftermath of violence and may suffer an impaired ability to recover.

Issues in counseling hate/gay violence victims will need not only to address the violence and any PTSD reactions, but also social hostility, isolation, stigmatization, and oppression. Assisting these victims to find supportive friends and available services will help them to feel accepted as human beings and help to reduce the stigmatization of being gay victims.

Helping victims to direct anger constructively is important. Gay victims feel targeted because of their sexuality, as opposed to random crime victims. This can produce overwhelming feelings of anger. Channeling anger into activities such as lobbying for antigay violence or helping other victims reduces anger and empowers the victim to feel constructive. Self-defense classes also can help victims feel they can reconstruct some avenues of safety in their life.

Conveying to victims' "significant others" and also to family members what victims are feeling is helpful in educating the family about postvictimization. However, do not overlook helping "significant others" and family members express their feelings about the crime. They are overlooked populations of secondary victims.

Client Concerns

- Disclosure of their sexual orientation;
- Fear of increased abuse based on disclosure of sexual orientation;
- Fear of impact of disclosure of victimization on gay community at large;
- Social hostility;
- Stigmatization;
- Isolation;
- Oppression;
- Overwhelming feelings of anger; and
- The effects of the crime on relationships.

Secondary Victimizations

- Prejudiced social services, criminal justice, and other systems designed to help;
- Significant others not being recognized or included in counseling or legal and medical procedures;
- Being "double victims"—victimized by the crime itself and being targeted because they are gay;
- Youths (and others) attempting/completing suicide because of the victimization surrounding their gayness; and

- Having to modify behavior and places they go to reduce risk of further attacks.

Social Services Needed

The social services utilized for any other victims of this type crime would be utilized for gay victims. However, in addition, you may need to check the availability of counseling, family therapy, support groups, and other services that may be available through the gay community.

LONG-TERM COUNSELING

Issues in long-term counseling may focus at length on victims' feelings of being singled out and targeted because of their sexual orientation. Educating them to understand their victimization in a social context will help them see that the crime was based more on a global hatred for gays rather than their being personal targets for the perpetrator (Garnets et al., 1990).

If victims felt forced into coming out only because of the victimization, this will increase their feelings of exposure, vulnerability, lack of control, fear of homophobia, and alienation. You may need to separate the experiences of the victimization from the coming-out experience and process them separately (Garnets et al., 1990).

The trauma associated with the violence may become internalized as being connected to the survivors' homosexuality or lesbianism. This can increase the psychosocial problems they already have that are associated with being gay, and can also lead to problems with their community involvement (Garnets et al., 1990).

Psychoeducation and general education surrounding PTSD and victimization are important treatment issues for victims. Helping survivors find constructive avenues for change regarding the way the world reacts to violence will help them construct a positive view of themselves and aid them in feeling they have some control over their lives. The community also benefits as former victims help make lasting changes in the way humanity treats and mistreats its members. Victims have always been the front-runners in prevention programming.

Those who are dying of AIDS also have had to contend not only with the agony of their death, but with the fear, reprisal, and hatred of the community and even their medical caregivers. Clearly, there are difficulties for gays that may not exist for other types of victims. There are different needs and considerations when working with those who have been victims of gay or hate violence.

Client Concerns

- Feelings of being singled out for victimization because of sexual orientation;
- Anger over victimization;
- Fear of retribution;
- "Coming-out" issues and fear of increased abuse because of disclosure;
- Vulnerability;
- Lack of safety and control;
- The effects of coming out on the family;
- How the violence will affect relationships; and
- AIDS contracted from sexual abuse.

Secondary Victimizations

- Effects of "coming out" on family and other relationships;
- AIDS scare from sexual abuse;
- Result of victimization on current relationships; and
- Prejudice of medical, legal, and psychological systems.

Social Services Needed

The social services that would be utilized for any other victims of this type of crime would be utilized with gay victims. However, in addition, you may need to consider counseling, social services, and family therapy that may be available through the gay community.

RECOMMENDED READING

National Association of Social Work. (1984, Summer). Working with gay and lesbian clients. *Practice Digest*, 7 (1).
National Gay Task Force. (1984, June). *Anti-gay/lesbian victimization: A study*. New York, NY: Author.

U.S. Commission on Civil Rights. (1983, January). *Intimidation and violence: Racial and religious bigotry in America.* Clearinghouse Publication 77. Washington, DC: Author.

NATIONAL REFERRALS FOR HATE VIOLENCE

Center For Democratic Renewal
P.O. Box 50469
Atlanta, GA 30302
404-221-0025

Human Rights Resource Center
30 N. Pan Pedro Rd., Suite 140
San Rafael, CA 94903
415-499-7463

National Institute Against Prejudice and Violence
31 South Greene Street
Baltimore, MD 21201
301-328-5170

NATIONAL REFERRALS FOR GAY VIOLENCE

National Gay & Lesbian Task Force
1517 U Street, NW
Washington, DC 20009
202-332-6483

	**Overview of Hate/Gay Violence**
Crisis Intervention Issues:	Targeted because different, targeted because of sexual orientation, fear, guilt, being blamed for their own victimization.
Short-Term Counseling:	Sexual orientation confusion, forced "coming out," feelings about "symbolic status," PTSD reactions, isolation, stigmatization, oppression.
Long-Term Counseling:	Understanding victimization in social context, lack of control, homophobia, alienation, psychosocial aspects of homosexuality, PTSD reactions, personal safety/self-defense.
Secondary Victimizations:	Society's homophobia, abuse ignored, changing the way they dress, places they go, how they act, significant others not included in social services/counseling, prejudice of systems providing care.
Social Services Needed:	The same type of services that would be offered to any other victims of that particular crime (see chapters on robbery, sexual abuse, homicide, etc.). In addition, you may want to find what services are offered by the gay community.

6

Domestic Violence

Patricia S. Gerard

- Battering is the single major cause of injury to women— more frequent than automobile accidents, muggings, and rapes combined (U.S. Surgeon General, 1984).
- As many as 15 million adult women have been victims of battering, rape, and other forms of physical and sexual assault (Crime Vicitims Digest, 1989).
- Each year, a million or more women are added to the total listed above for battering and other forms of violence (Crime Victims Digest, 1989).
- The recidivism rate for men who have had treatment for abusing their wives ranges from 30% to 40% (Saunders, 1988).

THE CYCLE OF VIOLENCE

Most domestic violence refers to rape, robbery, aggravated assault, or simple assault committed against a married, divorced, or separated woman by a relative or other person well known to the victim (U.S. Department of Justice, 1986). Contrary to popular belief and current myths, family violence cuts across all racial and economic lines. Victims come from all types of homes. Domestic violence has cut into the fabric of our community and touches lives of people of all ages and diverse occupations and professions (U.S. Attorney General's Task

Force on Family Violence, 1984). The major difference in family violence from other categories of violence is the relationship between the victim and the assailant.

Violence that is committed against a stranger is considered to be an assault. When violence is committed against a family member it is considered a family argument. Violence against a stranger usually ends in an arrest and the perpetrator is charged with assault and battery. Participants in family violence are told to "cool down" (U.S. Attorney General, 1984).

To understand any type of domestic or family violence, we must understand the cycle that violence inevitably goes through until it explodes and the physical act of violence occurs (see Figure 6–1). We will explain this as it pertains to domestic/family violence, although the same cycle would apply to any type of physical violence (child or elder abuse, or ethnic, hate, gay violence, etc.)

The battering cycle begins by an escalation of tension. Some victims recognize immediately the signs of impending violence. This could include screaming, yelling, blaming, demanding, and mild forms of shoving. The abuser will use almost any "excuse" as the trigger that sets him or her off: The victim didn't do the dishes correctly, answered the wrong way, said the wrong thing, looked stupid, cooked the food poorly, and so forth.

The trigger then sets into motion the actual violent event: hitting, punching, tearing, biting, tying up, beating, kicking, name calling, and sometimes murder. Some victims feel actual relief once the violent act is over because they know that built-up tension has exploded and the abuser will once again deescalate. Indeed, the abuser begins to deescalate, calms down, and usually will apologize, promising never to hit again. This is fondly referred to as the "honeymoon cycle." Passions are high as the abuser promises the victim "a rose garden." The honeymoon is followed by a cycle of hope in which the victim indeed hopes she has seen the last of the violence. However, the escalation of tension in the abuser begins again and they are soon on the merry-go-round of violence once more.

The statistics of violence point out the high probability that a couple or individual who seeks counseling for other presenting problems may also be engaged in a violent relationship. The counselor who is familiar with the dynamics of violent relationships will be in a position to identify the problem and to provide the most effective support and intervention to victims. Local battered women's programs can suggest

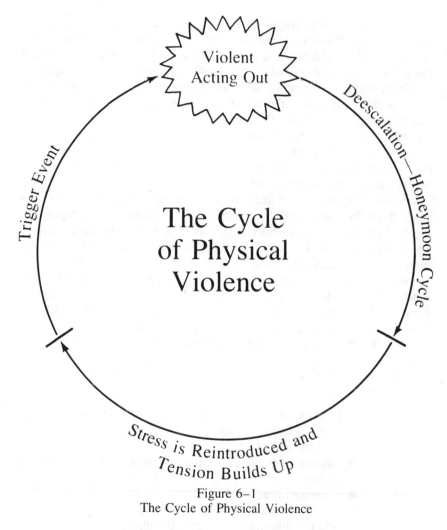

Figure 6–1
The Cycle of Physical Violence

books and other materials that will help the counselor to become more familiar with this common problem.

IDENTIFYING THE PROBLEM

In the initial evaluation of the client's problems, it is important that the counselor not rule out the possibility of domestic violence based

on the socioeconomic status, race, religion, age, or apparent relationship of the individuals concerned. Domestic violence is a problem that
cuts across all boundaries and affects all levels of our society. Although
there is a misconception that common stressors such as a lack of money,
children, and loss of employment are the causes of domestic violence,
the root problem is that the battering partner uses violence to obtain
and maintain control over the victim. Violence is a learned behavior,
a pattern of responding to others that is learned at a very early age.
Many batterers have experienced abuse from or witnessed abuse between their parents as children, and they play out the roles they have
learned when they reach adulthood.

Because a victim is not likely to volunteer information to the counselor about the violence in the presence of her batterer, it is important,
if you have reason to suspect abuse, that you arrange for a time to
speak with the victim alone and allow enough time for a complete
interview. It is common for a victim to minimize the violence or to
be unable or unwilling to identify what is happening to her as "violence." Direct, specific questions will help her to focus her thoughts.
It may help to have available a list of examples of the different types
of abuse (i.e., physical, emotional, sexual, etc.) and to ask the victim
to identify which behaviors have been used against her at any time in
her life, specifically in the relationship in question.

Some specifics in the assessment of the victim (Martin, 1987, pp.
54–56) are:*

- History of drug use, street or prescription, and any
  recent increase in use;
- History of lost pregnancies;
- History of medical injuries and trips to the emergency
  room;
- Repeated illnesses;
- Isolation from friends and family;
- Suicide attempts or other self-injury;
- Previous abuses and previous abusers;
- Previous legal action, including police protection;
- Previous separations;
- Inability to make decisions and choices;

---

*From G. Martin, *Counseling for Family Violence and Abuse*, RCC-Vol. 6, Dallas:
Word, Inc. © 1987.

- Any harm done to children by victim or abuser; and
- Ability of victim to harm abuser with weapons.

In addition, you may need to make an assessment concerning the abuser and how volatile the home situation seems. These questions can help in your assessment:

- Does the abuser have access to weapons?
- History of previous violent episodes, their outcome and severity;
- Is the abuser currently using drugs and alcohol?
- Does the abuser use intimidating behavior to control victim and children such as threatening family members, making threatening phone calls, or attempting to kill others?
- Is the abuser adept at utilizing and manipulating the legal system?
- Does the abuser have a previous mental illness history?
- Has the abuser physically assaulted others outside the immediate family?
- Is the abuser sexually abusing his wife or children?

Many victims of domestic violence have suffered abuse as children or have been in a succession of violent relationships. Most, understandably, have great difficulty with trust. The therapist must let the victim know that she is believed and supported in her disclosure and that the information shared will not be disclosed to her abuser without her express permission.

THE BATTERED WOMAN SYNDROME

Certain signs may be apparent as you speak with the victim that indicate that she is suffering from PTSD (or Battered Woman Syndrome, a term coined by Dr. Lenore Walker to describe the common effects of domestic violence on a woman) (Walker, 1979). Particularly if the relationship is longstanding, the victim may have developed mechanisms for coping with the emotional abuse and constant threat of violence that seem maladaptive or bizarre when taken out of context of the situation. She may abuse alcohol or drugs as a way of coping, or she may have severe mood swings, from euphoria to uncontrollable crying, dissociation, flattened affect, obsessive attention to others' moods and desires, nightmares, apparently irrational fears, inability to make decisions or act on her own behalf, and self-destructive tendencies as well as severe depression and apparent psychosis. In addition, it is typical for a battered woman to experience numerous physical reactions to stress such as headaches, unexplained rashes, gastrointestinal problems, fatigue, or insomnia. These symptoms often disappear quickly when the stress of the violent relationship is removed.

Because the violence that occurs within an intimate relationship may be sporadic and the victim may leave the situation only to return again later, there is no linear process in the development of the PTSD or the grief process and recovery. Repeated exposure to the trauma and the amount of control the abuser exerts over the life of the victim often produce a feeling of hopelessness in the victim that can be emotionally paralyzing.

Clearly, all victims are not female. Men are also battered by spouses and girlfriends. Abuse can carry devastating effects for men. Most abuse toward men is seen as preventable, and if it is not prevented, the man is considered to be "weak" or a "sissy." These perceptions are affronts to the man's sense of maleness and can impair his self-contruct, ego, and sexuality.

The needs of a family experiencing domestic violence are diversified and complex. If we are to salvage the family, many different aspects of the violence must be addressed, besides that of the offender. Effective community intervention that meets the needs of all family members requires that there be coordination among community services (U.S. Attorney General, 1984).

CRISIS INTERVENTION

The physical safety of the victim is the most important factor to address in the initial contact. Although the battered woman is in the best position to determine *when* the next incident of abuse may occur, she may underestimate the severity of past abuse and the potential for serious abuse in the future.

It is important that the counselor validate the victim's fears about the danger that she is in and help her to devise ways to feel in control again. The counselor can develop a safety plan with the victim including how the victim will escape during the next incident, where she will go, whom she will contact, what she will take with her, and so forth. The safety plan can help the victim to become more realistic about the likelihood of further violence and break through a certain amount of denial about the extent of the violence in her life.

The victim should be given information about legal alternatives she may have, such as calling the police and pressing charges, filing for restraining orders or injunctions, and gaining temporary custody of her children. She should also be referred to the local battered women's program so that she can learn about the availability of emergency shelter should she need it and where she may be able to attend a support group for women in violent relationships.

An important aspect to consider during crisis intervention counseling is that the victim is not likely to place much hope in law enforcement, police protection, or the criminal justice system. Victims who have engaged police assistance by calling may have received comments such as advising them to let the man cool down, or they may not have received the requested protection. Some domestic violence later ends in homicide. If the victim has had clashes with the police over the limited amount of protection provided, the police may be reluctant or unbelieving that a restraining order or other types of protection will be effective.

In many communities and in many parts of our society, domestic violence is still not recognized as criminal behavior but is seen as a "family problem." A popular sentiment is that if a battered woman wanted to, she could simply leave the relationship and end the abuse. This myth is believed and guides the response of law enforcement agencies and individuals despite facts to the contrary. The victim who does not immediately leave an abusive relationship, even though she has no place to go, no means of supporting herself, and no guarantee that the violence will stop, is labeled masochistic. Those who do not understand the dynamics of domestic violence assume that there must be a *reason* why the batterer is driven to acts of violence, and that if the victim were a good wife and mother, she would not be beaten. Little mention is ever made of why the batterer feels the need to use violence, but most of the focus is on the victim and why she:

- does not call the police;
- does not follow through on pressing charges;
- returns to the batterer;
- still loves her abuser;
- fails to protect her children; and
- seems unwilling to take the advice of family and friends.

All the above behaviors can be attributed directly to the fear of continuous violence and threats of violence. Secondary victimization also takes the form of a criminal justice system that is at times unresponsive to the needs and realities of the victim and her situation. In many jurisdictions, a woman is forced to press charges formally and to testify at various stages of the process against the person with whom she lives and who beats her on a regular basis. This of course is dangerous for the victim if she is still living with the abuser. When she fails to appear at a hearing or asks to drop the charges, she is accused of making a false report or of wasting the system's time. Many women follow through with the required legal procedures only to find that their charges are not taken seriously or that the system is reluctant to punish her abuser for what is still seen as a family problem.

These forms of secondary victimization serve to further isolate the victim of domestic violence and to make it more difficult for her to get the support she needs to break free. For some women, the failure of society and particularly the criminal justice system to provide effective support means that she will be forced to take matters into her own hands when her own or her children's life is at stake. Hundreds of women are serving prison sentences in the United States for defending themselves or retaliating against their abuser.

Client Concerns

- Physical safety of self and children;
- Fear of abuser locating them;
- Concern about how they will survive;
- Not having a place to stay away from the abuser;
- Not having money, a job, or work skills; and
- Having no transportation.

Secondary Victimizations

- Lack of protection from law enforcement agencies;
- Lack of services available to help with transition;
- Lack of work skills, money, or information about how to increase skills; and
- Stigmatization by label "spouse abuse victim."

Social Services Needed

- Crisis intervention counselor;
- Spouse abuse shelter;

- Victim advocate;
- Transitional services (housing, financial aid, job skills);
- Restraining order;
- Prosecutor/attorney;
- Group counseling;
- Police intervention;
- Child protection services;
- Transportation; and
- Emergency medical treatment.

SHORT-TERM COUNSELING

It is possible that the victim of domestic/family violence will not be ready to make any change in her situation at the time she first reaches out for help. The counselor who has not come to terms with his or her own attitudes and feelings about domestic violence may have a difficult time understanding how a victim could stay in the violent relationship, and will consciously or unconsciously convey a judgmental attitude about the battered woman's choices. Victim blaming is a constant in the life of a battered woman, and is one of the reasons why it is difficult for her to disclose. It takes many forms, from subtle statements such as "What were you fighting about?" (implying that there could be a justifiable reason for the violence), to "If that were me, I would leave him!" (implying that there must be something wrong with the victim because she chooses to stay). The effect of these statements is to reinforce the victim's own feelings of inadequacy and isolation and continue to keep her immobilized. Counselors must examine their own feelings and honestly decide whether they are the best agents for helping the victim or whether they should refer to someone with a more specific background in domestic violence. The victim's life may be at stake.

Empowering the woman to make choices on her own behalf is the most important goal of short-term counseling. Because domestic violence is basically a matter of power and control, and all power over her own life has been stripped from the battered woman, she must regain control in order to move forward. It is important to recognize that taking back power while she is with the batterer can be a risky procedure, and she must have some assurance of safety while doing that. Statistically, the most dangerous period in a violent relationship is when the victim takes back control and either leaves or starts making demands of her batterer. This is because the batterer has lost the control he previously had and, in some cases, will do anything to regain it. Many women have been killed because they asked for a divorce or otherwise threatened their batterer's status quo.

Encouraging the victim to make her own decisions can be a painstaking process. She may be reluctant to do so for safety reasons, may have forgotten how to be aware of what she wants, or may never have had the experience of making decisions for herself at all. Many battered women have moved from their parents' home to their abuser's home at an early age. They have never lived independently or learned how to support themselves financially or emotionally. These skills can and will be learned in an atmosphere of safety and unconditional acceptance with a support person who gently, but firmly, refuses to make decisions for the victim.

Issues surrounding low self-esteem (reinforced by the abuser), a sense of self, self-love, and a sense of purpose are important. Likewise, unrealistic hope, isolation, emotional dependence, and the need to repeat trauma are all issues that need to be challenged. Some of these issues will be dealt with in long-term counseing, if it is warranted.

Some women will recover rather quickly from the effects of violence when the threat is taken away; others, because of previous experiences with abuse or general psychological makeup, will take much longer and may need long-term counseling to recover.

Issues that may compound the problems of domestic violence include the victim's substance abuse; previous victimizations such as physical or sexual abuse as a child; family, cultural, or religious pressures to continue the relationship; or lack of economic resources necessary to maintain independent living.

Family or couples counseling with violent relationships should not be attempted until the counselor can be reasonably sure that the victim will be safe to speak honestly in a session. If the violence has not stopped, it is not safe for the victim to disclose information to the counselor that the abuser does not want disclosed, despite his claims to the contrary. Separating the partners will allow the victim the safety to explore her own feelings without fear of reprisal. At the same time, the batterer will be forced to focus on his own behavior instead of rationalizing his violence by focusing on what the victim did to provoke him. It should be the victim's decision when she feels ready, if ever, to enter into joint counseling with her batterer, not the counselor's or the batterer's.

Client Concerns

- When or how to disclose and to whom disclosures should be made;
- Regaining power and control over her life;
- Inability to make decisions;
- Separation;
- Divorce;
- Safety for self and children;
- Job/money/skills; and
- Future living arrangements.

Secondary Victimizations

- Counselor's bias concerning domestic violence;
- Victim-blaming from numerous sources;
- Lack of control in decision making;
- Lack of independent living skills;
- Substance abuse and other addictions; and
- Family/cultural/religious pressures to stay in relationship.

Social Services Needed

- Short-term counselor;
- Group counseling;
- Domestic violence shelter;
- Assertiveness training;
- Offender counseling (if desired);
- Job skills; and
- Housing, financial assistance, and food.

LONG-TERM COUNSELING

It should not be assumed that because a woman has been in a long-term violent relationship that she is in need of long-term counseling. As previously stated, the effects of the violence may quickly diminish when the threat of violence is taken away.

However, the violence may awaken the need to deal with:

- Previous victimizations including physical or sexual child abuse;
- Sexual assault;
- Substance abuse problems;
- Abandonment issues related to the death of a parent or divorce;
- Setting boundaries;
- Inability to have faith in her own feelings or judgment;
- Generalized loss of trust;
- Inability to develop close relationships;
- Childhood background;
- Shame;
- Loss;
- Poor self-esteem;
- Ego development;
- Codependency;
- Behavior patterns;
- Passive/aggressive issues; and
- Acting out.

The victim may also need help to deal with her rage or guilt feelings over her violent thoughts or actions in response to the violence, her inability to protect her children from abuse, and secondary abuses by those outside the relationship who failed to assist her in time of need. It can be very helpful for her to become involved with a support group of women who have been through similar experiences and who are now struggling with the same recovery issues. Most battered women's programs have such support groups available at no cost to the participants.

Client Concerns

- Finding available shelter;
- Returning to an abusive relationship;
- Unsure of pressing charges;
- Unsure charges will stick;
- Ability to survive and support children on her own;
- Loving yet fearing abuser;
- Fear of abandonment;
- Boundaries;

- Distrust in own judgment; and
- Rage.

Secondary Victimizations

- Substance abuse;
- Inability to develop close relationships;
- Loss of trust;
- Lack of protection by "systems";
- Societal bias surrounding domestic violence;
- Victim blaming; and
- Family/cultural/religious pressures to stay in relationship.

Social Services Needed

- Long-term counselor;
- Group counseling;
- Assertiveness training;
- Offender counseling (if desired);
- Housing, financial aid, and food;
- Occupational training; and
- Legal aid/advice.

Most communities in the United States are now served by a battered women's shelter or safe home network. The counselor who works with victims of domestic violence should be familiar with these programs and the services they offer.

Most shelters offer safe, confidential housing for women and their children, counseling by telephone or in person, and information about specific social service resources and legal remedies available for victims in that state.

In some communities, counseling services for the violent partner are offered through the battered women's shelter as well. If not, the shelter would be able to refer to a local counselor who specializes in batterer counseling.

RECOMMENDED READING

Bradshaw, J. (1987). *On the family*. Health Communications.
Bradshaw, J. (1988). *Healing the shame that binds*. Health Communications.

Clarke, R. L. (1986). *Pastoral care of battered women*. Philadelphia, PA: Westminster Press.

Finkelhor, D. (1983). *The dark side of families: Current family violence research*. Beverly Hills, CA: Sage.

Gondolf, E. (1985). *Men who batter: An integrated approach for stopping wife abuse*. Homes Beach, FL: Learning Publications.

Martin, D. (1976). *Battered wives*. Glide Publications.

Pagelow, M. (1984). *Family violence*. New York: Praeger.

Roy, M. (1982). *The abusive partner: An analysis of domestic battering*. New York: Van Nostrand Reinhold.

Sonkin, D., & Murphy, M. (1982). *Learning to live without violence: A handbook for men*. San Francisco: Volcano Press.

Walker, L. (1979). *The battered woman*. New York: Harper & Row.

REFERRALS

Clearinghouse on Family Violence Information
P.O. Box 1182
Washington, DC 20013
703-821-2086

National Coalition Against Domestic Violence
P.O. Box 34103
Washington, DC 20043-4103
202-638-6388

The National Council on Child Abuse and Family Violence
1155 Connecticut Ave., NW, Suite 300
Washington, DC 20036
800-222-2000

National Domestic Violence Toll Free Line
800-333-7230

NATIONAL REFERRALS FOR ORGANIZATIONS SPECIALIZING IN WORK WITH VIOLENT MEN

Amend
1445 Cleveland Place, Room 307
Denver, CO 80202

Bravo
Mid-Missour Men's Resource Group
707 Morningside Drive
Columbia, MO 65211

Brother to Brother
1660 Broad Street
Cranston, RI 02907

Commence
9656 Sycamore Trace Court
Cincinnati, OH 34242

Emerge
25 Hunington, Room 324
Boston, MA 02116

Men Stopping Rape
306 N. Brooks
Box 305
Madison, WI 53715

Men's Anti-Rape Resource Center
c/o George Marx
709 Orton Court
Madison, WI 53703

National Clearinghouse on Marital Rape
2325 Oak Street
Berkeley, CA 94708

RAVEN
665 Delmar Street, Suite 301
St. Louis, MO 63130
(Resource list of local groups working with male perpetrators and male
   victims of violence)

	**Overview of Domestic Violence**
Crisis Intervention Issues:	Physical safety of person, validation of fear of danger, safety plan for future victimization, safety contacts, legal aid, restraining order, temporary child custody, emergency shelters, support groups.
Short-Term Counseling:	Counselor's own attitudes about violence, empowering the victim to make decisions, encouraging her when she does make decisions, teaching independent living skills, unconditional acceptance, grieving, family counseling if abuse has stopped.
Long-Term Counseling:	Victim's own previous issues of child physical or sexual abuse, addictions, co-dependency, religious issues, handling economics, abandonment issues, divorce, boundaries, inability to trust self or others, inability to develop close relationships.
Secondary Victim-izations:	Not recognized as a crime, no place to go, no job skills, no money, lack of knowledgeable law enforcement officers or insensitive court personnel.
Social Services Needed:	Battered woman's shelter, victim advocate, restraining order, job skills training, vocational rehabilitation, General Education Degree schooling, counseling through all stages, battered woman's support group, welfare or public housing, food stamps, aid for dependent children, children's and woman's health care, medical attention.

7

Sexual Trauma

- One out four women will be raped or sexually assaulted at least once in her life (FBI, 1989).
- In 1985 there was one forcible rape every 6 minutes (FBI, 1989).
- One out of six women in college is raped by someone known to her (National Coalition Against Sexual Assault, 1989).
- One third of completed rapes occur in the home (U.S. Dept. of Justice, Bureau of Justice Statistics, 1985).
- Date rape accounts for 60% of all reported rapes (Date Violence Intervention Project Newsletter, 1989).

RAPE

Rape is one of the most frequently committed violent crimes and its incidence is steadily increasing. It is also underreported. Much of the focus on rape and rape crisis issues emerged in the 1970s. Thus, most of the theories surrounding treatment of rape victims also emerged in the 1970s and the 1980s. Current empirical research on rape victims includes a vast array of differing theories, methods, and opinions. While researching this chapter, for each study I read outlining successful treatments, another study existed to say those treatments may or may not be effective.

Therefore, this chapter will focus on historical theories as they relate to rape (Burgess & Holmstrom, 1974a, 1974b, 1976) and will also discuss newer theories currently being addressed. Interestingly enough, according to these authors, after the dust settled concerning the debates on theories and which worked and which didn't, the conclusion was that all theories provided measures of relief, none more so than the next.

I hope that this encourages us to believe that there is more than one way to help rape victims and that our approaches to them must be individualistic, keeping in mind the strengths and weaknesses of each approach. As mental health caregivers, we should become familiar with more than one technique in providing services. Our approach can become more global, with different available methods for differing needs of victims. Methods can be used interchangeably as the victim grows and changes. A mental health caregiver need not be locked and bound to one view of trauma.

In addition, one study remarked that having been a victim of rape in and of itself does not constitute a disorder. It is not the rape that is being psychologically treated but rather the specific symptomatology that the survivor develops as a result of the assault. Some women who were assaulted do not develop major symptomatic reactions and recover quickly without any type of professional treatment. Researchers and clinicians need to focus their attention on the specific types of symptoms that are manifested and tailor treatment to that symptomatology (Foa, Olasov, & Steketee, 1988).

DESCRIPTION OF SEXUAL TRAUMA

Sexual trauma incorporates the categories of rape, incest, sexual assault, and ritualistic abuse. They are all placed under a broad umbrella term of sexual trauma.

Rape

Rape occurs primarily during adulthood, consisting of penile penetration by another adult or gang of adults. Using instruments without penile penetration would be considered rape by instrumentation. Statutory rape is rape perpetrated by someone 18 years of age or older (depending on state law) against a minor (under 18 years of age).

Incest

Incest occurs during childhood, adolescence, or the teen years. Perpetrators are immediate family members, extended family, or close friends of the family. Incest can reflect the continuum between fondling and penile penetration.

Sexual Assault

Sexual assault usually occurs among adults. It does not involve penile penetration but consists of other types of sexual abuse such as fondling, oral sex, and digital penetration.

Ritualistic Abuse

Ritualistic abuse occurs when the victim is forced to participate in a worship-type service of cult members. Abuse can include forced sex with corpses, sex with dismembered body parts, sex by instrumentation, and various other types of abuse including forcing the victim to watch children being sacrificed. Most of this abuse is connected to various demonic types of worship.

In treatment, victims of the first three categories can be combined in group therapy. However, it has been our practice not to mix victims of acquaintance, stranger, or marital rape with survivors of incest. (Acquaintance rape is perpetrated by someone that is known to the victim. It may be a recent acquaintance or a well-known acquaintance. Stranger rape is perpetrated by someone unknown, or perceived as unknown to the victim. Martial rape is perpetrated by a spouse or ex-spouse.) The issues of incest and the dysfunctional family often demand intensive focus and can leave the rape victim feeling disconnected from the therapy group. The etiology of incest often encompasses different and extended issues than those of adult rape. We have placed rape victims in incest groups, but not with overwhelming success. However, we have also placed adult rape victims into incest groups and later found incest issues. Because it is not uncommon to find adult rape victims who were also abused as children (the continuation of trauma into adult years described in chapter 2 on the psychodynamics of trauma), it is sometimes beneficial to put an adult rape victim that you suspect was also sexually abused as a child into an incest group.

Victims of ritualistic abuse will need to be treated as a separate group. Their issues of torture and cult practices are not something they are willing to share with those who have not been tortured. Likewise, incest or rape survivors may be traumatized by the high level of torture in victims of ritualistic abuse.

The following are forms of sexual abuse:

1. Fondling of sexual parts or being made to fondle others' sexual parts.
2. Digital (finger) penetration in vagina or rectum or being made to penetrate another's vagina or rectum.
3. Being made to listen to age-inappropriate dialogue containing sexual jargon or pertaining to sexual acts.
4. Being made to read or talk about age-inappropriate subjects containing sexual jargon or pertaining to sexual acts.
5. Being made to watch or look at age-inappropriate literature, tapes, or people acting in sexual ways.
6. Being photographed in ways that make one uncomfortable.
7. Oral sex is either committed against the victim or victims are forced to perform oral sex with others.
8. Being looked at or leered at in ways that make one uncomfortable or making remarks about one's developing body.
9. Being penetrated orally, anally, or vaginally by any instrument or penis.
10. Being made to watch or to perform sex acts with animals.
11. Being made to watch or to perform sex acts with children.
12. Being made to watch or to perform sex acts with dead bodies or parts of dead bodies.
13. Extreme mixtures of physical abuse bordering on ritual abuse mixed with sexual abuse.

Sexual abuse is no respector of gender and is perpetrated against both male and female victims. There is a ratio differential between male and female victims, with female victims experiencing a higher rate of abuse. Some data support that women are about twice as likely as men to be targeted for childhood (Siegel, Sorenson, Golding, & Burman, 1987) or adult (Sorenson, Stein, Siegel, Golding, & Burman, 1987) sexual assault. In the majority of this chapter, the primary focus is on women. However, male victims of rape and some other issues are addressed later on in this chapter.

There is a wide continuum of effects from sexual abuse. However, we consider sexual abuse to have occurred when the person has suffered from its effects. We don't measure sexual abuse based on penile penetration alone, or any specific action of forced sex alone, or how we as counselors feel the victim should have reacted. Our diagnosis of sexual abuse is based on the trauma the victim has suffered. I have seen women seriously traumatized by fondling. I have seen women deal quite well with penile penetration. Therefore, it's not the act of sexual abuse alone we look to and measure, but the victim's reaction to that trauma. However, some studies indicate that higher levels of dissociation can be seen in those who have experienced penile pene-tration and acts of physical violence associated with sexual abuse (Wilson, 1989). Finkelhor (1986) indicated that the amount of violence experienced is a critical factor in trauma care. Thus examining the levels of violence experienced will be critical to treatment issues.

The victim's reaction to the trauma will often be affected and be related to the extent, intensity, and duration of abuse as well as the person's coping mechanism for emotional and physical pain. (See chapter 2 on the psychodynamics of trauma.) A U.S. Department of Justice booklet entitled *Child Sexual Abuse Victims and Their Treatment* (1988) states, "The finding that violence was a more important influence on a reaction than the type of sexual abuse is consistent with the literature on rape. Knowledge that the degree of violence in a sexual assault may be a potent influence on reactions has important implications for intervention."

CRISIS INTERVENTION FOR ADULT RAPE VICTIMS

As a mental health professional, you may be working with a client who was recently raped. Crisis intervention includes providing infor-mation and support so that the client feels at ease in expressing feelings about the rape, and helping the client develop new coping strategies to deal with the assault (Forman, 1980; Yassen & Glass, 1984).

One study indicated that if the reactions to a sexual assault are strongly negative, the majority of these negative reactions will diminish over time, but a minority of sexual assault victims (25%) will show continued signs of impairment more than a year after victimization (Siegel, Golding, Stein, Burnam, & Sorenson, 1990).

As many as 80% of assaulted women feel depressed after being raped (Norris & Feldman-Summers, 1981). The severity of the depres-sion has been found to subside after 3–4 months (Frank & Stewart, 1984; Kilpatrick, Veronen, & Resick, 1979; Atkeson, Calhoun, Re-sick, & Ellis, 1982).

Difficulty in sleeping is a common reaction in both male and female rape victims (Frank & Stewart, 1984; Goyer & Eddleman, 1984). Fear and fear-related actions such as the fear of being alone and restricted

behaviors because of fear seem to persist over a period of time (Calhoun, Atkeson, & Resick, 1982; Kilpatrick et al., 1979).

Sexual difficulties, adjustments, and changes as they relate to preas-
sault functioning are all prevalent. Areas affected are frequency of sex
(Ellis, Calhoun, & Atkeson, 1980), fear of sex (Becker, Skinner, Abel,
& Cichon, 1986), lowered sexual interest (Ageton, 1983), less pleasurable sex (Ellis et al., 1980; Feldman-Summers, Gordon, & Meagher,
1979), sexual difficulties (Briere & Runtz, 1988; Nadelson, Notman,
Zackson, & Gormick, 1982), sexual problems (Becker, Skinner, Abel,
Howell, & Bruce, 1982; Becker, Skinner, Abel, Axelrod, & Cichon,
1984), and sexual impairment (Bess & Janssen, 1982). These factors
could be affected by the victim's knowing the assailant (in particular,
a family member), having to experience an ongoing assault, the act
of penetration, verbal coercion, and the younger age of the victim
(Becker et al., 1982, 1984).

As mentioned previously, as a focus for rape crisis intervention, this
chapter segment will focus on historical documentation as seen through
the works of Burgess and Holmstrom (1976). Other more recent theories will be addressed briefly.

Burgess and Holmstrom (1986) indicated three phases in rape trauma:
impact, recoil, and recovery. You will find these dynamics to be similar
to the phases listed in the grief process in chapter 2. During the impact
phase (recoil and recovery phases will be discussed later in the chapter),
the victim will show a particular style of reaction following the rape.
One style could be hysterical (crying, confusion, agitation, faltering
in decision making, immobilization, helplessness). The second style
is acting numb or calm (composed, subdued, may joke about what
happens). This reaction of tranquility usually indicates a state of shock.
Victims' emotional upheaval is greater than their ability to cope. This
crisis stage is the shortest phase because it is a time of extreme stress.
A victim cannot tolerate its intensity too long. The most immediate
needs of a recent rape victim in crisis intervention are discussed next.

1. *Being at a safe place*. If attacked at home, victims' first instinct
may be to leave. This could put them in further danger as they wander
disoriented through the streets with no destination. If the assault occurred away from home, it can be harder for victims to find shelter.
A woman may be injured or unable to find her way out of an unfamiliar
area. The rapist may have taken her purse, car, or clothing. Arrange
for a family member of a friend to stay with the victim overnight.

2. *Calling the police*. No one should be forced to report. However,
filing a report will help in catching and convicting the rapist. Victims

should not be made to feel guilty if they do not report. Notifying the police does not obligate them to press charges or to go through criminal proceedings. A victim can stop the process at any point. This helps victims to regain control of their unorganized world. An account of the rape can also be given anonymously or through a third party.

The victim has a right to:

- Request that a female officer conduct the initial interview;
- Have a friend or legal advocate be present during questioning;
- Experience reactions to the rape—hysterics, shock, disorientation, or hostility—without these reactions being considered abnormal;
- Be treated in a considerate and sensitive manner regardless of the circumstances of the assault;
- Have the rape kept private and out of the news media; and
- Request that a female doctor handle any medical procedures, when possible.

3. *Medical attention.* It is advisable for victims to be hospitalized even if they feel they are not injured. They may be stressed and unable to recognize their injuries, particularly internal ones. Testing for pregnancy and sexually transmitted diseases may also be required. Although most victims don't think about prosecuting at this time, it is important to gather medical proof of the violation in case they do decide to press charges later. Medical evidence can be enough to convict a rapist, especially in light of the new DNA testing. Medical evidence not only includes the presence of seminal fluid, but the documentation of lacerations, bruises, pubic hair, clothing fibers, skin beneath a victim's fingernails, and DNA factors.

Some states have provisions for free HIV testing for rape victims. In the event the rapist is caught and prosecuted, some states have laws that can force the rapist to submit to an HIV test as well.

However, do not force victims into medical testing procedures against their wishes. Explain the benefits and allow victims the choice of doing so. Giving them control over choices helps reinforce empowerment. If they are struggling with making decisions, you may need to assist.

4. *Processing the experience.* Provide a secure place for the victim interview. Allow someone to be with victims as they talk with you.

This may take place immediately following the rape, or days, weeks, or even a few months later.

Pay attention to the victims' opening words. This will clue you to their real concerns and will include crisis requests as well as possible solutions. Let them ventilate about the experience and tell you what they wish you to know. It is important that you allow them to tell what's important to them. It may not even be the actual event itself, but something that led up to the rape or something that happened afterwards.

Help the victim to reduce guilt and self-blame. Do not phrase questions in ways that sound judgmental or put victims in a position of explaining or justifying their actions. Repeat often, "There is no reason for you to feel guilty. The rapist had no right to attack you."

If victims feel guilty about not fighting back or about giving in, indicate to them that survival is the most important aspect and that whatever they did to survive was the correct thing to have done at the time. The victim had good judgment, therefore the victim lived.

It is important that the rape victim have someone to talk to and someone to stay with after the event, usually a friend or a family member. The victim may be afraid to call a friend or family member because of the fear of being rejected or blamed. If victims are afraid to call, the crisis intervener may suggest making the call for them or talking to a friend/family member directly. Many rape victims are concerned about telling their husband/spouse or children. They should be assured that their children need not be told immediately. We usually suggest that children who are old enough to understand be told during the first 3 months following the rape. Spouses, of course, should be told, but allow the victim to discuss the pros and cons of telling the spouse with you prior to breaking the news privately.

Be able to provide a complete explanation of what the police investigation will entail and what the victim can expect at the hospital, what the procedures will be, why they are utilized, and what the court experience may be like, should the case advance to that stage. Minimizing these hard experiences the rape victim will have to face or "sugar-coating" them to protect the victim may result in the victim's loss of trust in you.

Additional theories not encompassed in Burgess and Holmstrom's discussion here but that you may want to consider in working from an individualistic approach are: dynamic psychotherapy (Cryer & Beutler, 1980; Evans, 1978; Fox & Scherl, 1972; Krupnick, 1980; Ledray, 1986; Metzger, 1976), supportive psychotherapy (Resick, Jordan, Girelli, Hutter, & Marhoefer-Dvorak, 1988), stress inoculation, assertiveness training, and systematic desensitization (Wolpe, 1958), cognitive therapy (Frank, Anderson, Stewart, Dancu, Hughes, & West, 1988), and constructivist self-development theory (McCann, Sakheim, & Abrahamson, 1988). All of these theories approach treatment of the rape victim from a posttraumatic stress disorder base (see chapter 2). The theories mentioned here would apply to the work done in short- and long-term counseling.

Client Concerns

- Should the rape be reported?
- Pregnancy;
- Sexually transmitted diseases;
- AIDS;
- Fear of rapist's return;
- Fear that friends/family will find out;
- Fear of being alone;
- Concern about impending procedures if rape is reported; and
- Need to process and ventilate anger.

Secondary Victimizations

- Medical costs;
- Time off from work;
- Replacement of car, clothes, credit cards, or whatever may have been taken during the rape;
- Media insensitivity;
- Abrupt law enforcement officers or medical attendants;
- Rapist may be caught and released on bond;
- Victim may have to take a polygraph test or psychiatric tests;
- Others may blame the victim; and
- Fear of being fired from job because of stigma of sexual assault.

Social Services Needed

- Crisis intervention counselor;
- Medical/rape exam;

- Victim assistance through police/sheriff's department;
- Bureau of Crime Compensation; and
- Prosecutor/attorney.

SHORT-TERM COUNSELING

You may begin the counseling of a rape victim at the time of impact/crisis, or you may begin after the initial crisis. Goals in short-term counseling will be geared toward the second phase of rape trauma, the recoil phase (Burgess & Holmstrom, 1986).

During this time, victims may seem to have made a satisfactory adjustment. They may no longer be acutely upset, and convince others that their life is back to normal. Usually, however, the problem is only suppressed. Victims must still deal with the upheaval of emotions such as guilt, anger, depression, and self-pity. Anxiety and fear also are significant problems for victims of sexual assault (Burgess & Holmstrom, 1974a, 1974b; Calhoun, Atkeson, & Resick, 1982; Kilpatrick, Resick, & Veronen, 1981; Kilpatrick & Veronen, 1984).

Victims usually are not willing to confront all these emotions at one time. The second stage of rape trauma is called recoil because it involves two distinct kinds of activity: denial and resolution (Burgess & Holmstrom, 1974b). Victims will struggle between periods of facing their inner trauma and periods of continuing to try to repress memories. They may relive the crime repeatedly in their mind, agonizing over what they could have done differently. Those who were numb during or following the rape may now experience its full, terrorizing emotion.

Many victims engage in various forms of distractions to avoid facing the pain. Some become compulsive about volunteer work, children, or jobs to escape the suppressed trauma.

They may go through mood swings and become easily depressed. They may feel the need to move or to change their schedules or jobs to avoid people and places associated with the rape. Adding security devices to the home, taking self-defense classes, and drawing on the support of friends can help regain confidence.

If victims do not get appropriate and professional support during this second crisis stage, their defenses may evolve into dysfunctional behavior and create psychological disorders later in life. Ambivalence toward men, low self-esteem, chronic depression, and sexual problems are some indications that the initial injury has not healed properly. Rape victims have significant depressive disorders 2 months following the rape (Atkeson et al., 1982) and up to 1 year following the rape (Kilpatrick & Veronen, 1984).

As a counselor, you may find yourself having to repeat similar information often to the victim. Part of the recovery process is educating the victim about distortions and rape dynamics.

Some of the distortions and myths about rape are: Rape is a crime of passion; women who are careful don't get raped; only bad women are raped; rape is impossible if the woman really resists; women secretly want to be raped; the rapist is usually a stranger; women invite rape by dressing or acting seductively; women falsely accuse men of rape; and most rapes are interracial (National Victims Resource Center, 1987).

Remember the other types of therapies listed previously in the crisis intervention section of this chapter if you are seeking a more individualistic approach.

Client Concerns

- How the judicial process will work, how they will handle it, will justice be served;
- How the rape will change their relationship with husband;
- Losing their job for time missed at court;
- Losing their job for the inability to be able to concentrate;
- Loss of privacy;
- Community stigma;
- Safety;
- Retribution;
- Fear of further or new victimizations;
- Loss of sexuality because of forced sexual violence; and
- Loss of relationship with spouse/lover.

Secondary Victimizations

- Legal costs;
- Time lost from work;
- Loss of job;
- Change in residence;
- Divorce;

- Rapist being acquitted or found not guilty;
- Being asked to corroborate or plea-bargain;
- Lack of information surrounding status of case;
- Cost of counseling;
- Pregnancy;
- Sexually transmitted diseases;
- AIDS; and
- Suicide attempts.

Social Services Needed

- Victim assistance from plice/sheriff's department;
- Short-term counselor;
- Group counseling; and
- Bureau of Crime Compensation.

LONG-TERM COUNSELING

The need for long-term counseling should be assessed based on the woman's prior victimization history, how well she resolved previous victimizations, and her ego strength. Particularly in cases of rape, if the victim has not undergone crisis intervention treatment and been allowed some sort of processing of the event, we can be sure that this victim will be seen in treatment later on in life. At Bridgework, we typically see women who come in years after a rape, finally recognizing that the event did affect their life and continues to affect their daily living. One study indicated that women who had been previously victimized years earlier (22 years ago on the average) were more likely to experience depression than nonvictims and still measure as PTSD reactive (Kilpatrick, Veronen, Saunders, Best, Arnick-McMullen, & Paduhovich, 1987).

Even after treatment, the victim will still experience various cycles throughout life that will bring to the surface issues about the rape that still need resolution. This could happen when female children approach the age of the mother when she was raped. If a woman was a victim of a campus rape at age 23, for example, she may find herself having to confront her rape issues again when her daughter is going to college, living on campus, and is about the same age as when she herself was raped.

Some issues to be dealt with in long-term counseling lead to the third phase of rape trauma, recovery. The overwhelming, intense feelings of mistrust, danger, and impaired intimacy are a source of great insecurity for the victim. Working toward stabilizing and empowering the victim's sense of safety is of help.

This may include continued self-defense classes, as well as cognitive restructuring of unrealistic statements about "impending danger" and "all men are rapists" thinking. It is common for rape victims to begin to feel that all men are going to hurt them or feel they will be revictimized. These thoughts need to be affirmed, yet challenged. Without cognitive restructuring and a more realistic and balanced view about men, "black-and-white" thinking can become prevalent. Rape groups help women in mirroring back images of themselves, watching others grow, conquering fears, and reentering dating relationships. Groups can also be instrumental in challenging black-and-white thinking.

Because rape victims experience depression, anxiety, fear, and sexual dysfunction, theory about techniques that treat these symptoms will be presented. Psychoeducation in these areas for the victim and the victim's family helps to reduce ideation of psychopathology. Continuing group therapy also allows the victim to see and hear similar responses from other rape victims. Attention to PTSD reactions that may be persisting and addressing those specific reactions will cut through to remaining core issues for rape victims.

Reorganization occurs when victims begin to integrate the rape experience into their life perspective and feel that the crime is not the only focus of their life. Feelings of anger and fear diminish, giving emotional energy to invest in other areas of life. Their mental state becomes more balanced. Although victims may still talk about the assault, it is with more composure. They recognize that the world is not as safe as they once thought and continue to take steps to ensure their own and their children's safety. They may see how to prevent a future attack but no longer blame themselves for the previous one/s. Rather than deciding to mistrust everyone, they selectively choose people they can trust.

Recovery can be delayed if there is no effective plan of action to follow, such as that provided in counseling. Victims' position is strengthened if they know that they are heading in the right direction, even if it may take them a while to get there.

The following suggestions, although they may seem simplistic, are effective in stabilizing the rape victim throughout the counseling process. Because some of the steps are basic, more paraprofessionals are now employed in this process. Nonetheless, the steps are viable throughout the three stages of counseling.

Suggestions for Long-Term Counseling Focus

1. Help victims accept that the rape will affect their life, not ultimately making it worse, but making it forever changed. Help them accept that relationships and the ways they perceive life, others, and themselves will also change.

2. Help victims to structure their days so as not to set themselves up for long-term depression. Make a list of things they want to get done for the day and suggest they do them one at a time. Advise them to stop to recognize and celebrate those small mountaintops and successes. Teach them to expect that not every day is going to be smooth. Reassure them that tomorrow may be better.

3. Educate victims how to nurture their inner child. Show them how to be good to themselves. Help them make a list of things that feel good to them and encourage them to go back to the list on bad days. Help them learn to say no to others' demands when they can't possibly meet them. Also help them to set strong boundaries and work through their codependency.

4. Remind victims to take care of themselves physically (eat, exercise, take vitamins, not abuse food, alcohol, drugs), emotionally (counseling, support group, a 12-step program, self-defense classes), spiritually (pray, go to a religious class, read books of encouragement), socially (go out with friends who understand where they have been, not to isolate themselves), and educationally (read books on rape, recovery, self-growth).

5. Help victims fight negative thinking. Remind them of what they did right and that the rape is not their fault. Help them to focus on their strengths and to direct their energies to positive outcomes in lobbying for victims' rights or rape prevention programs. Show them how to reach out to others who are not as far along in recovery as they are.

6. Teach victims how to express their feelings. Discourage repressing or denying. Encourage them to call their counselor, group member, friend, or write in their journal. Initiate them in drawing their fear, dancing their anger, sculpting their healing. Allow them to yell, cry, and ask questions.

7. Help victims to accept that no one has all the answers.

8. Stress that victims maintain a strong support group. Remind them that isolating themselves makes it harder and longer to heal. Instruct them not to rely on only a couple of people. Encourage them to expand their base of support to include family, friends, group members, 12-step members, church/synagogue friends, religious leader, counselor, and people from their self-defense classes or art classes.

10. Most of all remind victims to give themselves time to heal. Guide them to respect themselves for choosing to heal. Not all choose to begin the work of healing.

(Remember the other types of therapies listed previously in this chapter under crisis intervention if you are looking for a more individualistic approach.)

Client Concerns

- Safety of self;
- Safety of children;
- Mistrust of men/husband/dating;
- Frustration with impaired sexuality;
- Frustration with impaired emotional intimacy;
- Loss of self-esteem, self-respect, and level of functioning;
- Perceptual distortion;
- Marriage/dating problems;
- Divorce;
- Rapist being released/looking for them;
- Being revictimized; and
- Attempts at reentering dating/sexual relationships.

Secondary Victimizations

- Divorce;
- Loss of sexual desire;
- Cost of home safety equipment;
- Cost of self-defense classes;
- Cost of counseling (both victimization and marriage and family);
- Change of job;
- Lack of information about legal procedures; and
- Fear of AIDS.

Social Services Needed

- Long-term counselor;
- Group counseling;
- Bureau of Crime Compensation;
- Prosecutor/attorney; and
- Self-defense classes.

SPECIAL CONCERNS OF MALE RAPE VICTIMS

Often overlooked is the male rape victim. However, male rape is being reported more frequently and more victims are seeking psychological counseling. There is some stigmatization that only gay men are raped. This is also a myth. Although gay men are often targeted and raped because of their sexual orientation, "straight" men are also raped. (For more information on gay violence, see chapter 5 on assault.)

Most men who seek counseling do not do so based on an incident of rape, but often disclosure of the rape will come out in the course of counseling (McCann & Pearlman, 1990). Those who do seek counseling as a direct result of rape often struggle with shame and the belief that men should be able to ward off sexual assaults. It is an affront to their "maleness" to have experienced such a powerless and humiliating experience. If this becomes an internalized message, men may feel they collaborated with the offender and actually desired the assault. This may lead them to question their preferred sexual orientation and sexuality (McCann & Pearlman), especially if there was any physiological stimulation. Men need to be educated that sexual arousal is a normal physiological response. Some maladaptations in exerting power or dominance may result from the disruption in a man's power schemas (McCann & Pearlman).

CONCLUSION

Recent studies indicate that rape victims respond well to numerous types of counseling approaches. Study of the other types of effective treatments listed in this chapter will empower you as a counselor to reach out to rape victims in a global fashion and consider their individuality in the counseling process. Familiarity with the needs of rape victims will help you select appropriate approaches. Emerging theories that are now being researched will add to the dimension of counselors' choices. With the increasing amount of rape violence, the likelihood of treating rape victims will grow with the statistics.

Overview of Rape

Crisis Intervention Issues:	Shock, numbness, disorientation, PTSD, dissociation, impact phase of rape trauma syndrome, hysterical or calm presentation, medical attention, rape exam, processing the experience, reducing guilt/blame.
Short-Term Counseling:	Criminal justice system, pregnancy or STDs/AIDS, disclosure to family members, issues of fear and safety, attempts at repressing memories, guilt, anger, depression, ambivalence toward men, self-esteem, dispelling myths about rape, employment problems, stigma, recoil phase of rape trauma syndrome.
Long-Term Counseling:	Sexual problems, fear issues, male issues, damaged goods syndrome, safety, mistrust, danger, cognitive restructuring, interpersonal relationships, substance abuse, compulsions, recovery phase of rape trauma syndrome.
Secondary Victimizations:	Medical costs, time off work, replacement of articles stolen or damaged, insensitivity of caregivers, fear of rapists being released on bond, legal costs, loss of job, divorce, cost of security devices, loss of sexual desire, counseling costs.
Social Services Needed:	Medical exam, rape exam, DNA testing, Crime Compensation Bureau, victim advocate, crisis intervention counseling, short- and long-term counseling, social service money if victim cannot work for a while, job placement, legal aid if prosecuting, housing if leaving known abuser, temporary shelter.

INTRAFAMILIAL SEXUAL ABUSE (INCEST)

- One out of seven boys will be incest victims by the time they reach 18 (Russell, 1988).
- One out of four girls will be incest victims by the time they reach 18 (Russell 1988).

This segment will deal with adult incest victims, that is, those who were intrafamilially sexually abused.

COUNSELOR WARNING

This segment is written with a serious professional warning attached. Incest survivor counseling is not an area of trauma care and victimization to be entered into unadvisedly. It is a highly specialized area of counseling that deals with a complex population of victims.

The longer I work in the this area, the more I realize I don't know enough! It is the belief of many who work in this area that a counselor must have a solid understanding of trauma, trauma encodement, PTSD, personality disorders, dissociative disorders, and the willingness to accept the high possibility of working with clients who have multiple personality disorders.

You will hear the unheard of, the almost unbelievable, and will struggle personally with the concepts of humanity and the nature of evil. You may put yourself personally at risk, especially if you uncover a ritual/satanic abuse case and the case is prosecuted. When working in the area of sexual abuse, if you go beyond crisis intervention and decide to work with the client all the way through it, you have to be willing to hear it all, understand that you don't know what you may uncover, be willing to accept the danger that may be involved, understand your own transference and countertransference issues, be able to know that this is an irreplaceable loss for the victim, and be willing to do a lot of studying and reading about this area of victimization.

If you have bravely said yes to all the above, then carry on. . .

Courtois (1988) stated that "incest therapy is geared towards the special needs and is directed by feminist, traumatic stress, developmental, and loss theories." The feminist therapy is directed at reempowering the woman because abuse is disempowering. Traumatic stress therapy treats the trauma while acknowledging the victimization. The developmental therapy must be geared toward the "holes" that develop in the personality during the abuse stage, especially if it occurs over a period of time. This can be seen in trust issues, interpersonal relationships, and the imbalances in the personality. The loss therapy is focused on grieving things lost to victims such as childhood, stable upbringing, adequate parenting, virginity, and so forth.

Clinically we know that intentional trauma is worse than unintentional trauma, such as a natural catastrophe (Courtois, 1990). Any type of sexual abuse is intentional trauma. Intrafamilial abuse (immediate family) is more damaging to the child and more trapping than abuse by a stranger, especially if the abuser is a parent or sibling (Courtois, 1990; Greenwald & Leitenberg, 1990).

Incest trauma affects a victim in seven specific ways:

Emotional effects can include rage, grief, anxiety, depression, vulnerability, fear of loss of control, intrusive thought, hallucinations, auditory disturbances, and hyperarousal.

Self-perceptions and cognitive effects are seen in cognitive distortions, self-blame, and shame.

Somatic effects (physical reactions) are manifested in a host of physical problems seen with amazing frequency in women surviving sexual abuse, both directly and indirectly related to the locus of abuse.

Sexual effects are seen in problems of sexual emergence, sexual identity, arousal response, dissociation during sex, lack of sexual drive or satisfaction, and sexually transmitted diseases.

Interpersonal effects are seen in the ability to relate and function within relationships, especially in the areas of trust and intimacy.

Codependency and dysfunctional family effects are seen in victims' problems in relating to others, parenting, and setting appropriate and safe boundaries. It is sad to note that many of these effects will not be seen until the next generation, when the effects of poor parenting will emerge again in the victims' own children.

Social effects are seen in problems in functioning socially and occupationally. We are beginning to see the effects of sexual abuse in inmate populations, deviant juvenile offenders, and prostitutes. Studies suggest that two thirds of prostitutes were sexually abused as children (Courtois, 1990).

A recent study indicated that adults who were sexually abused as children are likely to manifest depression, self-destructive behaviors such as suicidal gestures or self-harm gestures, anxiety, low-self esteem, relationship problems, revictimization, sexual adjustment problems, substance abuse, and disturbed social relationships (Browne & Finkelhor, 1986). This clinical syndrome of symptomatology has been termed "postsexual abuse syndrome" (Briere, 1984). These symptoms are indicative of PTSD (Donaldson & Gardner, 1985; Frederick, 1986; Goodwin, 1985; Herman, Russell, & Trocki, 1986; Rychtarik, Silverman, Van Landingham, & Prue, 1984).

Some signs and symptoms of adult incest survivors are:

1. Depression;
2. Low self-esteem;
3. Social adjustment problems;
4. Sexual problems;
5. Eating disorders;
6. Self-destructive behaviors;
7. Revictimization;
8. Mental disorders, mostly similar to victims of MPD;
9. Anxiety;
10. Somatic symptoms, frequent surgery;
11. Drug abuse and other addictions;
12. Dissociation;
13. Lack of trust;
14. Impulse disorders/compulsive behaviors;
15. Feeling soiled, helpless, powerless;
16. Tendency to be workaholics, high achievers;
17. Problems with control issues, male issues;
18. Chronic feelings of betrayal, impostor syndrome (feeling their actions are committed by someone else—acting happy, successful, while actual being depressed or sick);
20. Night terrors and phobias;
*21. Epileptic type seizures;
*22. Mitral-valve prolapse;
*23. Digestive disorders;
*24. Chronic migranes; and
*25. Endometriosis and/or early hysterectomy.

(*There seem to be connections within the population to these types of somatic illnesses, but the concurrent proof is still lacking. More empirical research needs to be done, but don't be uncomfortable about asking the survivors about these symptoms.)

Establishing correlations with somatic illnesses and long-term chronic pain still demands more research. There are, however, connections proposed to actual physical symptoms in adult survivors. It stands to reason that those who were penetrated at an early age or over a long period of time can and will manifest, at the very least, female repro-

ductive disorders. Children's bodies are simply not made to accom-
modate an adult penis and other instruments. These internal injuries
are often permanent and lead to physical problems and diseases later
in life.

Some physical symptoms of sexual abuse are:

* 1. TMJ; chronic pain in the temporo mandibular joint;
* 2. Frequent urinary tract, colon, bladder, and yeast infections;
* 3. Lower back problems;
* 4. Migranes;
* 5. Undiagnosed chronic pain;
* 6. Strong gagging reflex;
  7. Weight problems;
* 8. Mitral-valve prolapse;
* 9. Digestive disorders; and
*10. Unexplained epileptic type seizures.

(*Many of these symptoms are seen with amazing frequency with adult
survivors of incest, yet concurrent medical proof is lacking. Empirical
studies need to be completed. However, do not be hesitant to ask about
these symptoms during intakes.)

Courtois (1988, 1990) further stated that denial and neglect of incest
have compounded aftereffects. These compounded effects and special
needs are brought to therapy.

1. Abuse within the family heightens the trauma while making escape
   and intervention more difficult.
2. Chronic trauma during the child's formative years alters the child's
   development.
3. Untreated trauma is seen in the victim-to-parent process.
4. Original effects, if untreated, spawn secondary problems (Courtois,
   1990).

The following acronym created by Jean Goodwin and cited by Courtois (1990) will help to remember the aftereffects of sexual abuse:

F = Fear and anxiety
E = Ego constriction: sexuality
A = Anger, lack of control
R = Repetitions, flashbacks
S = Sadness

Severe Symptoms:

F = Fugues and other dissociative symptoms
E = Ego splitting/MPD pathology
A = Antisocial behavior
R = Reenactments
S = Suicide

DISORDERS

Unlike other victimizations, because of its intensity, sexual abuse, especially in cases of incest that continued through most of childhood, or any ritual abuse, manifests in its victims various types of personality and dissociative disorders that are seen with amazing frequency. Just like grief and PTSD are seen on a continuum, so are the personality and dissociative disorders often manifested by these types of victims.

To understand this unconventional continuum that we have developed, we must again remember that we are assessing a person's response to trauma. The continuum that follows was created by Dr. Benjamin Keyes; it represents what a number of us in the field have found to be an example of the possible degrees of reaction to sexual abuse trauma. Although the continuum represents an unorthodox mixture of personality disorders and dissociative disorders, keep in mind that this continuum represents a variety of coping mechanisms and survival techniques. We readily recognize that the continuum given would not be considered a standard guideline under DSM-III-R classifications. We also readily recognize that we have mixed different types of disorders to create our continuum.

Bridgework, Inc., has seen over 100 sexually abused women and children. We compared observations of these victims with other professionals' observations in sexual abuse to find this continuum to occur with notable frequency.

We noticed that those experiencing a low-end (not severe or chronic) reaction to trauma frequently had a narcissistic personality disorder. We noted that most of the women who had been abused frequently had borderline personality disorders. Those with a high-end (severe and chronic) reaction to trauma were considered to have a dissociative disorder, although many women with borderline personality disorders also had some dissociative qualities; however, this high-end (dissociative) reaction far exceeded the borderlines' reaction. The ultimate reaction to long-term physical/sexual/psychological abuse was multiple personality disorder (MPD).

The narcissistic, borderline, dissociative, and multiple personality disorders are formed as a coping mechanism to long-term trauma and as a survival technique against other forms of psychotic breaks. Many types of diagnoses that have been given the sexual abuse victim have reflected more of the symptoms than an actual overview of the trauma. For instance, although a woman could be diagnosed with a depressive disorder, in actuality the depression is not the disorder but a symptom of the trauma. Over recent years, we have come to better understand traumatization, its long-term effects, and how that changes what we previously believed about people with borderline or dissociative disorders and those with multiple personalities.

In addition, within the four categories listed, many other types of disorders can be seen. For example, a person with a borderline personality disorder might also have adjustment or depressive disorders. We use the continuum to create a broader view of the most frequently seen personality disorders in incest.

TRAUMA CONTINUUM

1. *Narcissistic personality*: DSM-III-R states (301.81):*

A pervasive pattern of grandiosity (in fantasy or behavior), lack of empathy, and hypersensitivity to the evaluation of others, beginning by early adulthood and present in a variety of contexts, as indicated by at least five of the following:

1. Reacts to criticism with feelings of rage, shame or humiliation (even if not expressed).

2. Is interpersonally exploitative; takes advantage of others to achieve his or her own ends.

3. Has a grandiose sense of self-importance, e.g., exaggerates achievements and talents, expects to be noticed as "special" without appropriate achievement.

4. Believes that his or her problems are unique and can be understood only by other special people.

5. Is preoccupied with fantasies of unlimited success, power, brilliance, beauty, or ideal love.

6. Has a sense of entitlement; unreasonable expectation of especially favorable treatment, e.g., assumes that he or she does not have to wait in line when others must do so.

---

*Reprinted with permission from the *Diagnostic and Statistical Manual of Mental Disorders, Third Edition, Revised.* Copyright 1987 American Psychiatric Association.

7. Requires constant attention and admiration, e.g., keeps fishing for compliments.

8. Lack of empathy: inability to recognize and experience how others feel, e.g., annoyance and surprise when a friend who is seriously ill cancels a date.

9. Is preoccupied with feelings of envy. (American Psychiatric Association, 1987, pp. 349–351)

2. *Borderline personality*: DSM-III-R states (301.83):*

A pervasive pattern of instability of mood, interpersonal relationships, and self-image, beginning by early adulthood and present in a variety of contexts, as indicated by at least five of the following:

1. A pattern of unstable and intense interpersonal relationships characterized by alternating between extremes of overidealization and devaluation.

2. Impulsiveness in at least two areas that are potentially self-damaging, e.g., spending, sex, substance abuse, shoplifting, reckless driving, binge eating.

3. Affective instability: marked shifts from baseline mood to depression, irritability, or anxiety, usually lasting a few hours and only rarely more than a few days.

4. Inappropriate, intense anger or lack of control of anger, e.g., frequent display of temper, constant anger, recurrent physical fights.

5. Recurrent suicidal threats, gestures, or behavior, or self-mutilating behavior.

6. Marked and persistent identity disturbance manifested by uncertainty about at least two of the following: self-image, sexual orientation, long-term goals or career choice, type of friends desired, preferred values.

7. Chronic feelings of emptiness or boredom.

8. Frantic efforts to avoid real or imagined abandonment. (American Psychiatric Association, 1987, pp. 346–347)

The borderline personality, as seen in trauma victims, greatly stems from the mixture of parents/caregivers as addicts, codependency, dysfunctional family issues, fairly consistent physical abuse, or sexual abuse.

3. *Dissociative disorder*: DSM-III-R states:*

A disturbance or alteration in the normally integrative functions of identity, memory, or consciousness. The disturbance or alteration may be sudden or gradual, and transient or chronic. If it occurs primarily in identity, the person's customary identity is temporarily forgotten, or the customary feeling of one's own reality is lost and is replaced by a feeling of unreality. If the disturbance

---

*Reprinted with permission from the *Diagnostic and Statistical Manual of Mental Disorders, Third Edition, Revised.* Copyright 1987 American Psychiatric Association.

occurs primarily in memory, important personal events cannot be recalled. (American Psychiatric Association, 1987, pp. 269, 277)

As a defense to the abuse, the victims detach from their body so that the inner core/emotional self would not be injured during the act of abuse. They disconnect to avoid conflict and block memory that is too painful. Many victims call this their "out of body experience" because they will often project themselves out of their body to a safer place during the time the abuse is taking place.

At Bridgework, we see that about 75% of our women have the basic dissociative disorder. In this type of trauma, this disorder has worked quite well in childhood, allowing them to cope with the abuse, but this coping mechanism, when carried over to adulthood, becomes a defense mechanism. It is during adulthood that survivors begin to experience the dysfunction of dissociation. They begin to dissociate even when they no longer wish to. They dissociate during stress on the job, during conflict in relationships, and even during pleasurable sex.

In pathological dissociation, as we in see in trauma victims, especially those who have been sexually abused, the dissociation is used because the victim does not have other types of cognitive defenses. These must be taught during the counseling process.

In sexual abuse, the dissociation rate is higher than in physical abuse, based on the theory of participation. Because the child had to participate in sexual abuse on some level, the need to dissociate was greater than during physical abuse, which has no, or minimal participation basis.

Dissociation in the sexual abuse victim serves a number of purposes. It allows for analgesic numbing (which is the psychological numbing or absence of pain), allows the ability to create a fantasy and safe place psychologically, and helps to depersonalize the event (thinking this isn't happening, and providing a magical way of protecting). Also seen in the area of dissociation is psychological amnesia and psychogenic fugue states. These fall into the category of dissociation but represent different elements.

4. *Multiple personality*: This is the high-end reaction on the continuum. It goes further than dissociative disorder because victims don't just detach from their inner core or project themselves out of their inner core, but create another personality to "take" the various portions of the abuse they can no longer handle emotionally or physically. In a more animated sense I like to use the example of Tag Team Wrestling. Two men get in the ring to wrestle. The first man goes in and takes as much as he can take. When he can't take any more, he tags off and

the next man comes in. Most of the victims with MPD whom I work with state that is exactly how they view their personalities. The personalities are created to tolerate different aspects of the abuse: sexual, hatred, rage, physical abuse, dichotomies such as loving the abuser versus hating the abuser, father versus lover, protector versus abuser, and so forth.

DSM-III-R states (300.14):*

A. The existence within the person of two or more distinct personalities or personality states (each with its own relatively enduring pattern of perceiving, relating to, and thinking about the environment and self).

B. At least two of these personalities or personality states recurrently take full control of the person's behavior. (American Psychiatric Association, 1987, pp. 269–272)

The person with MPD will always be dissociative. In the DSM-III-R, MPD is listed as one of the dissociative disorders. The victim with MPD is on the high end of the continuum and this results from incredible amounts of abuse. The physical abuse factor is usually seen strongly in these victims and will border on, if not cross, the boundaries of ritualistic torture.

My cases have included knives inserted in the vagina for "episiotomies," the victim used in child sex rings, made to train other children how to perform acts of sex, made to perform sex with animals, have snake heads inserted in the vagina, made to drink blood, made to be impregnated at age 12 by others and sacrifice the baby, being tied up and watching bodies being dismembered, watching other children or adults tortured to death in various ways, and watching the manifestation of spirits.

The sexual abuse will be profound and incorporate many different types of sexual activity often with other people, animals, or instruments. Many people with MPD we now find, because we aren't afraid to ask, were used in cult worship services and were the actual instruments of breeding children for sacrifices and watching or participating in the sacrifice of their own babies.

If we view these four categories on the continuum of severity in reactions to trauma, coping mechanisms, and survival techniques, we can begin to see how trauma adversely affects the victim.

---

*Reprinted with permission from the *Diagnostic and Statistical Manual of Mental Disorders, Third Edition, Revised.* Copyright 1987 American Psychiatric Association.

CRISIS INTERVENTION FOR ADULT
SURVIVORS OF INCEST

The crisis intervention stage for an adult incest victim obviously occurs years after the incidents of abuse. The incest victim is usually involved in elaborate denial and repression that lasts many years (Courtois, 1990, Burgess, 1986). The defense mechanisms of repression add to the disorders so often seen in incest victims.

The victim who engages in counseling usually will not at first readily acknowledge or admit sexual abuse. Common presentations are:

1. Depression with complications of impulsive and dissociative elements (Courtois, 1990);
2. Either delayed or chronic PTSD showing signs of flashbacks, numbing, or memory leakage;
3. Problems with relationships—could include family, sexual, parental, employment, friendships, or any other type of interpersonal relationship;
4. Disclosure of a history of drugs and alcohol abuse, other addictions and compulsions, time loss (amnesia), frequent suicide attempts or self-mutilation, numerous counseling attempts, and revictimizations; and
5. Borderline diagnosis or borderline behaviors.

Many victims are unaware or seem ignorant about the possibility of sexual abuse existing in their background. Profuse denying of the possibility of abuse, justifying, or minimizing are common. However, the crisis intervention stage in counseling can start when the victim begins retrieval of new memories through abreactions (when memories begin to resurface or flood). Most women begin to have memory leakage, in which they begin to get flashes and fragments of memory, in their mid-to-late 20s and 30s, which brings them into counseling in a crisis state. For some, these are new memories presenting an unknown history of abuse; for others, it is confirmation of an assumed or vaguely remembered background.

Your contact with the victim may begin with memory leakage. Some victims present with childlike "uh-oh feelings" that often precede the actual memory.

Goals of Treatment

1. Development of a commitment to treatment and the establishment of a therapeutic alliance.

2. Acknowledgment and acceptance of the occurrence of the incest.
3. Recounting the incest.
4. The breakdown of feelings of isolation and stigma.
5. The recognition, labeling, and expression of feelings.
6. The resolution of responsibility and survival issues.
7. Grieving.
8. Cognitive restructuring of distorted beliefs and stress responses.
9. Self-determination and behavioral changes.
10. Education and skill building. (Courtois, 1988, 1990)

These 10 goals represent the overall goals of treatment for the adult incest survivor. Let's look at some specific treatment techniques for the crisis intervention/presentation phase you will be seeing in an incest survivor.

If the survivor is presenting with abreactions, flooding, and new memories, she will be highly charged, dissociative, and overstimulated. Your first goal will be to build a trusting alliance and defuse the activated memory to a level that she is able to handle emotionally. Do not attempt to work with past history at this time because it will add anxiety and overstimulate the victim. Work with the current problem of abreacting.

1. Help reduce stress and increase coping. Remove items or triggers that are inducing abreactions, such as interaction with abuser, photos of abuser, books on abuse, self-help books, or romance novels with high sex content.
2. Even if the victim is not abreacting, work toward teaching stress management and relaxation and building ego strength before moving on.
3. Safety: Is victim in an environment free from revictimization? Free from contact with abuser?
4. Strengthen resources: support persons, support groups, counseling programs, 12-step groups, religious groups, and so forth.

While strengthening resources, either you or a referral counselor of your choice should work with the victim for a reasonable amount of time before considering a group experience. Groups are an excellent form of therapy and should be utilized when working with this population; however, it is important for an alliance between the therapist and victim to have been formed and for crisis stabilization to have been completed. Encourage your clients to continue individual counseling while they are in a group. Peer support groups (as opposed to

therapy groups) should be utilized following therapy groups and relied
on for aftercare and maintenance.

Client Concerns

- To be able to stop or handle abreactions;
- Afraid he/she is "making up" memories of incest;
- Unable to stop or handle dissociation;
- Unable to stop or handle flooding of new memories;
- Afraid he/she will not be able to handle more memories
  or therapy;
- Afraid of interaction with family (abusers) or "rocking
  the boat"; and
- Afraid of having to confront abuser.

Secondary Victimizations

- Inability to maintain close relationships;
- Divorce;
- Medical costs for somatic illnesses;
- Counseling costs;
- Loss of employment;
- Drug, alcohol, and other addiction rehabilitation;
- Inability to care for their children;
- Lost childhood;
- Unhappy adulthood; and
- Revictimization in other areas.

The secondary victimizations in incest are not always apparent.
However, the victim has come to embrace them as part of her life and
her burden to bear. The incest victim has no doubt paid dearly for her
abuse in many ways. And she continues to pay until she decides to
heal. Then she pays throughout her healing process.

Social Services Needed

- Crisis intervention counselor;
- Psychiatrist (if medication is needed); and
- Drug/alcohol/addiction rehabilitation or groups.

SHORT-TERM COUNSELING

1. When abreactions subside, begin work with cognitive/behavioral therapies; deal with educating victim about abuse, depression, and managing elevated levels of stress.

2. Begin assessments: Incest History Questionnaire, Dissociative Experience Scale, Dissociative Disorders Interview Schedule, Trauma Symptom Checklist, Responses to Childhood Incest.

3. Challenge cognitive distortions and beliefs about abuse, themselves, the abuser, dichotomies.

4. Begin exploration/psychodynamics of memories and past history. Discuss the trauma and lead victims into understanding the trauma from sensory, perceptual, cognitive, and interpersonal views. Have them continue to work these over and over until it begins to integrate.

5. If memories begin to block, use items that will induce memory recall: photos of abuser or place of abuse, letters from abuser, or their own journal entries of prior memories. When staging memory retrieval, expect that abreactions may begin again.

Utilizing incest therapy groups will be appropriate at this time if both of you have regained control of the abreactions. Groups help to address stigma, shame, lack of sexual desire, interpersonal relationship problems, abuser confrontation, and ego building. The list mentioned above will be addressed somewhat in groups, but much of the work will need to be done in individual therapy. Do not overlook other types of effective expressive therapies that help the survivor connect to memories stored in other than cognitive areas. These are listed in chapter 3 on therapies for trauma victims.

Often, the list of five items above may need to be worked through many times. If abreactions come very quickly, slowing them down will be necessary. Once they are slowed down or stopped and the work of stabilization is completed, you may need to start the process again. Starting and slowing are normal. This can be seen even on a weekly basis. You may work very hard on a memory one week when a lot of memory is recalled during a session, and the following week focus on ego strength, stabilization, and preparing to hit it hard the next week.

Client Concerns

- Stigma and shame;
- Relationships;
- Trust;

- Emotional intimacy;
- Lack of sexual desire;
- Abreactions and controlling them;
- Confidentiality.

Secondary Victimizations

- Inability to maintain close relationships;
- Divorce;
- Medical costs for somatic illnesses;
- Counseling costs;
- Lack of sexual desire;
- Twisted self-image or sexual identification;
- Uncontrollable rage;
- Inability to nurture children;
- Drug, alcohol, or other addiction rehabilitation;
- Lost childhood; and
- Unhappy adulthood.

Social Services Needed

- Short-term counselor;
- Incest therapy group;
- Addiction therapy program;
- Eating disorders program;
- Financial assistance while undergoing therapy if unable to work;
- Attorney (if prosecution is desired);
- Psychiatrist (if medication is needed); and
- Job rehabilitation or career counseling.

LONG-TERM COUNSELING

Some adult survivors are sporadic in their consistency with ongoing counseling. They may seem committed only to leave short-term counseling for periods of time, reexperience crisis, and return for more ongoing counseling. Your long-term counseling attempts may be based on that sort of in-and-out treatment. Remember that many of these women also have personality disorders that add to the challenge not only of treatment itself but of keeping them in treatment!

Long-term counseling should focus on the following elements:

1. *Processing the trauma and memories that were retrieved.* This involves four aspects: sensory—learning techniques and exhibiting control over arousal of memories; perceptual—negative and positive cue identification of what ''sets them off'' in either memory or arousal; cognitive—learning to reframe dysfunctional and distorted beliefs; and interpersonal relationships—rebuilding and restoring old relationships and making new ones.

2. *Transferring trauma to past memory.* This process revolves around therapeutic forgetting and neutralizing emotions. This happens in stages and will have occurred, if therapy has been done correctly, through the course of treatment. As the memories are retrieved, experienced, and processed, they also become emotionally decharged. When they are decharged they can be moved from active memory, which is interrupting daily living, to past memory.

3. *Termination.* The victim begins to have a future-oriented stance. She begins to project and see herself in many activities in the future, has some anticipation for the future, and begins to set goals for herself.

For termination to be effective, the decision to terminate should be mutual. This will not always occur. Many survivors, as mentioned before, come in and out of therapy as they ''feel'' better (i.e., stabilized). This ''feeling'' of security is often short-lived. Their perception of when to terminate and yours will not always be the same. Expressing your concerns if you feel they are not ready is acceptable, yet if they do terminate, respect their choice to do so. I have an open-door policy should survivors decide to reconnect when the ''perceived stabilization'' wanes. Final and ultimate termination should be worked toward as an expressed goal and formulated early on in treatment. Often, asking the survivor to write out the goals that she or he wants to be able to accomplish to signify that termination is near is helpful to refer back to when premature termination is attempted.

Client Concerns

- Restabilization of self, their world, and relationships;
- Return of sexual desire;

- Strengthening of interpersonal relationships;
- Strengthening/establishing/reestablishing spiritual beliefs;
- Abuser/family confrontations;
- Future/further victimizations;
- Ability to protect their children adequately;
- Self-esteem, worth, and value;
- Career choices and options; and
- Life-style.

Secondary Victimizations

- Inability to maintain close, emotionally intimate, relationships;
- Inability to maintain close, sexually intimate, relationships;
- Cost of counseling;
- Addiction rehabilitation;
- Loss of trust;
- Loss of childhood;
- Loss of adult happiness; and
- Loss of virginity.

Social Services Needed

- Long-term counselor;
- Incest group;
- Career counseling;
- Eating disorders group;
- Addiction group;
- Attorney (if prosecution is desired);
- Financial aid (if therapy renders victims unable to work during abreactions); and
- Other community services to meet current needs.

CONCLUSION

Clearly the impact of childhood sexual abuse leaves its devastation on its survivors. In no area are the needs of survivors more pressing and the demand for knowledge, training, and professionalism so urgent on the part of counselors.

As the women's movement of the 1960s, the rape movement of the 1970s, and the mental health, child abuse, and sexual abuse movement of the 1980s have advanced, so has disclosure for adult survivors of childhood sexual abuse. We can well anticipate that as services become more prevalent and visible and the media continue to focus on this issue, and as survivors step forward to prosecute past offenders, mental health counselors will increasingly be receiving the byproduct of disclosure—the victims.

RECOMMENDED READING

Bass, E., & Davis, L. (1988). *Courage to heal.* New York: Harper & Row.

Burgess, A. W., & Holmstrom, L. L. (1986). *Rape: Crisis and recovery.* West Newton, MA: Awab.

Courtois, C. A. (1988). *Healing the incest wound: Adult survivors in therapy.* New York: Norton.

Herman, J. (1981). *Father-daughter incest.* Cambridge, MA: Harvard University Press.

Johnson, K. (1985). *If you are raped: What every woman needs to know.* Holmes Beach, FL: Learning Publications.

Ledray, L. (1986). *Recovering from rape.* New York: Holt.

Rencken, R. (1989). *Intervention strategies for sexual abuse.* Alexandria, VA: American Association for Counseling and Development.

Sgroi, S. M. (1988). *Vunerable populations: Evaluation and treatment of sexually abused children and adult survivors.* (Vol 1.). Lexington, MA: Lexington Books.

REFERRALS

Incest Survivors Resource Network, International
    Friends Meeting House
15 Rutherford Place
New York, NY 10003
P.O. Box 911
Hicksville, NY 11802

National Assault Prevention Center
P.O. Box 02005
Columbus, OH 43205
614-291-2540

National Center on Women and Family Law
799 Broadway, Room 402
New York, NY 10003
212-674-8200

National Clearinghouse on Marital and Date Rape
2325 Oak Street
Berkeley, CA 94708
415-548-1770

National Coalition Against Sexual Assault
2428 Ontario Road, NW
Washington, DC 20009
202-483-7165

Survivors of Incest Anonymous, Inc.
P.O. Box 21817
Baltimore, MD 21222
301-282-3400

	**Overview of Intrafamilial Sexual Abuse**
Crisis Intervention Issues:	Abreaction of new memories, reducing abreaction, depression, PTSD, relationship problems, addictions, self-mutilation, somatic illnesses, memory leakage, increasing coping, safety, stress management, strengthening resources.
Short-Term Counseling:	Establishing trust alliance, acknowledging incest, recounting incest, breakdown of feelings, stigma, expression of feelings.
Long-Term Counseling:	Resolution of responsibility, survival issues, grieving, cognitive restructuring of distorted beliefs, behavioral changes, education and skill building, transferring trauma to past memory.
Secondary Victim- izations:	Inability to maintain close relationships, counseling costs, medical costs for somatic illnesses, lost employment, addictions, ostracization by family members.
Social Services Needed:	Medical attention for somatic illnesses, attorney if prosecuting, rehabilitation training if new job skills needed, crisis, short- and long-term counseling, family counseling, addictions and/or compulsion programs, housing if leaving abuser, temporary shelter.

8

Violence Against Children

- Before puberty, one out of seven boys will be incest victims (Russell, 1988).
- By the time they reach 18, one out of four girls will be incest victims (Russell, 1988).
- Researchers found a significant rise in abuse. Physical abuse increased by 58% and sexual abuse occurred at more than triple its 1980 rate (National CASA Association, 1989).
- In 1989 1,100 children were reported as fatal victims of child abuse and neglect (National Committee for Prevention of Child Abuse, 1989.

PHYSICAL ABUSE

Child abuse has probably become the most widely recognized form of abuse. Many of us have sat in utter horror as we have heard the recounts of various types of children's deaths through child abuse. In Florida, our most recent devastation was the death of young Bradley McGee, just a toddler, who was killed when his stepfather made him eat his own feces and then dunked him by his feet headfirst in the toilet to teach him potty-training. Young Bradley died of extensive head injuries.

Probably just as frightening, though, we as a society must ask ourselves, "What if the child had lived?" The children who have survived neglect, and physical, sexual, and emotional abuse are emerging into society carrying with them a lot of unhealthy baggage.

When the next decade rolls around, we are going to see the proliferation in our society of adults abused as children. This will most certainly take a toll on our criminal, mental health, and social systems. It is a frightening thought that we as a society will not only face those adults abused as children but also victims who were born crack-addicted, those born unattached and unbonded to their parents, and those with other types of disorders. What does that mean for us as a society? What implications does that have for us as counselors?

It is not my intention to rewrite many fine books that address the issues of child abuse. Therefore, this segment will address only briefly the physical and behavioral indicators and recommended reading and national referrals. For more information on child treatment in child abuse, see the recommended reading list.

Education is paramount in the fight against abuse. Counselors, parents, teachers, and others must be aware of the impending signs of danger and that abuse, both physical and sexual, may be occurring.

TYPES OF ABUSE

Physical Abuse

Physical abuse includes violent assaults that utilize instruments that can cause injury to the child; assaults that injure the child and leave bruises, bites, welts, burns, breaks, or fractures; or spankings that yield bruises, welts, or burns.

Neglect

Physical neglect includes abandonment; refusing to seek or provide medical or psychological treatment for illnesses; the lack of adequate supervision to provide physical safety; the neglect of making the home safe for the child; and inadequate provision of nutrition, clothing, or cleanliness when these are within the means of the caregiver.

Emotional neglect includes emotional abandonment, the lack of encouragement or social interaction with the child, the lack of loving physical and verbal contact, and refusal to allow age-appropriate interaction with other children.

Educational neglect includes withholding school training, knowing about yet allowing chronic truancy, or not enrolling the child in school at all and not providing schooling at home or elsewhere.

Emotional Abuse

Emotional abuse inclues emotional and verbal assault; physical confinement that causes psychological damage such as being confined in a dark closet, tied to a bed, or other physical abuse of that nature; refusing treatment for a child's emotional illnesses; allowing the continuation of antisocial behavior in the child; and not responding by nurturance or by social service intervention to emotional/physical illnesses, such as failure to thrive in infants.

Sexual Abuse

Sexual abuse includes any type of molestation, penetration, fondling, assault, or exposure to age-inappropriate sexual materials, talk, or actions.

To identify a particular abuse or neglect, we must thoroughly look at the child's and parents' condition and behavior (U.S. Department of Health and Human Services, 1989).

BEHAVIORAL INDICATORS OF PHYSICAL ABUSE

- Radical mood swings;
- Sense of impending danger;
- Changes in eating habits;
- Nightmares, sleep disturbances, sleepwalking;
- Change in school performance, including radical improvement in grades (overachieving);
- Depression;
- Substance abuse;
- Hostile behavior or being overly withdrawn;
- Isolating self;
- Increased absenteeism from school;
- Being overcompliant;
- Bedwetting;
- Regressive or babyish behavior;
- Suicidal tendencies;
- Hints of physical abuse;
- Startle response when someone raises a hand/arm;
- Unexplained fears;

- Repetitive and rhythmic movements (such as rocking);
- Excessive attention to details; and
- Absence of verbal/physical/social communication with others.

PHYSICAL INDICATORS OF PHYSICAL ABUSE

- Bruising or bleeding on any areas of body;
- Unexplained, frequent injuries;
- Injuries not in normal areas for children (normal areas being knees, elbows, etc.);
- Any type of burns or bites;
- Frequent stomachaches or digestive distrubances;
- Somatic illnesses;
- Weight loss/gain;
- Unexplained "battle scars" around the back side of ears, inside mouth, and on scalp;
- Signs of malnutrition; and
- Injuries from lack of supervision (falling down stairs, ingestion of harmful substances, children cared for by other children).

Gauging the time frame and history of bruising may help to confirm or expose false stories. Colorations of bruising can only be approximated but may give you a guideline from which to operate:

- Red: immediate bruise, within a few hours of injury;
- Blue: from 6–12 hours prior to injury;
- Black-purple: from 12–24 hours prior to injury;
- Green tint, dark: from 4–6 days prior to injury
- Pale green to yellow: from 5–10 days prior to injury.

Bites and burns are serious injuries and demonstrate the seriousness of the abuse. These symptoms are usually signs of escalated physical abuse that has been occurring over a period of time, and they may indicate some pathology in the abuser. Get help at once!

Some children seem to be targeted for abuse based on high-risk factors associated with their families. These could include:

- Unwanted: too many children in family, too soon in marriage, illegitimate, difficult pregnancy;

- Non-normative: disabled, retarded, underweight, medical problems or diseases, "ugly," premature;
- Negative association: Remind parents of someone they do not like/hate (could be relative, spouse, another child); and
- Assertiveness: child may be highly needy, active, demanding, gifted, learning-impaired, or have other needs that engage the parents in providing more care than they think is "normal" or that is given other children in the family.

CHARACTERISTICS OF AN ABUSIVE FAMILY

Violence is a learned behavior that is transmitted by example from generation to generation. Those who were abused may go on to abuse their children, and those children will react and handle stress in the same way: violently.

Parents' Individual Characteristics

Parents may be emotionally needy or immature; isolated from friends or family for support; may have been personally abused or neglected as children or are being abused or neglected in a relationship; have low self-esteem; are addiction-oriented (drugs/alcohol); or may never have felt loved. Many parents who are abusing their children are remorseful about doing so. However, their parenting skills as well as coping skills for their problems are less than adequate. Persistence in intervention may override their resistance to treatment.

Intrafamilial Interactions

Each member of the family unit may affect negatively another family member, creating a chain of negative effect and dependence. Some families are not only socially isolated, but the adults attempt to have their children meet their emotional needs. This has been termed "emotional incest."

Environmental Atmosphere

Most dysfunctional families do not respond well to changes in their lives or environment. These changes can add to daily life stressors that may erupt in abuse toward the children. These can include financial problems, lack of employment, changes in the family structure due to separation, divorce, or added family members, having to move, or eviction.

Additional Factors

Inadequate family income seems to foster abuse. Data have shown that children from families with incomes under $15,000 per year experience maltreatment at a rate of five times higher than children from higher income families. In addition, families with four or more children revealed higher rates of abuse and neglect (U.S. Department of Health and Human Services, 1989).

Child abuse not followed by counseling interventions ultimately evolves into serious adult disorders, providing the children live to reach adulthood. These disorders can include depressive and anxiety disorders, codependency, learning disorders, and compulsive behaviors/addictions. They can also include borderline and narcissistic personality disorders. In extreme cases, they include dissociative and multiple personality disorders.

In most states, counselors do not have to prove child abuse to report it. We are mandated by law to report if we have a suspicion. Many counselors do not report because they fear they will have to prove their allegations. It is the state's responsibility to prove abuse. It is ours to report our suspicions. Not reporting places us at risk as an accessory to the crime.

CRISIS INTERVENTION

Child abuse is a family problem. Therefore, treatment must focus on each individual family member as well as the family as a cohesive unit. Treatment must be provided to the child, abuser, spouse, and siblings. Simply removing the child from an abusive situation creates an overload on the foster care system. HOWEVER, REMOVAL DURING ABUSE IS MANDATORY! It is during this time of removal that the counselor works with the family system during treatment. Removing the child to a foster system, working with the child on processing the events that occurred, strengthening personal and social resources, and working on prevention skills will only go so far when the child is returned to an infected environment. Likewise, removing one child from an abusive family may only put the remaining children at higher risk. The family remains sick and abusive, and other children are added to the list of statistics and the foster system.

During crisis intervention, mandatory reporting of the abuse to a state agency is foremost. The child may indicate a preference to remain in the family. This is not uncommon. Most children genuinely love their parents, but hate the abuse. Most children opt to be with the abusive family, hoping that the abuse will stop. Such optimism on the child's part may be unrealistic. Removing the child is the first priorty. Helping the child deal with feelings of loss, abandonment, guilt, fear, and stress is important. Helping the child develop positive coping mechanisms for placement in a new home may ward off acting-out behaviors, subsequent truancy, and other problems. Because abuse is a family issue, you may be involved in referral for the family or in doing some of the actual counseling with the family system.

Client Concerns (From a Child's Viewpoint)

- When the child will be reunited with the family;
- Will the family hold them to blame for disclosure?
- Will other siblings become the target for abuse?
- Adjusting to new environment;
- Stress from knowing they may have to testify in court;
- Loss of family/friends/familiar environment; and
- Healing from physical injuries.

Secondary Victimizations

- Removal from familiar environment;
- Loss of friends/support;
- Adjusting to new environment;
- Lack of adjustment to new school;
- Perceived abandonment from family;
- Hostility or blame for disclosure;
- Repeated interviews for court system; and
- Stigma of being a "foster child."

Social Services Needed for the Whole Family System

- Child protection services;
- Crisis intervention counselor;

- Guardian ad litem (for child victim);
- Prosecutor/attorney (for child victim);
- Defense attorney (for abuser/family);
- Offender treatment;
- Family treatment;
- Sibling treatment;
- If offender is arrested, may need financial assistance, new housing, job placement, etc.;
- Spouse counseling; and
- School guidance counselor (for child victim).

SHORT-TERM COUNSELING

Issues during this segment of counseling may be child or family oriented. Some issues may involve helping the child adjust to the new environment and dealing with the child's sense of blame, guilt, and low self-worth. Schoolwork, stress management, coping skills, loss issues, bereavement, anger, and acting-out behaviors may need to be addressed. Other issues involve how the child fits into the family system—these are dealt with in family systems work. In addition, issues of codependency, problems of children of alcoholics (if applicable), or drug addiction may be focused on as well. Teaching communication as a personal construct and how communication works in family systems is important.

The child (depending on age) may be ready for a group experience with other children of the same type of victimization. If the child is too young for that, play therapy or developmental play therapy may be helpful.

The family will need to engage in counseling as well and will need to focus on individual as well as family issues. If the offender is still in the home, offender counseling is paramount. Violence is a learned behavior, and new coping skills will need to be taught. Intervening in sibling abuse or their perception of the child victim's abuse is important. In addition, the spouse's reaction to the removal of the child and possibly the removal of the offender may involve a process of helping the spouse come to terms with any anger and resentment toward the child as well as the offender. Obviously, any addictions on the part of the offender, spouse, or siblings will also need to be treated.

Client Concerns (From a Child's Viewpoint)

- Loss of family;
- Continued feelings of blame or guilt;
- Abandonment;
- Difficulties in environment changes;
- Adjusting to new school, friends, etc.;
- Fear, nightmares, bedwetting;
- When child will be reunited with family;
- Will abuser be part of family; and
- Healing from physical injuries.

Secondary Victimizations

- Children may view themselves as criminals because they were removed and the abuser stayed (if applicable);
- Loss of familiar environment;
- Stigma of being a "foster child";
- Repeated interviews with court system;
- Inability to adjust to new environment; and
- Experiencing new abuse at foster home.

Social Services Needed for the Whole Family System

- Short-term counseling;
- Child protective services;
- Guardian ad litem (for child victim);
- Prosecutor/attorney (for child victim);
- Defense attorney (for abuser);
- Family counseling;
- Offender counseling;
- Sibling counseling;
- Spouse counseling;
- Group counseling for child victim;
- Financial assistance (if abuser is arrested), housing, etc.;
- School guidance counselor;
- Play or developmental play therapy; and
- Prevention skills.

LONG-TERM COUNSELING

Most child abuse cases are not geared to short-term counseling. When addressing the needs of a family unit that includes siblings, abuser, and spouse, short-term counseling may quickly become long-term. Issues dealt with in short-term counseling will be carried over into the long-term aspect of the process.

Additional factors that you will want to address include whether the abuser is incarcerated, any blame that is put on the child victim because of it, the effects of the court process on the child victim, reuniting the family if the abuser is returning home, or if the child is coming home. Teaching prevention skills to the child victim, siblings, and spouse will help to prevent revictimization by the same abuser or any subsequent abuser.

Careful monitoring of siblings and the child victim for any chronic pathology or acting out, as well as the precence of the victim syndrome will help ensure quick intervention in these areas. Likewise, monitoring of adjustment and affective and depressive disorders will help diagnosis in these areas.

Client Concerns (From a Child's Viewpoint)

- Being able to return home;
- Abuser returning home;
- Whether abuser has really changed;
- How the rest of the family feels about child since disclosure;
- Fear of retaliation; and
- Unsure of new coping/prevention skills.

Secondary Victimizations

- When returning to previous school, may be labeled as "foster child" or "abused child";
- Old friends may not renew acquaintance or may have made new friendships; and
- Stigma, shame, and guilt.

Social Services Needed for the Whole Family System

- Child protective services;
- Guardian ad litem (for child victim);

- Prosecutor/attorney;
- Court mediation services;
- Parenting classes;
- Offender reentry program;
- Long-term family counseling;
- Long-term sibling counseling;
- Long-term child victim counseling;
- Assertiveness training (child, siblings, spouse); and
- Prevention skills.

CONCLUSION

The future of society is in our youth's hands. If those hands have been burned, bruised, beat, and wounded, what will be society's fate? Working to help those wounded by child abuse and those who are the wounders is paramount to ending the cycle of generational violence that so well documents the genealogy of abusive families.

TREATING THE SEXUALLY ABUSED CHILD

Sexual abuse of children has been a widely covered area of research and publication. Again, it is not my intent to duplicate many existing books and articles on treatment issues, therefore, I will highlight those issues only briefly and recommend further study. There is no way for me to cover adequately this area of victimization in a portion of a chapter when it has been written about in voluminous detail in book format.

The magnitude of psychological problems that sexual abuse causes for children is vast. As disclosure seems to become more readily acceptable and as agencies, teachers, and the court system become more adept in treatment and response to new findings, sexually abused children are coming forth in waves. Research was recently conducted by the Crime Victims Research and Treatment Center (1989). The findings suggested that children who had experienced rape as part of their sexual abuse show significantly higher lifetime prevalence rates of psychological problems than a nonvictim group and have a 75% greater risk for major depressive episodes, five times greater risk for agoraphobia, six times greater risk for obsessive-compulsive disorders, have social phobias, a 50% greater risk for sexual disorders, a 50% greater risk for suicidal ideation, and are three times more likely to have made suicide attempts. Children who were molested are at greater risk than nonvictims for major depressive episodes, obsessive-compulsive disorders, sexual disorders, suicidal ideation, and suicide attempts. The Crime Victims Center study suggested that there may be severe, long-term mental health consequences for many victims. This study indicated that there are substantial anxiety and affective disorders related to child sexual abuse (Bagley & Ramsey, 1985; Briere, 1984; Conte & Berliner, 1987; Freidrich, 1986; Gomes-Schwartz, Horowitz, & Sauzier, 1985), and it indicated that if there could be intervention for treatment early on, a substantial number of these disorders could be prevented (Saunders, 1989). As mentioned in chapter 2, children who are abused by family members, those who witness a high level of violence in the abuse, and for the most part, those who are penetrated, show signs of great emotional distress.

In a recent study (Lipovsky, Saunders, & Murphy, 1989), children who were sexually abused displayed more internalizing, externalizing, and a higher number of behavioral problems than nonabused siblings in the incestuous family. The report also indicated that the victims had more behavioral dysfunction and greater levels of depression. Both victims and their siblings in the incestuous (dysfunctional) family had significant problems with self-esteem.

BEHAVIORAL INDICATORS OF SEXUAL ABUSE

- Sexually precocious, seductive, or sexual acting out;
- Abnormal knowledge about sex or sex acts;
- Radical mood swings;
- Sense of impending danger;
- Changes in eating habits;
- Boredom with same-age peers or activities;
- Nightmares or sleep disturbances;
- Change in school performance, including radical improvement in grades (overachieving);
- Depression;
- Substance abuse;
- "Damaged goods" syndrome;
- Hostile behavior;
- Fear of adults/adolescents;
- Fear of being photographed;
- Anxiety toward authority figures;

- Refusal to disrobe in gym class;
- Pseudomature;
- Overcompliant;
- Aggressive;
- Babyish or clinging behavior;
- Bedwetting;
- Attention-getting behavior, beyond normal;
- Recruiting other peers into involvement with adults;
- Suicidal tendencies;
- Inability to trust;
- Hints regarding sexual abuse;
- Unexplained fears;
- Self-mutilation or other self-injury; and
- Hyperactivity, inability to concentrate.

PHYSICAL INDICATORS OF SEXUAL ABUSE

- Sexually transmitted diseases;
- Bruising or bleeding on any area of body or sexual areas;
- Frequent stomach or digestive pain;
- Somatic illnesses;
- Urinary tract and yeast infections;
- Colon problems;
- Weight loss/gain;
- Purging;
- Foul odor from sexual organs;
- Discharge from sexual organs;
- Lubricant residues around vagina and rectum;
- Persistent sore throats;
- Strong gagging reflex;
- Unexplained gifts; and
- Exhaustion.

CRISIS INTERVENTION

I remember clearly one of my first sexually abused children, Matt. He was 4 years old when his mom and grandmother brought him. There were "concerns" about Matt and his sexual acting out on his younger brother, aged 18 months, and Matt's playmates.

They brought Matt hoping I could unravel the cord that would allow Matt to confess who was abusing him. Working with children is a challenge in and of itself. Add to that the complication of a language and concept deficit and dissociative factors, and you have a very complex matter. I, like some people, have always liked working with women/adults. I could ask them to sit down and in a rational manner explain why it is important, though painful, that they relay what happened to them. After fearful tears and squirming, they would tell me. Not so with children. Besides, the way you elicit information can be considered "contamination" in prosecuting the case.

Most children, when questioned directly or indirectly, begin the process of pushing memories further into their subconscious. Any mention of "strangers" or "touching" and I would see Matt taking his memories and burying them in a nest like a squirrel.

During one visit, Matt and I were playing on the floor together when I asked if I could read him a book. It was a book about strangers touching in the wrong way. As I read the book, Matt become hyperactive while playing on the floor. It became increasingly difficult for him to sit while I was reading. Soon he was buzzing all around the room, trying not to listen to the story. Afterwards, he looked at me and said, "You're trying to trick me into telling you. But now, I'm going to have to be twice as tricky as you to keep the secret." It was an eery feeling to watch a 4-year-old change strategies to keep the secret.

Because we suspected Matt's stepfather of the abuse and he was still living in the home, it was important that the facts come to the surface. For 6 weeks or more, Matt and I were building rapport. It became clear that his internal safe people were not his parents (mom and stepdad) but his grandparents. I asked his grandparents to bring him for his next visit. During that visit, his grandmother cradled him on her lap while we visited, telling him if he had anything to add to the conversation we would listen and would always believe him. Soon Matt began to whimper and cry. His grandfather compassionately asked if Matt would tell him why he was crying. Matt said he "couldn't" and then "wasn't allowed." His grandfather indicated that it was safe to tell us and perhaps we could start by Matt just giving us the reason for the secret, or the first name of the person who might know something about why he was crying.

Matt buried his face in his grandmother's shirt and said, "Maybe his name is Rick. He touched me." Rick just happened to be his stepfather's name. The grandfather asked, "You mean like your step-dad, Rick?" "No, another dad named Rick. This one is bad." (His splitting of good and bad became obvious.) "Matt, because this other dad Rick is the man, do you suppose you could tell us where to find him so we can get him some help?" "He's at work," Matt replied. "Where does he work so we can help him?" "I think he works at ABC Company." "You mean the ABC company where your stepdad Rick works?" "Yes." Matt buried his head in his grandmother's shirt again. Matt's disclosure had taken 6 weeks because he needed to know that he could trust me and know me, and was comfortable with his safe people, his grandparents, to disclose.

Until this point, Matt had first insisted that he had never been touched. Then when his mother and grandparents asked how he learned oral sex and other sexual acting-out behaviors, Matt changed his story. He alleged that he was playing outside his home when a man walked past his house and touched his penis, outside of his clothes, three times. Each time he told the story, it changed, becoming more or less elaborate, depending on Matt's willingness to discuss it.

When Matt named his abuser, authorities were notified. Unfortunately, the case was poorly handled by our local police department. A few days later, Matt was hauled down to the police department, put by himself in a room with three police officers with guns, and told to talk. He said nothing. The stepfather was brought in for questioning and released. The case was closed, stepdad filed for divorce, Mom signed the children over to the grandparents for adoption, and Matt failed kindergarten.

A year later, the grandmother placed Matt in a small children's group I was running. It had been a year and Matt's anxiety was very high. His hyperactivity was almost uncontrollable.

At any mention of the word "family" during group, Matt would start bucking like a bronco. When our group talked about feelings, Matt indicated he had only happy feelings. When the other children confronted him that that wasn't possible, Matt would run uncontrollably around the room. When the other children talked about "mad and sad feelings," Matt would hide behind the couch in a fetal position with all the couch cushions piled on top of him.

Although Matt has been removed from his abuser and an unstable home environment, he still harbors the remains of the abuse. His programming or repression of feelings will take some time to straighten out. But we feel certain that disclosure occurred because of taking those weeks to build trust and rapport, and by removing parents with whom he was uncomfortable and replacing them with his safe persons during the attempted disclosure session.

Sometimes this isn't possible when the identity of safe persons isn't clear and the family is in such disarray that finding the most stable, rational, and caring adult is difficult at best.

Disclosure is an area of great concern to those who work with children. How you elicit information, the kinds of questions you ask, how you get clarification, and any subsequent interviews you have with the child may well determine the validity of the case in court. If you are going to be seeing children who were abused, it is worth your while to receive training on how to interview children through your local child protection services or state attorney's office. With improper interviewing skills, the case could be thrown out of court for "contamination" because of your incorrect interviewing skills.

After disclosure, the same procedures apply that were mentioned under physical abuse (see previous segment of this same chapter). The state must be notified because of mandatory reporting laws. After the state has done an investigation or interview of the child, family, and others who know something about the case, the state may request or suggest a rape exam for the child. There has been much debate about the use and abuse of rape exams. Many children feel this is the second victimization because like for adult rape victims, to them the pelvic or anal exam feels like and represents the assault itself. Children can be traumatized by the exam. In some but not all cases, the evidence of the rape exam is crucial for the case. In cases where the child is young or has poor verbal or cognitive skills, medical backup information often is important. Counselors have complained that the exam is as devastating for the child as the abuse, and it often takes the counselor some time to help the child work through its aftermath.

Crisis intervention and stabilization would occur and focus on similar aspects, as mentioned in the physical abuse segment. But there are some additional factors or factors with a different focus. Many of these symptoms and feelings will be seen from crisis intervention right through short/long-term counseling.

During crisis, it is not unusual for children to feel as if they are "damaged goods." This refers to the societal, familial, and the child's self-perception of being weak, vulnerable, "used," and often partially to blame. For older children, the damaged goods syndrome reaches to thoughts of pregnancy, sexually transmitted diseases, and AIDS. Older children may act out sexually, "acting what they have been made to feel like.'' Some children, as they grow older, become apathetic toward their sexuality and choices about when and how to have sex. Joie, the multiple personality disordered victim, was forced to act out sexually by her father, the abuser. This included certain acts she performed for him, but also acts she performed for others while he watched. Even when Joie dated during high school and her father couldn't be there, he would ask when she got home if she ''gave him what he wanted and pleased him.'' Later, when she married and was having difficulty wanting and enjoying sex, Joie stated, ''I just lay there because that's all I'm good for anyway. That's all women were created for. I might as well do it or men will just take it from you and it's worse when they take it.'' Dede, another victim of abuse, had three pregnancies from abuse by her stepfather and was sure no one would want her sexually because of it.

The guilt in children who have been sexually abused seems to be slightly different than that of victims of physical abuse. Because of the level of participation that is involved in sexual abuse, children become guilt-ridden for not fighting harder, not fighting at all, or participating even under severe duress.

Guilt can be heightened if the abuser leads the child to believe the child asked for it, invited it, or seemed to enjoy it because the child did not fight enough. If victims become sexually aroused during the abuse, they may feel guilt, confusion, and anger toward their body for betraying them by responding.

Reducing fear and anxiety can be handled by decreasing arousal responses to cues and by teaching children how to neutralize their feelings about the fear and the cue that brought the fear back. Providing assertiveness training and teaching stress management and anger management techniques also help. Allowing older children a safe environment in which to talk about their fears and the specifics of the abuse will lessen the effect the memories have on them. Younger children may need help with safety procedures before bedtime to test if any abusers are present. This could be looking under the bed, helping to lock the doors, reading a story that makes them feel safe or empowered, and rehearsing safety/prevention skills or plans.

Finding out what the child's beliefs, assumptions, and attitudes about the abuse are will direct intervention, along with observing the symptomatology the child displays. In addition, what the child believes about the sexual abuse, how it was initiated, who is responsible, any role they may have had in its occurrence or continuance, and how they feel about themselves, the offender, and family is important.

Client Concerns (From a Child's Viewpoint)

- Removal from home/abuser;
- Removal from environment;
- Guilt;
- Fear;
- Disclosure;
- Finding safe persons;
- Rape exam;
- Testifying in court;
- Loss of friends/family; and
- Healing of physical/sexual injuries.

Secondary Victimizations

- Stigma from sexual abuse;
- Removal from home environment;
- Adjusting to new environment (if moved into foster system);
- Perceived abandonment;
- Insensitive treatment by court system;
- Constant interviews; and
- Rape/medical exams.

Social Services Needed for the Whole Family System

- Child protective services;
- Rape/medical exam;
- Guardian ad litem (for child victim);
- Crisis intervention counselor;
- Prosecutor/attorney (for child victim);
- Defense attorney (if abuser is family member);
- If abuser is removed from home, family may need financial assistance, housing, etc.;
- Family counseling;
- Sibling, spouse, offender counseling; and
- School guidance counselor.

SHORT-TERM COUNSELING

During short-term counseling, building trust and rapport with the child and family will strengthen the commitment to familial treatment. Often this is difficult when the family as well as the children suffer from PTSD. When family members, parents, and abused children struggle with trust issues, role confusion, and blurred boundaries, beginning treatment can be difficult.

Amy, 7, Fay, 5, and Robby, 3, were brought in by the mother insisting that they were abused in a day-care satanic ring. After spending time with Amy and Fay, it was clear from their intense, specific drawings of commonly used satanic practices that they had indeed been abused.

From a series of the children's drawings, we concluded that all drawings revealed serious disorders. Drawings are often utilized to convey subconscious conflicts, intrusive thoughts, and other information that may not be cognitively relayed by children. Fay, 5, called herself by numerous names. After dissociative testing, she was found to have MPD. We were still unsure if Amy had MPD. It did not exist in Robby. The children would not discuss any abuse on any level with me. They would, however, draw for me in my presence, and then draw pictures at home that mom later gave me. Their abuse, as displayed in their drawings, consisted of food deprivation, drugging, sexual abuse, penetration, possible electric shocks, watching other children being physically tortured or killed by being put through a wood chopping machine, watching babies being buried, being made to drink blood, being forced to take part in ritual worship services, and being subjected to severe threats and elaborate mind control.

The family had been on the run for a few years since they had reported the abuse to the police and were being threatened by other satanists. The original operators of this day care, were, according to the family, "assisted out of the country." The family had to flee at night a number of times from threats. The family had gone to hospital psychiatrists and other counselors, none of whom believed them. They sought help from a church hoping the clergy would have had more exposure to this type of victimization.

Mom, as you can well imagine, was near a nervous breakdown. The children, during the course of the day, would drop "disclosure bombs" on her, telling her specifics of torture incidents. They would, however, not tell counselors. Mom was suffering from severe PTSD. I asked for her and her husband to come in. He indicated that they would never be able to prove this occurred and he wanted to forget it and go on with his life. Mom, on the other hand, was insistent that someone find out that Fay was suffering from MPD (undiagnosed at this point). She seemed determined for that to be Fay's diagnosis. Dad didn't want the children in treatment nor cared to be in treatment himself. He did, however, want treatment for his wife. They had no family locally and were isolated, with no friends except church acquaintances.

The children were suffering night terrors, were hyperactive, and played off mom's tension. Following sessions with the children, Mom and I would talk. But by the next day, she had retained nothing of what we discussed in terms of the children's treatment. Her agitation grew as she perceived nothing was being done with treating the children. Her history of utilizing counselors and facilities was extensive.

Finding an adult in the children's lives who would commit to long-term treatment proved to be impossible. Dad, who was less stressed and more capable of making long-standing decisions, wasn't interested. Mom, who was the only one interested in having treatment for the children, was in a difficult position because of her own PTSD for maintaining the longevity of treatment that would be required of the children.

Working with these three children would take months of rapport building before any significant verbal disclosure would occur. Mom, however, removed the children from our services, saw two other counselors and left them, hospitalized Fay and Amy, and when they were released, the family fled again. Unfortunately, such incidents are not uncommon in families who have experienced high levels of trauma. It is our hope that the children and family will find treatment someday.

Finding key safe persons for the child and building personal rapport and trust are key elements in the beginning stages. Sometimes this person is a parent. Sometimes a parent is the abuser and the other parent is in significant denial. You will need to look for and utilize another safe person as your bridging tool for rapport and trust for the child. Rencken* (1989) indicated that the safe person can bridge the rapport building during early treatment stages by five steps:

1. *Preparing the child for the counseling experience.* The safe person can tell the child he or she will be meeting new grownups (or children if in group) for talk and play concerning events happening in the family. If the child asks directly about abuse events, the safe person should tell the child the truth that those events will also be discussed.

---

*From Robert H. Rencken. (1989). *Intervention Strategies for Sexual Abuse.* Alexandria, VA: American Association for Counseling and Development.

2. *Accompanying the child*. The safe person can bring comfort to the child by telling the child he or she will stay with them during the sessions or wait right outside the door. The safe person can also suggest the child bring "security" items along such as a toy, blanket, or doll. The child can be reassured that the safe person will be there physically and emotionally throughout the sessions.

3. *Supporting the child*. The safe person can support the child emotionally not only during sessions but at home in the family environment. When the abuser is one of the parents, often the other parent will display some displaced anger toward the child; take on therapist duties of interpreting play, art, or conversation; take on duties of a police caseworker by drilling the child or husband for answers; and consequently not assume the role of supporting the child through this trauma. Undoubtedly, the child will feel the tension and stress between caregivers and any verbal exchange of accusations.

4. *Being there*. The child's fear of abandonment is heightened during this time. Amazingly so, most children will not opt for the abusing caregiver to leave the home, go to jail, or get divorced. The fear of abandonment is more significant than the fear of abuse. The child's wish is for the abuse to stop and the parent to stay.

5. *Therapy*. The safe person may also consent to be in therapy sessions to work out the feelings and concerns surrounding the abuse. In families where a child has been sexually abused, it is 10 times more likely than in nonabusive families that the mother was also sexually abused. The mother, or safe person consenting to therapy, gives a message to the child that counseling is OK and that the mother or the safe person cares about the child enough to work on the abuse problem.

I would like to add one more item to this list:

6. *Protecting the child*. It never ceases to amaze me that even when the safe person (most often the mother) knows the abuse is happening, the child or abuser is not removed from the situation. The family is so dysfunctional, and perhaps the safe person was abused as a child as well, that the messages of abuse are not as critical as in a previously nonabusive environment. Although the child may not opt to have the abuser removed because of abandonment issues, we ask the safe person to remove either the child or the abuser. However, be aware that the safe person may also have abandonment issues and may not provide the safety required. Protective services may need to be contacted.

Poor social skills become noticeable during short-term counseling. Children could have been isolated from others or programmed to not enter into relationships with others. Evidence of their helplessness, lack of control, and powerlessness is common.

Children's inability to trust becomes increasingly important as you begin any work on intrafamilial issues. Trusting the abuser (if a family member or parent) has become risky business for them. Trusting the other parent to stop the abuse proved to them to be a fruitless investment of trust. Some children begin not to trust adults at all, (if the abusers were adults), and reporting the incident to adults in the criminal justice system seems futile to them. Because of their low trust levels, it could take time to build a relationship with children in which they feel comfortable in surrendering information.

Some children exhibit pseudomaturity. In actuality, they have not completed some fundamental developmental tasks for their age. Children who are abused are thrust very quickly into methods and ways of coping that do not allow them to be children for long. Development can be delayed in areas of affect and cognition. The oldest children in the family may have to move into roles of pseudoadults taking care of younger children, meeting the needs of the adult/parent, cleaning, cooking, and anticipating and fulfilling needs.

Sherry began her pseudoadult role when her mother died during childbirth. She was only 7, yet took care of a 2-year-old and a newborn as well as having almost nightly intercourse with her stepfather. She even shared his bed. Sherry was fully developed at an early age and shows signs of early sexualization.

Sharla, on the other hand, was penetrated at age 9 over the course of 2 years. Developmentally she was delayed, which was revealed in emotional, psychological, affective, cognitive, interpersonal, social, and educational areas.

She had an inability to concentrate in school, was failing, and was unable to get along with peers or teachers. She was released from school a number of times. She was placed in a girls' residence but lacked the emotional maturity to relate to troubled girls her own age. Interpersonally she was acting out aggressively at home with the family, which kept the family focused on her "unwillingness to get better." She was unable to express any emotion except anger and rage. She had destroyed her bedroom furniture numerous times by smashing it to pieces, and had set the apartment on fire. Her behavior became sexualized. She was caught repeatedly with boys, and exhibited chronic masturbation. This behavior revealed deep levels of turmoil and incompleted developmental tasks for her age. Whereas Sherry had a pseudomaturity and had learned the adult skills of housekeeping and caregiving, Sharla had not developed along a mature line and lacked skills even in basic areas.

Because sexually abused children have experienced very little control and mastery in their life, much of therapy may need to focus on assisting children to choose options that empower them. Despite outward manifestations of pseudomaturity, the children are still very dependent and will need to be taught how to make healthy decisions. Assertiveness training, communication, prevention skills, and self-esteem need to be focused on as well.

Client Concerns (From a Child's Viewpoint)

- Inability to trust others;
- Removal from home or removal of offender;
- Guilt, shame, and stigma;
- Disclosure;
- Loss of family/friends;
- Healing from physical/sexual injuries;
- Misunderstanding of what is happening to them emotionally; and
- Helplessness, lack of control.

Secondary Victimizations

- Court system, interviews;
- Media coverage that may identify child as victim;
- Stigma of sexual abuse;
- "Damaged goods" syndrome; and
- Trouble in school/grades/acting out.

Social Services Needed for the Whole Family System

- Child protective services;
- Guardian ad litem (for child victim);
- Short-term counselor;
- Prosecutor/attorney (for child victim);
- Defense attorney (if abuser is family member);
- Financial assistance (if abuser is removed from home), housing, etc.;
- Family counseling;

- Spouse, sibling, offender counseling; and
- School guidance counselor.

LONG-TERM COUNSELING

Treating children differs from treating adult survivors. Different issues must be considered for male victims and female victims. Many varied specifics will change the direction of counseling when working with abused children. Assessing the trauma to determine counseling direction can be accomplished by referring back to chapter 2 on psychodynamics of trauma. Using methods other than cognitive therapies is often necessary. Reviewing chapter 3 on effective therapies will help you gather insights for other types of expressive therapies to use with children. Recommended books are listed in a referral section for further techniques.

Certainly anger, rage, and hostility are long-term issues that need to be focused on to teach the child to direct anger at the appropriate person and issues. Aggressive behavior, anger, guilt and shame, running away, and inappropriate sexual behavior are frequent and represent attempts to cope with the anxiety produced by the traumatic stress (Browne & Finkelhor, 1986). Children may try to cope either through approach strategies (their ways of approaching and dealing with their sexual abuse) or through avoidance and denial (Roth & Cohen, 1986). If they lack direction in this area, their anger becomes deflected and turned inward, or is misdirected and used on innocent others.

Young juvenile offenders who had been victimized exhibit a great deal of anger. Much research is being done regarding early intervention that can deactivate much of the anger and rage that turns children into juvenile offenders, or becomes debilitating when they reach adulthood.

The anger directed to mom is just as strong for her ''perceived'' knowledge of the abuse and her lack of intervention. Our women spend a great deal of group time working through ambivalent feelings toward their nonabusing caregivers who, they feel certain, knew or had a ''hunch'' that something was happening.

If you are working with the family unit, family therapy and approaches to codependency and addictions will need to be incorporated in treating the family as a whole. Groups can be utilized as a resource for offenders, spouses, siblings, and child victims. Creative therapies such as music, art, play, movement, and journaling are ways of helping noncognitive, nonexpressive children give voice to their pain and inner conflicts.

Client Concerns (From a Child's Viewpoint)

- Reuniting with family (if removed);
- Wondering whether offender has really been rehabilitated;
- Abuse from others;
- Fear;
- Blame; and
- Stigma.

Secondary Victimizations

- Stigma of sexual abuse;
- Loss of familiar environment;
- Trouble with schoolwork; failing school;
- Acting out aggression/sexuality;
- Repeated court hearings; and
- Exposure by media coverage and being identified as a sexual abuse victim.

Social Services Needed for the Whole Family System

- Child protective services;
- Guardian ad litem (for child victim);
- Prosecutor/attorney (for child victim);
- Defense attorney (if offender is family member);
- Long-term counselor;
- Family counseling;
- Sibling, spouse, offender counseling;
- School guidance counselor; and
- Counseling to bridge child back into home.

CONCLUSION

You will need to identify your own feelings regarding pedophiles who are reunited with their families and cases that remain unprosecuted. It can be a difficult issue for counselors. Many of us feel we are able to distance ourselves professionally, yet when faced with the criminal justice system or family dynamics, we feel frustrated about the possible outcome and the child's future.

Monitoring transference and countertransference in cases such as these is important. Supervision can help keep you focused and point out any transference if it is beginning.

In closing, children are our most vital resource. If we want to enter the 21st century with some semblance of order, balance, and national productivity, we need to intervene and help the children who are the victims of child abuse.

RECOMMENDED READING

Crewson, J. (1988). *By silence betrayed: Sexual abuse of children in America*. Boston: Little, Brown.

Finkelhor, D. (1979). *Sexually victimized children*. New York: Free Press.

Finkelhor, D. (1984). *Child sexual abuse: New theory and research*. New York: Free Press.

Finkelhor, D. (1986). *A sourcebook on child sexual abuse*. Beverly Hills, CA: Sage.

Herman, J. L. (1981). *Father-daughter incest*. Cambrige, MA: Harvard University Press.

Sgroi, S. M. (1987). *Handbook of clinical intervention in child sexual abuse*. Lexington, MA: Heath.

Walker, L. E. A. (1988). *Handbook on sexual abuse of children*. New York: Springer.

REFERRALS

Child Abuse Hotline
1-800-962-2873

Childhelp USA
National Campaign for the Prevention of Child Abuse and
    Neglect
Woodland Hills, CA 91370

Children's Rights of America
Exploited and Runaways
1-813-593-0090

Children's Village USA
1-800-4 A CHILD

Compassion Connection
P.O. Box 36-C
Denver, CO 80236
1-303-985-HOPE
Abuse Data Bank

National Center on Child Abuse and Neglect
Administration for Children, Youth and Families
U.S. Department of Health & Human Services
P.O. Box 1182
Washington, DC 20013
1-301-251-5157

National Coalition Against Sexual Assault
2428 Ontairo Road, NW
Washington, DC 20009
1-202-483-7165

National Committee for Prevention of Child Abuse
332 S. Michigan Ave., Suite 950
Chicago, IL 60604-4357
1-312-663-3520

National Council of Child Abuse & Family Violence
Plaza La Reina
6033 W. Century Blvd., Suite 400
Los Angeles, CA 90045

	**Overview of Violence Against Children**
Crisis Intervention Issues:	Mandatory reporting, child safety, protective services, providing service/referrals to family unit, transition of being placed in new environment, helping children understand why they are removed, treatment for physical injuries, affirmation of feelings.
Short-Term Counseling:	Sense of blame, guilt, low self-worth, stress management, acting-out behaviors, how child fits in family system, codependency, education on physical/sexual abuse.
Long-Term Counseling:	Prevention skills, communication, acting-out behaviors, anger management, self-blame if abuser is incarcerated, family systems counseling, preparing child to return home (if applicable).
Secondary Victimizations:	Removal feels like punishment, adjustment to new environment, loss of family/friends, stigma, physical injuries and treatment.
Social Services Needed:	Protective services, guardian ad litem, prosecutor, family counseling, group counseling, medical treatment, offender treatment, school guidance counselor, state financial services for children.

9

Murder

- There was one murder every 25 minutes in 1988 (FBI, 1989).
- Approximately one in three murders is committed by one family member against another (Domestic Abuse—Families in Trouble, 1989).
- Thirty percent of female homicide victims are killed by their husbands/boyfriends (FBI, 1989).
- Homicide is the leading cause of injury-related death among children younger than 1 year of age. ("The Hunt for Crime Starts," 1989).

In looking at the recent levels of escalating violence, murder is at the top of the continuum. Professionals who work specifically in homicide and those who work in death education/counseling have agreed that homicide is the highest bereavement known to man. Added to that is the parental loss of a child through a homicide death. To understand the dynamics of murder, one must keep the theories of grief and posttraumatic stress clearly in mind.

A Crime Victims Research and Treatment Center (1988) preliminary research data paper on PTSD following murders and drunk driving crashes concluded that:

- It is significant to note that 4.5 million adults have experienced this type of indirect victimization.
- The percentage of homicide survivors who developed PTSD was substantial.

- About 1.4 million adults develop PTSD after the homicide of a family member and about 280,000 currently have homicide-related PTSD.
- Among homicide survivors, 74% felt the judicial system should be responsible to see they get emotional or psychological counseling, but only 17% indicated they had received adequate access to such services.

Someone once said, "Death is not the greatest loss in life. The greatest loss is what dies inside us while we live." And such is the encapsulation of murder.

Few things in life evoke such terror as the image of murder. Today, there are many types of murders to fear. We face the violence of murder daily in this country as gunmen fire into playgrounds and kill children, as we see drive-by shootings on the highways, and as our neighborhoods turn into six-gun territories with full-blown gun battles and shootouts. This violence evokes fear not only to society at large, but to those professionals who must help survivors pick up the pieces.

In the United States there are about 21,000 murders a year (FBI, 1989). Each murder produces about 10 persons in need of counseling. That totals 210,000 clients per year. Over a 5-year period, that totals over 1 million persons! Today as I listened to the news, the announcer reported that the murder rate is expected to increase by at least 8% over the past year's rates, which would be the highest increase ever. We can only speculate that the increase is linked directly to drugs and drug violence.

Although many victimizations are readily growing in "acceptance," murder still holds its social stigma. Even though murder is portrayed on television and in the movies, in social reality we have a long way to go in accepting the survivors left behind. Many counselors must struggle with their own personal feelings about murder and its stigma before they will feel comfortable doing this work. The stigma is based on the myth that "bad people are murdered." Our denial helps to protect us from the reality that we too may be murdered. If drug dealers or pimps are not the only people murdered, then we as a society also are vulnerable. A murder of a young child, elderly person, or business professional carries much more impact than the murder of a suspected "drug lord."

Our own personal terror about murder increases when we hear about serial murders or mass murders. They evoke images (rightfully so) of crazed killers stalking innocent, unsuspecting people. Ritualistic murders surrounding satanic killings evoke Edgar Allen Poe images of evil and full-mooned nights. More and more campus rapes and other types of rapes are evolving into murders. Yet even a lay person's terror of the most dreaded kinds of killings cannot compare to victims' reality when *their* loved one has been murdered in the most heinous of ways.

Homicide survivors have found solace in group therapy in dealing with the murder of their loved ones. Homicide survivors who participate in group therapy listen to other group members' stories. Some survivors have indicated that it isn't difficult to listen to others' stories because others listened to theirs. No one winced or seemed shocked. However, some wondered how rookie counselors took it. Survivors listened to stories of a young man who was stabbed through the heart in the bathroom of a bar; of a girl who was raped by kids she knew from school, her body dragged to a field and then set on fire; a woman whose head was blown off at close range by her fiancé's shotgun, leaving her brain matter on the ceiling; a mother who was stabbed 42 times all over her body; a father who was shot down in his own home, Mafia style, on a contract killing; a father who was shot in the back in the parking lot of his apartment complex; a daughter who was abducted by a convicted and released pedophile who slit her throat and then crushed her face out of her skull by using a post set in concrete.

I tell you the stories of these survivors' agony not for shock value, but because this is what you, as a counselor, can expect to hear if you choose to treat those who have been touched by murder. Much of survivors' personal therapy may focus around processing the picture that is still embedded in their minds of the murder scene that they had come across. Counselors must be able to help victims work through these images of violence. One survivor arrived the day of the murder and went to the murder site where her father had been killed. No one told her that the crime scene had not been cleaned up.

There was his blood, fluorescently red, sprayed against the building and the gutter. Big, thick red runs of his blood had poured down a parked car, where his hand prints revealed that he had struggled in vein to stand up. It was an eery sight, one that Alfred Hitchcock movies were made of. But those were her Daddy's handprints—the evidence of his remaining moments alive.

Some of the hardest trauma does not result from the murder alone, but is inflicted by counselors who open up a wound they cannot close. Some elicit information from a particular type of victim that they have never been trained to handle. Much like the complex issues of sexual abuse, homicide is not a victimization to be entered into without prior extensive training.

TYPES OF MURDER

All murder is heinous and violent. All types of murder leave incredible devastation in their wake. Some types of murder have a greater impact than others. Basically we will be talking about six types of murder: Mass/multiple murder, serial murder, ritualistic murder, single incident murder, vehicular homicide, and accidental homicide or manslaughter.

Mass/Multiple Murder

These murders are committed by the same person(s), involve more than one victim, and are committed during one incident. These murders are "blitz" in style and are referred to as massacres. The Palm Bay massacre is an example where a gunman opened fire in a shopping center. The Charles Manson murders were mass murders. He went in and killed a number of people at one time.

Serial Murder

Serial murders are committed by the same person(s), involve more than one victim, but are not committed all at the same time. The Boston Strangler and Ted Bundy were serial murderers. They killed numerous people over a period of time. Generally serial murders are similar in style, technique, and victim orientation.

Ritualistic Murder

Ritualistic murders are committed by people involved in cult or satanic worship in which the victim is used as a device of torture or sacrifice to their deity. Ritualistic murders can be mass or serial type murders, involving many people either at once or over a period of time. Many victims are children and infants born to "breeders" in their cult. (See chapter 10 on cult, satanic, and ritual victims.)

Single Incident Murder

These murders are heard about most on the nightly news. They involve crimes of passion, rapes and robberies, and one-on-one killings. They can be random or premeditated.

Vehicular Homicide

Vehicular homicide occurs as the result of negligent or reckless driving, or driving while intoxicated or drugged. This type of homicide is now considered intentional in most states. It is based on the belief that a car is a weapon that can kill a person through the driver's usage or neglect.

Accidental Homicide or Manslaughter

This type of murder is committed without malice. It is either accidental in nature, or the courts cannot prove malice and the sentence is reduced from first- or second-degree homicide to manslaughter.

When working with homicide cases, your client/victim will obviously be the family member/friend of the murdered loved one. The most direct victim is dead. It has been noted that family members not only of homicide but crime victims in general who are not directly themselves victimized are a neglected and overlooked population of people (McCann & Pearlman, 1990). Family members left behind suffer the effects of trauma (Figley, 1983, 1986). Figley (1986) indicated that the empathy that families expend in suffering the loss of a loved one or watching a loved one suffer is the process that makes them vulnerable and susceptible to psychological distress.

Because of the finality of death, and usually the violence that surrounded the death, victimization as a result of murder is qualitatively different and separated from other forms of victimizations and life experiences. This type of victimization produces a severe shattering of life schemas in all areas, resulting in a state of acute psychic disequilibrium and distress that disrupts the entire self (Bard, Arnone, & Nemiroff, 1986; Masters, Friedman, & Getzel, 1988).

Survivors in immediate crisis feel like they, too, have died. It is perceived as injury to self. Yet, even when survivors experience a highly emotionally charged state of perceiving the injury as an injury to self, often counselors and "systems" (medical, mental health, criminal) do not perceive the survivors as being victimized.

Family members may not fully comprehend how the death occurred but may not be able to ask for further details in fear of worsening their own scattered and wounded self/safety schema. Because of this, family members may develop a disturbed schema surrounding their safety issues and frame of reference and not have an opportunity to explore and repair these disturbed schemas (McCann & Pearlman, 1990). Because of their reluctance to ask questions about the murder (in fear of more psychic injury to self), they are left with bare pieces of information that can lead to constant obsessions of "what really happened/ what could have happened/what didn't happen." On the other hand, knowing the details provides victims with the "weapon" to replay the event over and over again, focusing on the final moments of terror and pain. These "reruns" of the tortuous end of their loved one's life produce great waves of helplessness and rage.

Any theories or training you have had on death, dying, and bereavement will come to mean a great deal to you when working with this population. It is important to remember that a homicide survivor's grief will bypass the normal grief period. From murder to recovery is an estimated 5 years, whereas in other types of death, recovery can be seen in approximately 2 years. This should give you an example of what PTSD can do to the grief process and just how severe homicide reactions can be.

INJURIOUS SYSTEMS

In homicide, just as in domestic violence or child or sexual abuse, systems inflict secondary injuries that are equal or greater than the original abuse. Although I have mentioned secondary injuries in other chapters, I want to outline some that are seen with frequency in homicide.

Media

The public's right to know usually overrides the survivors' right to privacy. Murder is the highlight of most newspapers, TV news coverage, and rag mags. The media can intrude at the most inopportune times, such as at the moment the survivor is told that a loved one is dead, as the survivor emerges from the funeral or trial, or when the survivor gets the news of the jury's verdict.

A large amount of domestic violence, child abuse, and sexual assault goes unreported, and when it is reported, it is becoming common practice for the press to handle it with confidentiality and to withhold victims' names. This is not true with murder. Murder is commonly reported and is considered an act against the state, not a private loss, therefore the survivors are identified publicly.

Every move the court makes is reported in the news. Private details of the murder victim's life and the surviving family's life are made public, either through the trial, media coverage, or court documents.

The emphasis throughout the media coverage is on the crime, the criminal, and the outcome. Survivors are rarely interviewed. The victim of the murder may be portrayed as "asking for it," "at fault," "bad," "on drugs or alcohol," or somehow responsible for his or her own death. The victim's family can be portrayed as heathens for wanting the death penalty for the offender or for not offering to forgive the criminal publicly (Redmond, 1989).

Criminal Justice System

Murder is considered a crime against the state, not a private crime against a family. Because this is a "depersonalized" crime, interaction between court and family can be limited, or information can be given without concern of its impact.

The community at large has been raised to believe that the world is basically safe, and in those rare occasions when it isn't, that the courts will bring justice, that the person who performs the act of violence is the offender and is given the smaller amount of rights, and the one who suffers the act of violence is the victim and is innocent and is given the larger amount of rights. The survivor soon finds this is not the case.

Laws vary from state to state, but many prohibit the surviving family of a homicide from being in the courtroom during the trial, except at the sentencing, and in some cases from supplying the judge and jury with a victim impact statement defining their personal loss through the act of violence. The defense attorneys usually opt to "invoke the rule" that excludes family members on the chance they may influence the jury with their emotional reactions. The criminal's family, though, may stay and show emotion.

The survivor may not be notified accurately about hearings or arrests. The criminal may be released on bond without the family's being notified. If the case goes to trial, they can be assured of delays and continuances. Some trials don't even start until 9 months after the murder. Most will go through at least three to six delays or continuances, pushing the actual trial to a year or more after the murder. (Many homicide survivors purposely put off the grieving process until after the trial. Most do not realize how long that will take. You can see the possible complications when the survivor waits for more than a year to grieve!) When they do get a trial date, the survivors are left outside the courtroom doors, unable to participate in the judicial process.

During the trial, survivors may see the murderer pass them in the hall. This incident may be the first time they see the murderer. If they are allowed to be present at the trial, they may hear defense attorneys attacking the character of their loved one, trying to make the victim the criminal. They may listen to character witnesses speak favorably of the criminal. If they are allowed in the courtroom, they may hear and reexperience in great detail the events and violence of the murder. If they are allowed in the courtroom they are instructed to show no emotion. They may not have been given proper notification and may miss the trial altogether! The criminal's sentence may be plea bargained with or without the consent of the family.

Once the trial is over, most survivors think they will begin to feel normal. Actually, the grieving process will usually begin then, if it is not interrupted again with other court procedures. Survivors may become distressed to find that they do not begin to feel relief.

The hope of a death sentence is farfetched in most homicide cases. Fewer than a double-digited percentage ever receive it and less than that are ever executed. A life sentence averages about 8 years. Most survivors recognize that the victim/survivor is the only one who serves a true life sentence.

The criminal will probably appeal the case, perhaps more than once. The average appeal process takes 9 years. Survivors will be in and out of repeat trials for 9 years. If the appeal is overturned, survivors have to wait for parole hearings, and at their own expense, travel to these hearings in hopes of blocking the criminal's release on parole. That is, if the survivors are notified of the parole hearings at all!

If the criminal is released on parole, the family lives in constant fear of retaliation and revenge. Most families feel they have been failed by a system that neither protected their loved ones from violent people while they were alive, nor protected their character during the court process, nor was successful in keeping a violent criminal behind bars.

Law Enforcement System

Survivors have described detectives and police who have been part of the crime scene as reporting the news of their loved one's murder as if they were reciting their rank and serial number. The officials focus on the formality of the occasion and the evidence that needs to be gathered. Often the traumatized survivors' questions and demands for answers are overlooked. Details are often withheld from the family because the investigation is still pending or ongoing. Prized possessions of the murder victim can be held as evidence for years.

Fortunately, much education has been and is being provided to law enforcement officials to help them deal with homicide survivors. Awareness and sensitivity training as well as psychoeducation is now often provided. Because of this educational process, homicide survivors are receiving better and more sensitive treatment from law enforcement officials.

Probate/Estate System

Probating a will of someone who was murdered often takes longer than probating the will of a person who died nonviolently. Some families wait for months for the trial, the decision of the mode of death, and other elements surrounding the death. The actual estate settlement may occur more than 2 years after a death.

Some families have to bear many financial burdens such as the final hospital bill and funeral, cremation, and burial costs. One survivor, upon the settlement, found that the attorney who handled the case had overcharged and double-charged. The survivor had to take the attorney to court to have a reasonable amount established for his services! Families often are not in agreement with settlements, which causes family system problems. Grieving families can also be targets for financial exploitation by attorneys, doctors, and others.

Medical System

Survivors may hold hostility toward those who cared for their murdered loved one. The family may have been treated insensitively by doctors,

ambulance workers, fire rescue workers, or hospital staff. Some survivors find hospital billing practices incredibly cruel. Some are charged
for services that were never performed for their loved one, yet they
are emotionally unable to fight the battle with the hospital and they
pay the bill. Survivors sometimes are asked to pay anesthesiologists'
bills or operating room charges even though the coroner had pro-
nounced the victim dead on arrival.

Some survivors have difficulty with elements disclosed in the au-
topsy reports that are later used by the defense against the murder
victim. For instance, most defense attorneys will use an AIDS diagnosis
to indicate a character defect of the victim even though the victim's
medical condition had nothing to do with the murder event. The same
holds true if the victim was a drug user or a prostitute, for example.
The survivor may be treated insensitively by personnel at the funeral
home, crematory, or cemetery. For example, they may unadvisedly
open a casket that should be closed because of severe mutilation of
the victim, thus causing further emotional trauma to the family.

Mental Health System

On a national level, there are very few counselors trained to work with
homicide survivors. Until recently, homicide survivors were not even
recognized as "victims" by the government or its programs. Within
the past 4 years, therapy geared toward homicide survivors has been
developed, and mutual support groups are forming nationwide.Yet,
there are so few trained counselors in this area that the homicide
survivor is victimized again just by the mere lack of qualified, trained
professionals.

Survivors who have seen therapists often have been put through
severe psychometric testing. Some have been hospitalized, highly med-
icated, and even given shock treatments as a means to deal with the
aftereffects of murder. If we ever hope to move past this barbaric
revictimization of homicide survivors, counselors must receive specialized training.

OTHER STRESSORS FOR HOMICIDE SURVIVORS

The National Organization for Victim Assistance (1985) listed seven
additional stressors. The first stressor is the notification process. Most
survivors well remember how they learned of the murder—receiving

incomplete or inaccurate information over the telephone, or learning about it through the media. Insensitive notification causes additional pain. Survivors should be notified appropriately by law enforcement officials, a victim advocate, a crisis counselor, or clergy.

The second stressor is the fact that the murder affects other life changes or intensifies problems such as an impending divorce, illness, or financial difficulties. These problems do not go away while dealing with the homicide.

The third stressor is that any violent death produces unforeseen demands on the family such as identifying the body, making funeral arrangements, handling medical bills, notifying the rest of the family and making arrangements for them, and dealing with the media. These tasks can be overwhelming in the midst of incredible emotional pain.

The fourth stressor is that death necessitates role changes in the family. The wife may become the breadwinner, or the husband may become the caregiver to the children. An older child may become head of the family.

The fifth stressor is that death causes financial burdens, especially when the victim was the sole breadwinnner. There is an immediate loss of income, combined with medical and funeral expenses. If the victim was murdered at home, items might have been stolen during the murder that must be replaced.

The sixth stressor is the reaction or treatment by the survivors' religious community. Many churches have outreach programs to jails and prisons but do nothing for the survivors in their own congregations. who are left behind. Some offer pat scriptures on forgiveness or God's will.

The seventh stressor is that people don't perceive murder as an acceptable manner of death. Because it is a frightening way to die, others may try to blame, at least in part, the murder on the victim so they can sustain the illusion that murder couldn't happen to them.

SITUATIONAL FACTORS THAT AFFECT TRAUMA

Certain elements will affect survivors' reactions to the trauma and their ability to cope. These, of course, as we have seen in other types of victimization, depend on their relationship to the victim (spouse, parent, child, grandparent, extended family member, or friend).

Witnessing the event or seeing the aftermath leaves lasting impressions. Those who witness a murder usually feel more self-blame. Those who were not witnesses fantasize there was something that could have been done to save the victim.

Witnesses, either family members or others, may fear retaliation and may not want to testify. This is a normal reaction that may add additional conflict about mustering the ego strength to give testimony and relieve the sense of guilt for having seen the murder and not having been able to prevent it.

Relationship to the assailant is a factor in trauma. Many murders are intrafamilial, which adds complexity to loyalties, prosecution, and family systems dynamics. One mother whose son murdered her new husband asked me, "Which side of the table do I sit on? Prosecution or defense? I know he did it. He needs to be punished, but he's my son and I love him and I don't want the death penalty. But I can't guarantee that, can I?"

Survivors react differently to different types of murder. These include vehicular homicide, murder accompanied by sexual assault, murder accompanied by torture, murder preceded by kidnapping, or murder in which the body is violated after death.

Attributes of the assailant(s) affect survivors' trauma. Was there more than one murderer? What was the assailant's age (juvenile, adult, elderly), race, and marital status? Does the assailant have children?

Attributes of the victim also influence reactions. How old was the victim (infant, child, adult, elderly)? What was the victim's sexual preference and race, marital status? Did he or she have children or other dependents?

The geographic distance between the survivor's home and the murder scene can have a financial impact for the survivor—he or she may not be eligible for victim compensation because of state laws if more than one state is involved. Survivors may feel less safe when they live in close proximity to the murder scene.

In addition, consideration needs to be paid to a survivor's personal coping style and mechanisms, previous crisis experiences, current and potential support systems, family dynamics and structure, the relationship with the murdered loved one, religious beliefs, and any existing or previous emotional disorders.

OVERALL NEEDS OF HOMICIDE SURVIVORS

Homicide survivors, in the course of a 5-year recovery period, will require different types of therapies. Homicide survivors' needs are not complicated but are basic to humans anywhere. What they have survived is horrendous but it does not make working with them horrendous.

They need to feel support from others (either family, a group, or a counselor). They need validation that their feelings, no matter what they are, are appropriate for what they have lived through. This includes murderous impulses, guilt for surviving, or rage. These feelings are not bad or wrong, and survivors can't and shouldn't be rushed through experiencing them to appease others who are uncomfortable with the survivors' having these feelings. They are normal for the abnormal event experienced.

Survivors need to feel they can live their life again, that they have some control over their own environment and life, and that all life and living isn't dangerous. There are some things they can control and some things they can't, but life is still worth living even when there are things beyond their control.

They need to understand the role of the various entities that are involved in the aftermath of a homicide. These can include hospitals, coroners, police, criminal justice system, mental health system, mass media, and the legalities of probate, wills, and settling an estate. They may need assistance maneuvering through these systems or support in tolerating these systems. They may need help in understanding the jargon, principles, or even necessity of these systems.

Survivors need most of all to be able to grieve—for all that entails for them, for whatever meaning it has for them, and in whatever manner it feels right. Short of hurting themselves or others, there are no right and wrong ways to grieve.

They need to resolve the murder enough psychologically to move it from present (active) memory and stimulus to past (still remembered but less activated) memory. No one "forgets" the murder or a loved one who was murdered. No counselor should ask or suggest that. But living can get a lot less painful when the memories begin to be deactivated.

Survivors need to feel complete again and to live a satisfying life despite the murder. Murder isn't all there is in life, but for a long while it feels like that's all there is. The survivor will eat, drink, and dream the homicide. Soon life does not feel like living—it feels like slow death. Murder takes more than just a loved one. It often takes a survivor's marriage, finances, relationships, health, and the very will to live.

The needs of the homicide survivor can be met in different types of therapies, such as individual, group, and peer support group programs. Other expressive therapies can be helpful (see chapter 3 on effective therapies). However, DO NOT UTILIZE PSYCHODRAMA! I was horrified to hear that some counselors utilize that technique with this type of population. The homicide survivor does not need to reenact the event to "get in touch with" his or her feelings. The feelings are there. Psychodrama can be abusive and traumatic, adding to the PTSD instead or relieving it. Long-term damage can be done to different schemas when utilizing this practice. It is wise to follow more traditional grief practices when working with homicide survivors.

CRISIS INTERVENTION

You may come into contact with the homicide survivor following the murder or months later when he or she comes for counseling while still in crisis. This segment in crisis intervention will focus on how to work with a homicide survivor immediately following a murder.

If your homicide survivor was not referred through a victim advocate, get one! A victim advocate will save you a lot of time in social service placement, keep you posted on the status of the case in the criminal justice system, and assist in matters of confrontation with the system. A victim advocate is an employee of your local police or sheriff's department whose sole purpose is to assist victims through the criminal justice system and to offer appropriate referrals for their practical needs throughout this process.

Following the murder, the survivor is obviously in shock and denial. This state can last for a number of months. In addition, the homicide adversely affects the family system. Many homicide survivors come in not only for help to cope with the loss and to integrate the image of violence, but because they do not know how to function within a fractured family system. A murder will blow a closed, dysfunctional family system apart. In a well-knit open system, it will certainly cause strains and stresses, but, overall will draw the family closer. Clinical experience shows, however, that the majority of family systems will be blown apart.

During crisis, homicide survivors are overwhelmed not only with the immediate loss, but with the incredible overload of systems they must deal with. Much of your work as a mental health provider will focus on helping them navigate through systems, not only technically and physically, but emotionally and psychologically. That is why a victim advocate is a great benefit. Murders attract media while they repel friends, coworkers, and those from whom the survivor seeks comfort. Survivors are thrown into a whirlwind of reporters, inadequate and insensitive reporting, lack of information available about their case, calls from prosecutors and defense attorneys, state agencies, the hospital, morgue and funeral home, police or sheriff's department, and homicide and crime scene investigators. Soon survivors begin to feel trapped within the systems. They also begin to feel the murder of their loved one is not a human tragedy but just a part of a large cycle within an inhumane system.

All these demands begin while the survivor is still in shock and denial. Most have not perforated the lining of denial, whereas personnel of all these systems are saying that their loved one was, in fact, murdered. The survivor needs the time to allow the reality of this violent death to become real. The overwhelming needs of the system force the survivor to push grieving aside, thus contributing to the possibility of delayed, chronic, or exacerbated grief.

The survivors' grief process will continue to be interrupted again and again by the systems—a court hearing, trial, bond hearing, parole hearing, and so forth. Survivors must stop their grieving and focus on the tasks at hand. These stops and starts in the grieving process explain why it usually takes about 5 years to complete the process.

During the crisis, survivors are not only stunned but they may suffer anxiety attacks, anger outbursts, or the opposite—be sullen and withdrawn. Their functioning level is greatly reduced, attention span is shortened, and thinking is confused. This comes at a time when most of the preparations for the funeral and estate must be handled. They feel very disconnected from the world. Most survivors say that they floated through these times, that they felt very animated, as if someone else were doing and saying everything.

This type of psychological numbing and disconnecting is a protective measure for the ego. The survivor will accept the reality only in pieces that can be integrated at a particular time. The acceptance of the whole reality of the death, the violence, and the totality of all that was lost will come over a long period of time.

If you are in a position to assist survivors with funeral arrangements and other tasks, encourage their participation in the funeral, such as attending, helping with the arrangements as much as possible, and viewing the body (except if the body was mutilated). All these activities increase survivors' acceptance of the reality of the finality of the death and help penetrate denial, shock, and numbness. Those who have attended the funeral seem to have a smoother transition in their grieving process and also experience and express less remorse about not participating or not attending to "unfinished business."

Survivors must struggle not only with what has occurred immediately but what this means for the present and the future. This may cause an overload that is demonstrated by inappropriate affect. They may laugh when it is more appropriate to cry, or be remourseful or show other signs of not reacting to events with what would be termed "appropriate" emotion.

You may be asked to help repair the walls of the family at this time. Family members may react to the murder in widely different ways. Some may refuse to be part of the court process, whereas others need and want to be present. Some may openly grieve while others remain stoic. Some may need to talk repeatedly about the murder event, but others refuse to acknowledge it. These types of coping styles reap havoc with a grieving family system where one family member will judge another for having different reactions, feelings, and needs.

In one survivor's family system, this dynamic caused an estrangement of one of the family members for 6 years. In her grief and disorganization, the survivor turned inward and internalized. A family member wanted help to grasp their personal loss. But she couldn't reach out beyond herself as she struggled to integrate the image of violence. This caused a 6-year split that was only repaired last year.

Following the death notification you can support survivors in several ways:

1. Inform survivors what their rights are concerning media representatives, interviews, photographing, and so forth. This includes telling the media to leave, writing their statement in a letter, or designating someone else as spokesperson. Tell them what to expect so they are not shocked when they see graphic details of body bags on the 6 o'clock news.

2. Assist survivors with funeral arrangements if they need help. Give them information about options for funeral homes, services, crematories, and cemeteries.

3. If the victim was murdered in the home, comprehensive cleanup services will be needed. Not all cleaning services will clean up homicides and suicides. Call first. DO NOT ALLOW THE SURVIVING FAMILY TO CLEAN UP THE MURDER SCENE! Much of survivors' focused therapy can be around the image of the murder scene that they happened to see. One survivor was forced to scrape her

daughter's brain matter from her ceiling tiles. No one ever should be exposed to this level of further traumatization. It is indescribable what it is like to see or have to clean up the blood of your loved one.

4. Provide survivors with as much information as possible concerning the process of the criminal justice system. If you can't supply the details, talk with a victim advocate. It is wise for you as a counselor to learn about the process also.

5. Assist with the financial consequences of the murder. This could include probating the estate, filing insurance claims, and filing for victim compensation program benefits or social security death benefits.

6. Help survivors reconstruct their lives in practical, emotional, physical, and spiritual ways.

Client Concerns

- Was the murder preventable?
- Has the murderer been apprehended?
- Will the murderer go to trial?
- Dealing with the media;
- Dealing with the investigation;
- Return of family possessions taken as evidence in the investigation;
- Funeral arrangements;
- Family problems;
- Explaining the death to children; and
- Inability to work.

Secondary Victimizations

- Loss of income;
- Paying funeral expenses, medical expenses;
- Counseling costs; and
- Insensitive media, criminal justice system, law enforcement.

Social Services Needed

- Victim advocate;
- Trained crisis counselor;
- Homicide detective or private P.I.;

- Prosecutor/attorney;
- Bureau of Crime Compensation (financial aid);
- Life insurance company;
- Homicide cleanup crew (if appropriate); and
- Clergy (if trained!).

SHORT-TERM COUNSELING

Short-term counseling is geared toward normal progressive grief issues. In the case of homicide survivors, however, it may be geared to non-progressive grief issues that have become complicated, exaggerated, or chronic.

These complications can be seen in survivors' sudden murderous impulses, which are frightening for counselors and others as well; phobic-like fears, intense survivor guilt, and irrational other-oriented blame (that is, blame toward anyone not directly involved in the murder); violation of primary beliefs and values concerning safety, the world, and human behavior; and severe emotional withdrawal and cognitive distortion.

During this time, survivors may be heading toward or already be in the "searching and yearning" phase of the grief process. Therefore, a therapy-focused group can be of great benefit. No groups should be offered until survivors reach this point because shock, denial, and numbness interfere with any group therapeutic process. During the searching and yearning phase, the shock and numbness begin to fade and the reaction to the ultimate violation begins to manifest itself.

Some particular difficulties are usual in death but highlighted in murder: depersonalization, hallucinations both visual and auditory, some dissociation, a high focus on the violent murder event, the beginning of survivors' own murderous impulses, and survivor guilt, which can be of long duration and intensify family system problems. All these are common elements in homicide survivors and in and of themselves do not constitute pathology.

When choosing to utilize a group format, it is suggested that you select groups that are set up for a focal psychotherapy format and not for mutual support at this time. Using mutual support groups before the completion of psychotherapy can be disastrous as it perpetuates the symptomatology without bringing resolution. It can be discouraging for a new homicide survivor to go to a mutual support group (whose members have not received therapy first) and find homicide survivors who are still utilizing the support group as a therapy group 10 years after the murder and showing no signs of improvement.

A counselor focus during short-term counseling is often the below-the-surface, boiling rage of the survivor. Most therapists don't know what to do with it, so they ignore it, avoid it, or try to dismantle it—all of which can be harmful.

In group and individual therapy, it is common for survivors to discuss their rage and link it to their own murderous impulses. Survivors have indicated that they appreciated very much when the counselor of the homicide group said to them, "Are you angry inside? Are you raging?" Survivors may deny it because everyone else had either been afraid of their rage or had tried to remove it. When the counselor saw one survivor who was denying her rage, she stated, "I am not going to take your rage from you. It's yours. You keep it. You earned it." As the survivor kept her rage and brought it to group, others also brought theirs. The group had enormous energy, as you can imagine, but as they shared their rage and recognized that no one there was going to take it, deny it, minimize it, judge it, nor justify it, their rage lowered to anger, and the anger lowered to motivation, and soon a mutual support group was born. Ten homicide survivors worked together to open an office and start the nation's first focal psychotherapy homicide survivors support group. This positive outcome would not have happened if the counselor really believed that the survivors' murderous impulses were going to be acted out, or that their rage needed to be extinguished instead of expressed.

Counselors also have struggled with listening to the survivors' meticulous plans of a revenge murder. Most survivors have mental images of what they would like to do to the criminal. Some include quite detailed plans of chopping the criminal up for fishing bait, or electrocuting, castrating, or torturing the criminal. This is a normal phase for homicide survivors. Listening to and affirming their anger and rage is helpful. Watch to make sure they do not act on impulses. Most do not. Just as essential as listening to the homicide survivors' own story of their loved one's murder is that the counselor also listen to their murderous impulses. If you can't take all of this, don't take the case.

During the short-term counseling process, track the survivors' grief process to make sure it is moving. Remember, however, that their movement may be slower than what you are accustomed to because they have a lot to process.

In short-term counseling, it will be helpful to see the survivor in both individual and group format, as well as seeing the family, if they are willing. Most family systems will be falling apart, and the survivors' level of functioning during this time and during individual and group counseling will be decreasing.

Helping a victim holistically cannot exclude the need for a victim to question and even hold accountable an omnipotent God who "allowed" or "did not prevent" this tragedy. Because I am a person of the clergy, I am extremely aware of the lack of training most clergy have in this instance. A person's faith is a personal and intimate thing. Sometimes help from clergy feels abusive and forceful. Sometimes scriptures said (even if they are appropriate) are not encouraging and uplifting but short, clichéd, and painful. Sometimes they go against the grain of humanity, rubbing salt into a bleeding wound. Sometimes they are against what survivors believe about who God is, what He does, and what He doesn't do. This area is a shaky ground to walk on. One survivor's previous pastor showed up to tell her that it was "God's will" her father was murdered and that "he must have had some hidden sin in his life." That one statement sent her whirling from the arms of the church, which could have been a support for her, to a gutter of despair and suicidal ideation. Had even her God left her? Had even her God wanted a person she loved murdered? What kind of God is this? Tread carefully, my friends. . . .

It is important for the counselor to utilize "death" words that help the survivor grasp the finality. America has not been at the forefront of death education. We seem to want to shelter instead of acknowledge. Utilize words such as "murdered, dead, died, killed, homicide." We pass gas, we pass the salt, but we do not pass away. We die, or in this case, we are murdered. Teach the survivor grief education and the corresponding symptomatology. Be sensitive, however, to respect the idiosyncrasies of each person's grief.

Client Concerns

- Still obsessed with the murder if it was preventable;
- When the trial will start/or murderer will be apprehended;
- Inability to work or complications with work;
- Is their grief progressing as it should?
- Phobias and fears about safety;
- Survivor guilt;
- Murderous impulses and rage; and
- Wondering where God was.

Secondary Victimizations

- Loss of income;
- Counseling costs;
- Insensitive media and law enforcement;
- Delayed trial dates;
- Withdrawal of social support from friends and family; and
- Clergy asks them to forgive or offers insensitive counsel.

- Wondering where God was.

Secondary Victimizations

- Loss of income;
- Counseling costs;
- Insensitive media and law enforcement;
- Delayed trial dates;
- Withdrawal of social support from friends and family; and
- Clergy asks them to forgive or offers insensitive counsel.

LONG-TERM COUNSELING

As survivors move into disorientation/disorganization, their lives become even more chaotic. A highly difficult time for survivors is from 6 months after the murder to 2 years after the murder. The reality of the murder has set in, their previous coping mechanisms are wanting in the face of such a brutal event, their outside support systems will be fading as most feel they should be over it, the trial has probably begun with its many continuances and hearings, the media have been hot on their trail for months now, their family system has almost completely shut down if the system has not been helped, their physical health is deteriorating, marriages are suffering, finances are crucial because of the inability to work or absenteeism from work, previous spiritual connections are broken (Rinear, 1988), and they are fast approaching holidays, death anniversaries, and birthdays of the deceased, all of which are difficult and may elicit original trauma symptoms.

Self-blaming becomes prevalent, even when it was feasibly impossible for the survivor to have any part or blame in the murder. It is important to not challenge victims' self-blaming prematurely. It may be painful for you as a counselor to watch the person in great agony over a perceived connection to the personal responsibility for the murder. When the survivor is able to process fully the attendant meaning and attached emotion, these schemas will change and the person will move closer to acceptance (McCann & Pearlman, 1990).

Individual treatment may be sporadic. Survivors may come for a few weeks and then feel they don't need further help, only to call again. If they have completed group therapy, they will have gained some new support persons from the group, some coping mechanisms, and the knowledge that they are on track in their healing. Individual treatment should continue, and continued contact with group members should be encouraged on both a social and a support level.

During the actual trial, relapses may occur where survivors manifest severe PTSD reactions. Reutilization of principles used previously will help them to reconnect to what they have learned and experienced through group. Support from group members during the trial and afterwards greatly helps survivors. Do not be surprised if survivors lean more toward other survivors during this time than depending on therapeutic alliances.

Over long periods of time, the devastating effects of this type of intense trauma can be seen in the wreckage of a survivor's family life and relationships, social skills, occupation, and own self-constructs. If therapy was not provided, severe effects could have resulted in divorce, no contact with the rest of the family, self-isolation, and loss of job or the inability to stay at a high-functioning position. With the loss of family relationships and support, isolation from friends and social outings, and the reduction of career opportunties, victims perceive these losses to be self-induced and representative of their own value as human beings. Severe self-esteem and motivation deficits can be the long-term effects of not treating homicide survivors. A pervailing hopeless, hapless, and helpless feeling may reside over them like a dark cloud.

After stabilization has occurred after the trial, holidays and death anniversaries, and the grief phase of disorganization, it may be time to consider mutual survivor support groups. In our program, those who completed the focal psychotherapy group went on to develop, form, and operate a monthly mutual support group. No one could enter or join the mutual support group except those who had completed therapy groups. This assured some sort of stabilization and proved that the mutual support had at least jumped the first hurdle in healing.

You may want to check mutual support groups already existing in your community. However, be aware that the those who are in the mutual support group may not have completed therapy and may be at an entirely different level than your survivor. Many survivors choose peer support programs in lieu of therapy because therapy is too painful. As long as they stay attached to the peer support program, they avoid therapy. If they haven't completed therapy, it would be wise to indicate to your survivor that he or she may see people in various levels of healing, and some who could have been in the support group for years without progress. Personally, the only problem I sometimes encounter with peer support programs is that if the survivors haven't worked through even some basic issues, it becomes a cesspool of complaining and bitterness with no progressive movement. After 5 years, you will literally see them discussing the same issues, over and over again, with little or no resolution.

Some mutual support programs have gone on to be national champions, such as Parents of Murdered Children (POMC), who have set up support programs all over the United States. They have influenced legislation, increased support work, accelerated community awareness, and have been a blessing to homicide survivors at large.

Client Concerns

- The need of increased coping skills;
- The need of varying types of support;
- Help in dealing with media, trial, etc.;
- Family system falling apart;
- Physical health problems;
- Spiritual problems; and
- Approaching holidays or death anniversary dates.

Secondary Victimizations

- Loss of income;
- Loss of physical health;

- Counseling costs;
- Court delays;
- Intruding media; and
- Loss of family support or lost relationships.

Social Services Needed

- Victim advocate;
- Long-term counselor;
- Group counseling (psychotherapy);
- Mutual support groups (following psychotherapy);
- Prosecutor/attorney;
- Clergy; and
- Vocational rehabilitation (if new job is needed).

CONCLUSION

Clearly, homicide survivors are wanting in both service providers and those who advocate, understand, and support in paraprofessional roles. Training for this population needs to expand to law enforcement; criminal justice personnel including judges, prosecutors, and defense attorneys; clergy; mental health workers; and hospital staff. This population has been unnoticed, undiagnosed, and untreated for many years. Their pain is so raw and so fresh that it cannot continue to be shelved. For those who feel called to work with this population, the work is difficult and arduous, but oh how the survivors need it and thank you for it!

RECOMMENDED READING

Bowlby, J. (1969). *Attachment and loss*, Vol. 1. New York: Basic Books.

Bowlby, J. (1980). *Attachment and loss*, Vol. II. New York: Basic Books.

Lifton, R. J. (1979). *The broken connection, On death and the continuity of life.* New York: Simon & Schuster.

Rando, T. A. (1984). *Grief, dying and death. Clinical interventions for caregivers.* Champaign, IL: Research Press.

Rando, T. A. (1986). *Loss and anticipatory grief.* Lexington, MA: Lexington Books.

Rando, T. A. (1988). *Grieving, How to go on living when someone you love dies*. Lexington, MA: Lexington Books.

Redmond, L. M. (1989). *Surviving: When someone you love was murdered: A professionals' guide to group grief therapy for families and friends of murder victims*. Clearwater, FL: Self-published. You can order this book by writing to: Lu Redmond, P.O. Box 6111, Clearwater, FL 34618-6111.

REFERRALS

Children of Murdered Parents
P.O. Box 9317
Whittier, CA 90608
213–699–8427

Committee to Halt Useless College Killings (C.H.U.C.K.)
P.O. Box 188
Sayville, NY 11782
516–557–1130

The Compassionate Friends, Inc.
P.O. Box 3696
Oakbrook, IL 60522
708–990–0010

Parents of Murdered Children
P.O. Box 9802
Whittier, CA 90608
213–699–8427

REFERRALS ON VEHICULAR HOMICIDE

Mothers Against Drunk Driving (MADD)
669 Airport Freeway, Suite 310
Hurst, TX 76053
1–800–GET-MADD

RID-USA
P.O. Box 520
Schenectady, NY 12301
518–327–0034

	**Overview of Murder**
Crisis Intervention Issues:	Shock, numbness, PTSD, dealing with funeral arrangements, estate management, media, handling crime investigators, family interpersonal relationships, site cleanup services.
Short-Term Counseling:	Family interpersonal relationships, criminal justice system and treatment, beginning of grieving process, fear and safety, survivor guilt.
Long-Term Counseling:	Fear, anger, rage, family relationships, continuation of criminal justice problems, grieving process, job dysfunction, addictions and compulsions.
Secondary Victim- izations:	Loss of income (if primary income producer), final medical costs for victim, time off work, murderer may be released on bond, case may not go to trial, insensitivity of criminal justice system, lack of information given by crime investigators, slow payment by insurance company, funeral expenses, counseling costs, intense media coverage.
Social Services Needed:	Crime Compensation Bureau, victim advocate, legal aid, crisis, short- and long-term counseling, private investigator, trial attendants.

10

Cult, Satanic, and Ritual Victims

COUNSELOR WARNING

I have received calls from mental health counselors who have quite accidentally stumbled across cult, ritual, or satanic abuse. They call to obtain instructions for working with cult survivors. Most refer them on.

Cult, ritual, and satanic work is incredibly long and intense. It can also be dangerous. Those of you who opt to work with these survivors must be willing to accept the high possibility of multiple personality disorders and also must recognize that you may see psychic phenomena.

If you have never witnessed psychic phenomena, it will be difficult for you to accept the stories of the survivors when they talk about seeing spirits, manifestations, and moving objects. When I began teaching and lecturing on satanism, I witnessed more and more psychic phenomena. When I began to take cult survivors on as clients, psychic phenomana increased in my presence as well as in the lives of the survivors.

Some envision cult participants as teenage dabblers who play Dungeons and Dragons. The reality is that high-level cult members and satanists are White-collar executives. They are bankers, lawyers, doctors, military, judges, cops, and teachers. They are BMW drivers, Sunday school teachers, and charity volunteers. They work at your bank, your hospital, and your office. They have nice houses in nice suburbs. They do not do nice things. They play for keeps and their thrill is torture and death. Their activity is not so obvious. They don't rob graveyards—most of the dabblers do that. They don't just skin cats. They do untold torture to their own children bred from other cult members. And they hope to do it to our children as well.

Steele (1989, pp. 19–25) stated:

As therapists, we are increasingly confronted with survivors of severe abuse
and are being pushed to build new and personal frameworks within which to
fit the impact of their experiences. All the therapists I know who do this work
have been blindsided at least once by the horror of it. Their own vulnerability,
their helplessness in the face of such abuse is staggering. So is the evil. I
don't know another word for it. Science has failed us here, so I draw on a
spiritual vocabulary.

What you will read will shock you, anger you, and sicken you. But
what you will read is also the truth that many of us work with on a
regular basis. And one day, you may too.

CULTS, RITUALS, AND SATANISM

Not all cults are satanic, that is, their primary focus is not Satan, as
we know him. Their focus can be many other types of perceived
"deities." Cults are considered cults when they bypass the norm of
the Judeo-Christian faith. Jim Jones and Charles Manson were thought
to be cult-type leaders, enticing their followers into their own morality
and standards not condoned by the rest of society. Other cults don't
seem to focus on a particular "deity" but are more involved in psychological mind control to meet their own financial needs. Some cults
mix both "deity" worship and psychological mind control.

Ritual abuse can be seen in cults, satanism, and non-cult related
sexual abuse. Sexual abuse, in and of itself, can be a ritual. Ritual
describes a pattern of events that lead up to and are often included in
the abuse itself. We see ritual consistently in cults and satanism.

Satanism is the worship of Satan, the devil. It is the opposite of
Judeo-Christian faith and contains elements diametrically opposed to
the Christian faith. Satanists believe in God and know who Jesus is,
but they work against both, using Satan as their master and using
rituals that mock and ridicule Judeo-Christian practices. God is life.
Satan is death. Satanists focus on glorifying death. And they do it
through various means, including animal and human sacrifices, and
perhaps even worse, untold types of human torture.

MEANS OF ABUSE

The facts are all the same from coast to coast, from young survivors
to old survivors. We know they are true because they are seen with

continuity, because survivors don't manifest MPD from slight abuses, and because deep inside, we know this human evil exists.

We also know because others are coming forward to tell, including those who were witnesses to it and even the abusers—ex-satanists. We frequently see abuse such as physical torture using torture chambers and tools; sexual abuse; sexual mutilation; bestiality; starvation; force-feeding of human excrements, body parts, and blood; sleep-deprivation; brainwashing; drugging; binding and leaving victims in darkness for extended periods of time; inserting animal parts into sexual organs; and watching and often participating in killings. Victims may have been buried with corpses, raped on the altar as part of the worship service, taught to respond to torture by asking for more, and experienced all these practices repeatedly and sometimes since birth. Some were born for this deliberate purpose. Their mother may have been a "breeder" who bore children for death sacrifices or for indoctrination into the cult and its rituals of torture. Some breeders are given fertility drugs so they will produce twins. The preference is for a son for sacrifice and a daughter to be kept for rituals.

Orthodox satanists, as opposed to self-styled dabblers, have elaborate means of abuse targeted to a specific end. This result is the emotional, physical, spiritual, social, and sexual slavery of the cult's victims, rendering them extremely dissociative and ultimately multiple personality disordered.

These effects, coupled with drugging, hypnotic suggestions, and brainwashing, render victims poor witnesses should they try to report or prosecute the cult. Many involved in memory retrieval recall their experiences in a drugged-like, entranced state, or coupled with brain-washing messages.

Some cult victims who have wanted to prosecute have not done so and cannot, because prosecutors shy away from the unbelievable (which ritual abuse is) and especially from those who suffer from multiple personality disorder. Some satanists have become experts at creating not only dissociation and multiple personality disorder, but polyfrag-mented multiples. This entails memory being "shared" or spread out among many personalities, making congruence of the story and memory retrieval from all segments of the personality difficult. "Alter" personalities are "other" personalities that coexist inside the multiple. These could be younger children, adults, opposite-sex alters, blind, deaf, or dumb alters, or alters who are ageless (as old as time, existing from the "beginning").

A description of the types of abuse satanists use to achieve dissociation and multiple personality disorder follows.

Drugging

Most drugging begins when victims are children (for generational satanism). Many drugs are administered by legal medical doctors in the cult. Drugs are used for dissociation purposes and to obscure memory retrieval, but they also have a symbolic and spiritual representation. Most satanists also freely use street drugs before or during a ritual. Survivors talk frequently about drugged experiences, and they experience memories in the same drugged state. Drugs are also used when young breeders give birth. A survivor bore a "bred" baby at age 12, was drugged through the entire pregnancy, and was heavily drugged during delivery and the subsequent sacrificial death of the male child.

Cognitive Distortion

A primary teaching universally seen is the reversal of truths. Good is bad, bad is good, Satan is good, love is bad, hate is good. Children learn that the non-cult world is the opposite of what they believe; they are confused by it and do not fit in. When told they are loved, they are often beaten or sexually abused to change the context of that meaning. As they are instrumentally raped, scripture is quoted and they may be told, "Jesus loves you this much." Other scriptures are utilized to reinforce the association between abuse and God and focus on the helplessness of the situation. Scriptures about submission are utilized—obeying parents, honoring parents, "giving" unto others, serving others, and so forth. These concepts enter into the bonds of slavery often inflicted on the victim.

Forced Consumption of Body Waste Materials

These materials include blood, urine, feces, body parts, and semen. This forms a part of the ritual service, just as we would have wine and bread for communion. Survivors recalling these memories will often vomit and gag and reveal a past history of eating disorders.

Physical Abuse/Torture

Survivors (including children) have told me about being cut, hung similar to the way Jesus was hung, electrically shocked in the "Chair of Life," burned, mutilated by others and later by self, tied up, beaten, tortured with torture chamber-type devices, having hot curling irons inserted in the vagina and rectum, having live snake heads inserted in the vagina, being laid on the altar and gang raped or raped by instrumentation, and being tattooed or marked by cuttings on the body for Satan. Some physical torture involves methods that bring the victim to near-death experiences to enhance dissociation and produce "out-of-body experiences." Constant exposure to near-death experiences not only enhances dissociation but also speeds the process that leads to fragmentation and multiplicity. Some specific types of abuse are utilized to bring about multiplicity. Cult members desire multiplicity in their victims because it is difficult to prosecute or even believe someone with as many as 68 personalities.

Mind Control

Snowden (1988) indicated in her training materials that mind control/ brainwashing is often used in conjunction with drugs. This sophisticated hypnosis involves the associative pairing of induced pain/terror plus the cult message plus the trigger cue(s) that will reassociate victims (when they see/hear the cue) back to the actual abuse event. Trigger cues are planted in the unconscious and are utilized by cult members to control the survivor without his or her conscious awareness. The cues can be flowers, common hand gestures, and any common everyday events. These triggers stay planted for years and can reconnect the survivor, even when an adult, to the original trauma. Some cult members can retrigger events over the phone by utilizing certain phrases, or by seemingly innocent letters to the victim.

Sexual Abuse

Ritual abuse does not occur without sexual abuse. Sexual abuse occurs almost continuously with different abusers of both sexes and of all ages, including children, and with trained animals. One woman with MPD was cut vaginally almost daily for "blood letting" and now, when extremely stressed or cued, will cut herself vaginally. Sexual abuse is part of the ritual worship service in which rape by instrumentation on the altar is common. Some victims are then used as trainers to train other children how to perform certain sexual acts. Some cults are associated with child pornography rings and child abduction. These children are later used as child prostitutes in child sex rings.

Lockup

Victims are often locked up to reinforce their helplessness and the cult's ultimate control. Certain types of lockup are used to invoke terror, are used to bring about dissociation, or they can be part of different ceremonies or rituals. Some survivors with MPD remember being locked up and sometimes chained. One remembers and will often draw herself in a cage. Two children with MPD also drew themselves caged. Others have been locked in closets, coffins, graves, and other small spaces.

Sacrifice

Most cults offer some type of blood sacrifice through a ritual worship service. This type of ritual is usually similar to blood sacrifices described in the Old Testament of the Bible. Blood both in Judeo-Christian and in cult aspects is a sign of covenant. Covenant is the closest and ultimate relationship that exists and cannot ever be broken. Blood sacrifices are also described in the Old Testament as a means of remission of sin. These Judeo-Christian practices are mocked and reversed in cult worship.

In cult worship, blood sacrifices are offered as a means of showing a covenant relationship with Satan or a deity. Blood sacrifices are also a mockery of the blood of Christ. In the New Testament, Jesus Christ was nailed to a cross, shedding His blood (the sign of covenant) so that we no longer had to offer blood sacrifices for remission of sins. Cults continue to shed blood as a sign of ridicule against Christ, who met the final need for "bloodshed or blood letting." Cult blood sacrifices are also a way of showing the power and control of the cults' deity and the weakness of the human race.

Some survivors, including child survivors, have indicated watching and participating in both human and animal sacrifices. Some cult members are made to perform the actual murder or they are tricked into believing they committed the murder, even if they did not. Cults will use this as a way of keeping victims in the cult, threatening to turn them in to the authorities as murderers if they leave.

Multideprivation

Victims are deprived of food, sleep, water, love, touch (except abuse), social contact, and any other human need you can think of.

CULT ENTRY AND ENTRAPMENT

Snowden (1988) indicated in her training materials that people enter an orthodox and generational satanic cult by:

1. Being born into cult (generational);
2. Are given to Satan at an early age by relative (whole family is not cult-involved);
3. Extrafamilial preschool abuse;
4. Teenagers/young adults are lured by progressive entrapment (promise of power, rebellion, etc.);
5. Individuals of all ages are kidnapped and used by a cult; and
6. Criminals who are not cult members are paid for "hits."

Three main values of the child victim's belief system are targeted and destroyed repetitiously:

1. *God.* God is mocked at rituals. Children are forced to desecrate religious items by urinating or spitting on the Bible and other religious articles. They may also be asked to defecate on Bible pages and to consume them. They may be sexually abused with religious items, including having crosses inserted vaginally/anally. Some of their abusers may wear clerical robes or articles of the Christian faith. During the abuse, scripture is recited in order to induce association of the memory of the abuse with a particular scripture. One victim with MPD I work with drew elaborate pictures that contained a list of scriptures used over and over again, including "honor thy father and mother," "love thy neighbor," "give whatsoever you have," "all things work together for good," and others.

2. *Country.* Patriotism is destroyed through practices such as sexual penetration with articles that represent our country, such as small flags or other items that represent love of country. Patriotic music may be played in the background during abuse, and the victimizer is sometimes

dressed in a military uniform to increase the child's association of patriotism with the abuse.

3. *Family*. The child is told that "they," the abusers, are the child's new family. Sometimes the abusers are truly the child's biological family. The child may be asked to draw a picture of his or her natural family and urinate or defecate on it. Some children are ritualistically married to another child victim or to an adult member of the satanic coven. Some are then sexually abused by the "married partner," and if a girl, may be told that she is going to have a baby.

Brainwashing and mind control keep the child subservient by the following means:

1. *Participation*. Participation by the child victim is one of the most effective means of keeping that child continually connected to the abuse setting. If the child has been forced to kill, mutilate, or harm another person, or has been forced to participate or made to believe that he or she participated in sexual activity with another child, adult, or animal, then the child no longer identifies as a victim but becomes a participant in the offense. The child is made to take on the role of a victimizer. The child believes he or she is bad and evil and assumes the guilt of having acted out sexually and harmfully to others. Once children feel guilty, they become an integral part of the abuse act. Their guilt and their perception of having participated are used manipulatively to keep them active in the cult and engage in further abusive acts.

2. *Repetition of phrases*. "Truth phrases" are designed to keep a child from telling. Examples are "My spirit guide is watching me. My spirit friend will report me if I tell." It took many months before a victim with MPD with whom I work felt safe enough to tell me that she had been told she had spirit guides who heard everything she said and watched all things. If the spirit guide found out her disclosure to me, I could have been injured.

3. *Trigger words*. The use of trigger words known only by the abuser and the child recalls events of terror or specific threats made by the abuser. Trigger words may be simply taught to the child or put into the child's subconscious mind while drugged or in a hypnotic, trancelike state. Trigger words are often linked to a specific abuse act, and when the trigger word is spoken, it will reconnect the child or adult to the act of violence and to the cult message, "If you tell, others die," and to the assignment of the trigger, "Each time you hear the word, 'daddy,' you will remember this act of abuse and this message, 'If you tell, others die.' " Memories retrieved from times when triggers

were placed may come to the victim in drugged states or may be repeated aloud in a mind-controlled manner.

4. *Pictures or drawings.* Just as truth phrases and trigger words have hidden meanings known only to the abuser and the child, pictures and drawings are used to remind children of abusive episodes and threats of what will happen if they tell. This is an especially common practice in preschool and day-care centers where ritualistic abuse has occurred.

A picture of an animal with large eyes or ears often means that the eyes see the children and the ears hear them. A picture of a rabbit or a turtle may remind the children of a small animal that they either saw killed or one which they were forced to stick a pin or knife into. A drawing with a sentence or a poem beneath it may contain trigger words. A picture of someone in a costume or uniform may remind the children of their abuser who wore an identical costume or uniform.

Often innocent everyday items are used as triggers so that the child is constantly exposed to repeating internal/subconscious messages of abuse/don't tell. These triggers can literally be set out many times a day as a child sees greeting cards with bunnies, sees a magazine with flowers on it, hears songs about "daddy," or hears any other innocent word or sees a picture or item that has been set as an internal trigger.

INDICATORS OF RITUAL ABUSE

Chapter 8 on violence against children included physical and behavioral indicators of abuse. Those are good indicators for assessment. However, the following indicators are indigenous to ritual abuse and supplement those on physical and sexual abuse.

1. Talking to unseen persons victims insist are real; talking about spirit friends or guides;
2. Performing satanic, spirit, or unfamiliar dances, songs, chants, or prayers;
3. Fear or unusual preoccupation with the number 6 or multiples of the number 6. (Sometimes children are frightened of their 6th birthday because they have been told they would die then);
4. Verbal or written words that are strange (not known or understandable to you), or verbal or written words that are backwards (not to be confused with children who have dyslexia);
5. Fear of the colors red, black, or purple;

6. Sudden, unexplainable fear of small spaces. Victims may have been shut in coffins, cemetery field grave holes, or closets;
7. Sudden fascination with or abhorrence to urine or feces. Putting body waste into the mouth may indicate the child has been made to consume urine or feces;
8. Murderous impulses to kill siblings, parents, or others expressed verbally or with a weapon;
9. Preoccupation with drawing pentagrams, crescent moon with five stars, and dominant colors of black, red, and purple; and
10. Sudden fear of religious objects or persons.

WORKING WITH SURVIVORS

I believe that many survivors have attempted to get help but are not believed by therapists, who cast them off as psychotic. It would be much easier if they were. It takes unbelievable courage on our part as counselors to listen and hear the unbelievable recounting of evil.

What do we do when we are slapped in the face with unfathomable thoughts of torture by parents toward their own children whom they are supposed to love? How do we as counselors integrate that for ourselves, process it, and then help the survivor do the same? How do we resolve the extreme dichotomies of life and death, good and evil, abuser and parent, God and Satan? What happens when we realize that there is more to healing than ''processing the events of the abuse,'' that there is a spiritual element here, a soul so shattered and blown apart by human and inhuman evil that we don't know how it could possibly be made whole? When we look at the survivors' pain so clearly displayed in their eyes, and yet they can't name the pain or the abuser, how do we ward off our own helplessness, our own sense of incredible ineptness? How do we look at their legacy of pain, their haunting heritage, and offer anything, anything that will bring a moistened drop of healing to them? Inside, they suffer silently, remembering in a drug-enduced state the atrocities and hearing the brainwashed message of never telling.

What we do is deny it. We focus on their relationship problems, the lesser sexual abuse issues that we can handle, their substance abuse and eating disorders, their depression and anxiety. We rationalize that they can't really prove any of this. And we refer them out.

If we do keep them, we also will initially suffer our own form of PTSD when working with and responding to the severe abuse. We may have nightmares and other sleeping problems, anxiety, and psychological numbing, and become preoccupied with the events of the abuse and turn into vigilantes. Yet Steele (1989, pp. 19–25) stated:

Eventually, most of us are able to move from reacting to the content to being with the process. We discover that as we become part of the survivors' process, that experience in turn becomes a piece of our own personal process. And if we are willing to attend to our own process we can move from reaction to action, from helplessness to hopefulness, although this may only evolve slowly over time, and it may be painful and frightening.

Working with generationally involved cult survivors is far more difficult than working with non-cult MPD victims. Generationally involved cult survivors may still be under the control of the cult, may continue to participate in the cult even during therapy, and may relay information given during your sessions to the cult. Cult survivors most certainly bring to treatment the implants of brainwashing and programming. Therapy becomes difficult because some will go into a trance as you begin to work with them.

CRISIS INTERVENTION

It is totally beyond the scope of this chapter to describe how to work with cult survivors of any sort. It is a detailed process that has been the subject of volumes of research about multiple personality disorder and cult work.

Cult survivors are one of the most difficult populations to work with. Therefore, these outlines on crisis, short-term, and long-term counseling give a few basic tenets but in no way focus on all that is encompassed in caring for these individuals. It is suggested that if you have discovered MPD victims or cult survivors that you STOP and contact another therapist who has worked with them. Then decide if you are going to research and learn the techniques or refer the clients out. This chapter is meant to give you background information that will offer substantiation to horrific stories and details you may hear. In offering this information, I hope you will get a more realistic view of what this type of counseling entails. Then, if you decide to proceed, you will need a realistic assessment of the necessary training, education, and supervision.

Cult survivors, like other types of victims, do not come into therapy stating, "I was tortured in a cult." Most come in bearing the same types of complex issues that other victims present, only more so. It is to our utter amazement when we begin to retrieve flashes and fragments of undescribable acts.

We should not become so involved in attaining information on all the criminal acts perpetrated that we further traumatize the survivor. When digging for facts is not in pace with the progress of the survivor, many will pull away or become so overwhelmed that they might panic. They also believe that the spiritual aspect need not be a focus of treatment.

Because I am also a minister, I differ with many mental health counselors in believing that the spiritual aspect should be dealt with outside the need for exorcism/deliverance. I see it as a vital and intricate part. Yet, its timing and practice must be done by someone skilled in that field so that the event itself does not further traumatize the victim. Recognizing that we are triune (body, soul, and spirit), it is hard for me to fathom that ritual abuse affects only the body (physical) and the soul (mind and emotions). Perhaps the mental health field has not had success with treating cult victims because of the lack of skilled practitioners in this highly specialized area. Treating the spiritual aspects offers a more holistic approach in offering help and healing to this population.

Whether or not we as mental health counselors believe in God, Satan, or nothing, it is important to realize when dealing with ritual abuse that *this is their religion*. It is *their* belief system. It is the way in which they *worshiped*, at least in some ways. Whether or not we recognize satanism as a form of worship is not the issue. The issue is that the survivors do. And they have been permeated in their body, soul (mind, emotions), and spirit.

A word about the difficulty of prosecution: A number of us who work with cult survivors have found that many people to whom we report cult activity and from whom we seek help are involved in cults. Cult members and satanists are in all walks of life. Cult cases are difficult to prosecute because law enforcement and the judicial system are laced with practicing satanists. Why is this?

People involved in satanism and in cults seek ''control'' and ''power.'' Therefore they usually seek out professions that allow the exercise of power and control. Likewise, we have seen many cult survivors who were raised in military homes.

In one case I am currently working on, the survivor's dad was high-ranking military. When he retired, he went into law enforcement. Her brother is also in law enforcement. We are trying to prosecute this case in the same town that her father (abuser) and brother (victim and abuser) are working as cops. These cops have friends who are judges (and who may be practicing satanists). And the difficulty continues on. . .

Client Concerns

- Their story will not be believed;
- The cult will find out they have given information;
- The cult will kill them;
- The cult will torture one of their loved ones for telling;
- If they turn in information, the law enforcement system will not be able to convict them and secure their protection;
- They will be prosecuted for their part in the cult;
- Buried bodies or parts of bodies will not be able to be located for evidence; and
- Their lack of stability to withstand prosecution (especially if they are MPD victims).

Secondary Victimizations

- The fact they may have MPD;
- Untrained caregivers may not believe them;
- An unbelieving court system;
- Many medical problems they now suffer;
- The difficulty of prosecuting cult cases;
- The long-term treatment they may have to endure because of their horrific abuse; and
- The possibility of being killed for turning in evidence.

Social Services Needed

- A TRAINED counselor who has worked with cult survivors;
- Cult investigator;
- Witness protection program (may need it); and
- Prosecutor who believes in cult survivors.

SHORT-TERM AND LONG-TERM COUNSELING

Because of the nature of the emotional, physical, and spiritual injury inflicted in cult abuse, short-term counseling is not enough. Because of the abuse and the victims' inability to trust and anchor to persons or treatment, DO NOT BEGIN if you are not prepared to stay with them over the course of a few years.

Because treatment issues for ritual abuse and MPD are so extensive, we will not attempt to cover aspects of long-term treatment here. However, similar techniques of anchoring, building ego strength, managing abreactions, healing the inner child, and other types of integration work are all common. (These techniques have been listed in chapter 2 on psychodynamics of trauma and in chapter 7 on sexual trauma). For details on long-term treatment issues, see the recommended reading list at the close of this chapter.

Client Concerns

- Their story will not be believed;
- The cult will find out they have given information;
- The cult will kill them;
- The cult will kill a loved one for telling;
- The cult will kill their therapist/counselor;
- The inability to prosecute the case or fear that the case will be dismissed;
- They will be prosecuted for their part in the cult;
- Evidence such as bodies or body parts will not be able to be retrieved; and
- Their lack of stability to withstand the judicial process (especially if they are MPD victims).

Secondary Victimizations

- Developing MPD;
- Unbelieving caregivers;
- Unbelieving court system or jury;
- The difficulty in prosecuting cult cases;
- Many medical problems they may now have;
- Fear of being killed for turning in evidence;
- The long-term counseling they will have to endure because of their horrific abuse;

- The possibility of satanists being involved in the law enforcement and judicial systems in which they are trying to prosecute.

Social Services Needed

- A TRAINED counselor who has worked with cult survivors;
- Witness protection program;
- Cult investigator;
- Cult support group;
- Rehabilitation counseling; and
- Long-term counseling and support.

CLOSING

The decision to work with cult survivors is a serious one. It is incredibly intense work, certainly not without its hair pulling and frustration. It entails uncertainty in prosecuting and personal danger. The dichotomy of being the most interesting and challenging work versus the most draining and uncertain work has kept me on the edge of my "counseling chair" throughout this type work. Yet there is something so dear in those who have been so abused. For all the heartache, frustration, and lack of finances, I wouldn't refuse the challenge!

RECOMMENDED READING

Cultic Studies Journal: A Journal on Cults and Manipulative Techniques of Social Influence. Weston, MA: American Family Foundation.

Hassan, S. (1988). *Combatting cult mind control*. Rochester, VT: Park Street Press.

Healing Hearts, an organization of ritual abuse survivors which publishes a newsletter, resource and referral list. Albany, CA.

Hollingsworth, J. (1986). *Unspeakable acts*. New York: Cogdon & Weed.

Pazder, L., & Smith, M. (1980). *Michelle remembers*. New York: Pocket Books.

Pulling, P. (1989). *The devil's webb*. Lafayette, LA: Huntington House Press.

Ross, C.A. (1989). *Multiple personalty disorder diagnosis, Clinical features and treatment*. New York: Wiley.

Terry, M. (1987). *The ultimate evil: An investigation into America's most dangerous satanic cult*. Garden City, NJ: Doubleday.

Wedge, T. (1988). *The satan hunter*. Canton, OH: Daring Books.

REFERRALS

American Family Foundation
P.O. Box 336
Weston, MA 02193
617-893-0930

Bob Larsen Ministries
P.O. Box 36A
Denver, CO 80236

Cult Awareness Network
2421 W. Pratt Blvd., Suite 1173
Chicago, IL 60645
312-267-7777

Overview of Cult, Satanic, and Ritual Victims

Crisis Intervention Issues:	Physical safety, fear for life, reduction of abreactions, affirmation of cult abuse, suicide and mutilation prevention, control of dissociation.
Short-Term & Long-Term Counseling:	Finding an experienced and believing counselor, overcoming dissociation, memory retrieval, working through abreactions, inner child work, spiritual guidance, rebuilding ability to trust, trauma treatment techniques, treatment for addictions (drug, alcohol, sex, crisis, work, food).
Secondary Victimizations:	Development of MPD, disbelief from caregivers and court system, medical problems, difficulty of prosecuting case, need for long-term treatment, possibility of violent retribution (including murder by cult members).
Social Services Needed:	Trained cult-survivor counselor, cult investigator, witness protection program, prosecutor who believes in cult survivor, cult support groups, rehabilitation counseling.

11

Conclusion: Crime Fighters or Crime Repairers?

Each of us as social beings has had to come to terms with the increase of crime. We have had to measure it against our own feelings of safety, what it means for the future of our children, the increase in drug trafficking and drug crime, the social systems that need to be developed and funded by our government, and the building of prisons and the release of unreformed criminals.

Over 25 years we have watched serial and mass murderers like Manson and Bundy. When they were locked up, we felt safer only to find a new serial or mass murderer following in their footsteps. We have watched the rise of spouse abuse and the emergence of shelters. We have watched the enactment of legislation for vicitms. We have seen the atrocities of the day-care child abuse cases. We have listened in horror as our child protective services have failed to protect children who were killed by parents or foster parents. We have witnessed lots of hate, ethnic, and gay violence since the diagnosis of AIDS. We have listened with suspicion about tales and rumors of emerging satanists and their eery practices of death and doom. We have watched a new breed of victim emerge from our calculated and violent society: the multiple personality disordered victim.

Politically we have long argued about treatment versus incarceration. Prevention, especially in the area of crime, is relatively new. It has taken us years of research to understand the changing complexities of an increasingly violent community, and the characteristics of programs that have been unsuccessful.

As counselors, we have avenues available to make huge strides and impact in the field of victimology. With the increase of random violence and the emergence of campus-related crime, our services for victims are needed more than ever. We will have influence regarding research on victim programs and their effectiveness as well as child abuse prevention programs. Our voices will be heard by the government about new programs for new types of victim populations that are emerging. We will be partially responsible for future developments in victim-offender programming and its success, as well as for further development in expressive therapies and other types of psychotherapy geared toward victim populations. We will be responsible for increasing services for victims, and if we are educationally conscious, we will make a notable impact in educating and passing on training about victims to other counselors, clergy, and community.

Yet, working with victims is not without its sacrifices. As we forge this new frontier we are aware of the vast need for various types of training in specialized areas of psychotherapy. Victimology encompasses individual counseling for adults and children; group work for offenders and their families and victims and their families; and substantial knowledge of social work and the criminal justice parole and child protection systems. We need to be familiar with marriage and family therapy, dysfunctional families, addictions and compulsions (drugs, alcohol, sex addictions, eating disorders), sex therapy, spiritual inner healing of memories, women's issues, personality disorders, grief therapy, and death education.

Never has there been a greater need for us to grasp the reality of the intensity of a growing population of untreated victims. And most certainly, the future holds scores of those yet to be victimized who will stumble through our doorways hoping we will bring comfort to their shattered souls.

The women I have helped have forever changed my life. Especially Dede. I will always remember and love her. My hope in writing this book was to fill in some of the cracks Dede fell through while she was in search of treatment. I hope you will be one of those mental health providers who will begin to fill in the cracks of a system laced with holes.

If you are an agency director, won't you consider adding victim programs? Government grants are available in some areas for that purpose. If you are in private practice, could you see a few victims a week? Some services to victims can be billed to the Bureau of Crime Compensation in some areas. If you are a leader of a religious organization, could you not offer your place of worship for other agencies for running evening programs or offering 12-step victim programs for indigent victims?

If you are already a victim provider, is there a way to expand your services? We have recently joined forces with other therapists to open our area's first trauma recovery clinic for victims. We are developing it into a day treatment model, which for insurance purposes is considered partial hospitalization. This treatment facility is in a normal office space and services are offered to those victims who need counseling more than once or twice a week. Most of these represent extreme cases of abuse—they are highly dissociative. They come for 5 hours a day and are given various types of group and 12-step experiences as well as individual and expressive therapies. You could do it also.

If you are a hospital administrator, do you have a trauma tract that is offered to incoming victims? Can you add a women's issues tract in addition to what you are offering? Do you have and are you involved in a victims' coalition of services in your area? Are you joining with other victim providers to help shape and form legislation? Are you networking with other providers to find out about new services in your area?

Are you sharing the wealth of your own personal knowledge and experience by training others? Bridgework has chosen to focus on educating religious leaders. We have trained over 600 persons. Are you involved in receiving training yourself from other professionals? I have traveled from my home in Florida all over the United States for professional training. Are you reading victim material as it comes out? I read at least a book a month on some type of victimization. I try to choose a subject I am not familiar with. Then I hunt down training in that area.

Are you documenting and assisting research? Our research will change the direction of intervention and treatment. Can you help lay/peer volunteers begin grass-roots organizations or support groups? I regularly speak at peer-run support groups and help train lay volunteers to operate 24-hour crisis lines. Can you teach a few segments of a class at a local college or seminary? I regularly teach at public and private, secular and Christian colleges in their crisis intervention classes. Can you speak at your children's PTA, at church groups, or at civic associations?

I believe we can all do something. I am not "Super Counselor," but over the course of 4 years, I have done all those things. It helped me immensely to get an overall picture of victimization by seeing not only the grass-roots organizations but by being part of training and a judicial debate sponsored by the Department of Justice.

How can we affect victims' lives unless we understand their inner dynamics? Until we've participated in a grass-roots organization or lobbied ourselves, how can we possibly voice feelings of inequality in legislation and service programs? Until I stood before a judicial debate team with my knees shaking, I couldn't understand the fear and feeling of being ostracized within the political framework of our system.

I challenge each and every one of you to take seriously the recommendations listed in this chapter and to target some for this year. At the end of 1991–1992, will you have reached out to a victim and assisted in healing? In a decade, at the turn of the century, where will you be in providing services to the multitudes of vicitms? With your help, we will see a reduction in the number of pathological problems associated with unresolved trauma as we enter the 21st century.

References

Adam, B. D. (1987). *The rise of a gay and lesbian movement*. Boston: Twayne.

Ageton, S. S. (1983). *Sexual assault among adolescents*. Lexington, MA: Lexington Books.

American Psychiatric Association. (1987). *Diagnostic and statistical manual of mental disorders, third edition, revised*. Washington, DC: Author.

Anderson, C. L. (1982). Males as sexual assault victims: Multiple levels of trauma. *Journal of Homosexuality, 7*, 145–162.

Atkeson, B. M., Calhoun, K. S., Resick, P. A., & Ellis, E. M. (1982). Victims of rape: Repeated assessment of depressive symptoms. *Journal of Consulting and Clinical Psychology*, 96–102.

Aurand, S. K., Gross, L., & Addessa, R. (1985). *Violence and discrimination against lesbian and gay people in Philadelphia and the Commonwealth of Pennsylvania*. Philadelphia, PA: Philadelphia's Gay and Lesbian Task Force Report.

Bagley, C., & Ramsey, R. (1985). *Disputed childhood and vulnerability to sexual assault: Long term consequences with implications of counseling*. Paper presented at Conference on Counseling the Sexual Abuse Survivor, Winnipeg, Canada.

Bard, M., & Sangrey, D. (1979). *The crime victim's hand book*. New York: Basic Books.

Bard, M., Arnone, H. C., & Nemiroff, D. (1986). Contextual influences on the post-traumatic stress adaptation of homicide survivor-victims. In C. R. Figley (Ed.), *Trauma and its wake: The study and treatment of post-traumatic stress disorder, Vol. 2* (pp. 292–304). New York: Brunner/Mazel.

Becker, J. V., Skinner, L. J., Abel, G. G., Axelrod, R., & Cichon, J. (1984). Sexual problems of sexual assault survivors. *Women and Health, 9*, 5–20.

Becker, J. V., Skinner, L. J., Abel, G. G., & Cichon, J. (1986). Level of post assault sexual functioning in rape and incest victims. *Archives of Sexual Behavior, 15*, 37–49.

Becker, J. V., Skinner, L. J., Abel, G. G., Howell, J. M., & Bruce, K. (1982). The effects of sexual assault on rape and attempted rape victims. *Victimology, 7*, 106–113.

Berk, R. A. (1972). The emergence of muted violence in crowd behavior: A case study of an almost race riot. In J. F. Short & M. E. Wolfgang (Eds.), *Collective violence* (pp. 309–328). Chicago: Aldine Atherton.

Berk, R. A. (1990). Thinking about hate-motivated crimes. *Journal of Interpersonal Violence, 5*(3), 334–349.

Berrill, K. (1990). Anti-gay violence and victimization in the United States. *Journal of Interpersonal Violence, 5*(3), 274–294.

Bess, B. E., & Janssen, Y. (1982). Incest: A pilot study. *Hillside Journal of Clinical Psychiatry, 42*, 437–438.

Blanchard, E. B., Kolb, L. C., Pallmeyer, T. P., & Gerardi, R. J. (1982). A psychophysiological study of post traumatic stress disorder in Vietnam veterans. *Psychiatric Quarterly, 54*, 220–228.

Block, M. R., & Sinnott, J. D. (1979). *The battered elder syndrome: An exploratory study*. College Park, MD: University of Maryland, Center on Aging.

Bourque, B. B., Brumback, G. B., Krug, E. E., & Richardson, L. O. (1978). *Crisis intervention: Investigating the need for new applications*. Unpublished manuscript. Washington, DC: American Institutes for Research.

Briere, J. (1984). *The effects of childhood sexual abuse on later psychological functioning: Defining a "post sexual abuse syndrome."* Paper presented at the Third National Conference on Sexual Victimization of Children, Washington, DC.

Briere, J., & Runtz, M. (1988). Post sexual abuse trauma. In G. E. Wyatt & G. J. Powell (Eds.), *Lasting effects of child sexual abuse* (pp. 85–99). Newbury Park, CA: Sage.

Browne, A., & Finkelhor, D. (1986). The impact of child sexual abuse: A review of the research. *Psychological Bulletin, 99*, 66–77.

Buchanan, S. H. (1979). Haitian women in New York City. *Migration Today, 7*, 19–25, 39.

Burgess, A. W., Hartman, C. R., & Kelley, S. J. (1990). *Assessing child abuse: The TRIADS checklist*. An instructional handout sheet from a Conference by Forensics Mental Health. Tampa, FL.

Burgess, A. W., & Holmstrom, L. L. (1974a). *Rape: Victims of crisis*. Bowie, MD: Robert J. Brady.

Burgess, A. W., & Holmstrom, L. L. (1974b). Rape trauma syndrome. *American Journal of Psychiatry, 131*, 981–986.

Burgess, A. W., & Holmstrom, L. L. (1976). Rape: Its effects on task performance at varying stages in the life-cycle. In M. J. Walker & S. L.

Bordsky (Eds.), *Sexual assault: The victim and the rapists* (pp. 23–33). Lexington, MA: Lexington Books.

Burgess, A. W., & Holmstrom, L. L. (1986). *Rape: Crisis and recovery.* West Newton, MA: Awab.

Burman, M., Stein, J., Golding, J., Siegel, J., Sorenson, S., Forsythe, A., & Telles, C. (1988). Sexual assault and mental disorders in a community population. *Journal of Consulting and Clinical Psychology, 56*, 843–850.

Butler, R. N., & Lewis, M. L. (1983). *Aging and mental health.* St. Louis: Mosby.

Calhoun, K. S., Atkeson, B. N., & Resick, P. A. (1982). A longitudinal examination of the reactions in victims of rape. *Journal of Counseling Psychology, 29*, 655–661.

Carmen, E. M., Rieker, P. R., & Mills, R. (1984). Victims of violence and psychiatric illness. *American Journal of Psychiatry, 141*, 378–383.

Chaplin, J. P. (1972). *Dictionary of psychology.* New York: Dell.

Cherry, D., & Allen, M. (1983). *Elder abuse: Planning for services and prevention activities in Flint, Michigan.* Flint, MI: Task Force on Elder Abuse.

Clearinghouse on Child Abuse and Neglect Information & U.S. Department of Health and Human Services, Office of Human Development Services, Administration for Children, Youth and Families, Children's Bureau, National Center on Child Abuse and Neglect (1989, March). *Child abuse and neglect: A shared community concern paper.* Washington, DC.

Coates, D., & Winston, T. (1983). Counteracting the deviance of depression: Peer support groups for victims. *Journal of Social Issues, 39*, 169–194.

Coates, D., Wortman, C. B., & Abbey, A. (1979). Reactions to victims. In I. H. Frieze, D. Bar-Tal, & J. S. Carroll (Eds.), *New approaches to social problems* (pp. 21–52). San Francisco: Jossey-Bass.

Conte, J. R., & Berliner, L. (1987). The impact of sexual abuse on children: Empirical findings. In L. Walker (Ed.), *Handbook on sexual abuse of children: Assessment and treatment issues.* New York: Springer.

Cook, R. F., Smith, B. E, & Harrell, A. (1987). *Helping crime victims: Levels of trauma and effectiveness of service.* Washington, DC: U.S. Department of Justice, National Institute of Justice.

Courtois, C. A. (1988). *Healing the incest wound: Adult survivors in therapy.* A paper presented at the American Association for Counseling and Development Conference, Cincinnati, OH.

Courtois, C. A. (1990). *The world of the sexual abuse survivor: A clincal spectrum.* A paper presented at the Second Annual Eastern Regional Conference on Multiple Personality and Dissociation, Washington, DC.

Crime Victims Digest. (1989, January). *6*(1).

Crime Victims Research and Treatment Center. (1988). *PTSD following murders and drunk driving crashes*. Department of Psychiatry and Behavioral Sciences, Medical University of South Carolina. A paper presented at the National Organization of Victim Assistance Conference.

Crime Victims Research and Treatment Center. (1989, January). Department of Psychiatry and Behavioral Sciences, Medical University of South Carolina. *Treating families of child sexual assault*. (Dr. Benjamin E. Saunders).

Cryer, L., & Beutler, L. (1980). Group therapy: An alternative treatment approach for rape victims. *Journal of Sex & Marital Therapy, 6*, 40–46.

Dating Violence Intervention Project Newsletter. (1989, Summer). Reported in *Action Ohio Newsletter*, October 1989.

Domestic Abuse—Families in Trouble. (1989).

Donaldson, M. A., & Gardner, R. (1985). Diagnosis and treatment of traumatic stress among women after childhood incest. In C. R. Figley (Ed.), *Trauma and its wake* (pp. 356–377). New York: Brunner/Mazel.

Ehrlich, H. J. (1990, September). The ecology of anti-gay violence. *The Journal of Interpersonal Violence, 5*(3), 359–365.

Ellis, E. M., Calhoun, K. S., & Atkeson, B. M. (1980). Sexual dysfunction in victims of rape: Victims may experience a loss of sexual arousal and frightening flashbacks even one year after the assault. *Women and Health, 5*, 39–47.

Evans, H. I. (1978). Psychotherapy for the rape victim: Some treatment models. *Hospital and Community Psychiatry, 29*, 309–312.

Falk, P. (1989). Lesbian mothers: Psychosocial assumptions in family law. *American Psychologist, 44*(6), 941–947.

Federal Bureau of Investigation. (1989). *Uniform crime reports, 1988*. Release date August 6, 1989.

Federal Council on Aging. (1976). *Bicentennial charter for older Americans*.

Feldman-Summers, S., Gordon, P. E., & Meagher, J. R. (1979). The impact of rape on sexual satisfaction. *Journal of Abnormal Psychology, 88*, 101–105.

Ferguson, D., & Beck, C. (1983, Sept.–Oct.). H.A.L.F.—A tool to assess elder abuse within the family. *Geriatric Nurse*, pp. 301–304.

Figley, C. R. (1983). Catastrophies: An overview of family reaction. In C. R. Figley & H. I. McCubbine (Eds.), *Stress and the family: Coping with catastrophe, Vol. 2* (pp. 3–20). New York: Brunner/Mazel.

Figley, C. R. (1986). Traumatic stress: The role of the family and social support. In C. R. Figley (Ed.), *Trauma and its wake: The study and treatment of post-traumatic stress disorder, Vol. 2* (pp. 39–56). New York: Brunner/Mazel.

Finkelhor, D. (1986). *A sourcebook on child sexual abuse*. Beverly Hills: Sage.

Finkelhor, D., & Browne, A. (1985). The traumatic impact of child sexual abuse: A conceptualization. *American Journal of Orthopsychiatry, 55*, 530–541.

Florida Child Advocate Newsletter. (1989, April-June). *3*(2).

Foa, E., Olasov, B., & Steketee, G. (1988, September). *Treatment of rape victims*. Paper presented at NIMH Conference "State of the Art Workshop on Victims of Sexual Assault," Charleston, SC.

Forman, B. D., (1980). Psychotherapy with rape victims. *Psychotherapy: Theory, Research and Practice, 17*, 304–311.

Fox, S. S., & Scherl, D. J. (1972). Crisis intervention with victims of rape. *Social Work, 17*, 37–42.

Frank, E., Anderson, B., Stewart, B. D., Dancu, C., Hughes, C., & West, D. (1988). Efficacy of cognitive behavior therapy and systematic desensitization in the treatment of rape trauma. *Behavior Therapy, 19*, 403–420.

Frank, E., & Stewart, B. D. (1984). Depressive symptons in rape victims: A revisit. *Journal of Affective Disorders, 7*, 77–85.

Frederick, C. J. (1986). Post-traumtic stress disorder and child molestation. In A. W. Burgess & C. R. Hartman (Eds.), *Sexual exploitation of patients by health professionals* (pp. 133–142). New York: Praeger.

Freidrich, W. (1986). Behavior problems in sexually abused young children. *Journal of Pediatric Psychology, 11*, 47–57.

Friedman, K., Bischoof, H., Davis, R., & Person, A. (1982). *Victims and their helpers: Reaction to crime*. New York: Victim Services Agency.

Frieze, I. H., Hymer, S., & Greenberg, M. S. (1987). Describing the crime victims: Psychological reactions to victimization. *Professional Psychology: Research and Practice, 18*, 299–315.

Garnets, L., Herek, G., & Levy, B. (1990). Violence and victimization of lesbians and gay men: Mental health consequences. *Journal of Interpersonal Violence, 5*(3), 366–383.

Gibson, P. (1989). Gay males and lesbian youth suicide. In *Report to the Secretary's Task Force on Youth Suicide, Vol 3. Prevention and intervention in youth suicide* (pp. 110–142). Washington DC: U.S. Department of Health and Human Services.

Giller, E. L. (Ed.). (1990). *Biological assessment and treatment of post traumtic stress disorder*. Washington, DC: American Psychiatric Press.

Gomes-Schwartz, B., Horowitz, J. M., & Sauzier, M. (1985). Severity of emotional distress among sexually abused preschool, school-age and adolescent children. *Hospital and Community Psychiatry, 35*, 503–508.

Goodwin, J. (1985). Post-traumatic symptoms in incest victims. In S. Eth & R. S. Pynoos (Eds.), *Post-traumtic stress disorder in children* (pp. 157–168). Washington, DC: American Psychiatric Association.

Goyer, P. F., & Eddleman, H. C. (1984). Same-sex rape of nonincarcerated men. *American Journal of Psychiatry, 141*, 576–579.

Greenwald, E., & Leitenberg, H. (1990). Posttraumtic stress disorder in a nonclinical and nonstudent sample of adult women sexually abused as children. *Journal of Interpersonal Violence, 5*(2), 217–228.

Grimshaw, A. D. (1969). Three views of urban violence: Civil disturbance, racial revolt, class assault. In A. D. Grimshaw (Ed.), *Racial violence in the United States* (pp. 385–396). Chicago: Aldine.

Gross, L., Aurand, S., & Adessa, R. (1988). *Violence and discrimination against lesbian and gay people in Philadelphia and the Commonwealth of Pennsylvania*. Philadelphia, PA: Philadelphia's Gay and Lesbian Task Force Report.

Groth, A. N. (1990). *Forensic Mental Health Conference notes*, Tampa, FL.

Groth, A. N., & Burgess, A. W. (1980). Male rape: Offenders and victims. *American Journal of Psychiatry, 137*(7), 806–810.

Harry, J. (1990). Conceptualizing anti-gay violence. *Journal of Interpersonal Violence, 5*(3), 350–358.

Henton, J., Cate, R., & Emery, B. (1984). The dependent elderly: Targets for abuse. In W. H. Quinn & G. A. Hughson (Eds.), *Independent aging* (pp. 149–162). Rockville, MD: Aspen.

Herek, G. (1990). The context of anti-gay violence. Notes on cultural and psychological heterosexism. *Journal of Interpersonal Violence, 5*(3), 316–333.

Herek, G. M., & Glunt, E. K. (1988). An epidemic of stigma: Public's reaction to AIDS. *American Psychologist, 43*, 886–891.

Herman, J., Russell, D., & Trocki, K. (1986). Long-term effects of incestuous abuse in childhood. *American Journal of Psychiatry, 143*, 1293–1296.

The hunt for crime starts. (1989, January 22). *USA Today*.

Hunter, J., & Schaecher, R. (1990). Gay and lesbian youths. In M. Rotheram-Borus, J. Bradley, & N. Oblensky (Eds.), *Planning to live: Suicidal youths in community settings* (pp. 297–317). Tusla: University of Oklahoma Press.

Janoff-Bulman, R. (1979). Characterological versus behavioral self-blame: Inquiries into depression and rape. *Journal of Personality and Social Psychology, 37*, 1798–1809.

Kahana, B., Harel, Z., & Kahana, E. (1988). Predictors of psychological well-being among survivors of the Holocasut. In J. P. Wilson, Z. Harel, & B. Kahana (Eds.), *Human adaptation to extreme stress: From the Holocaust to Vietnam* (pp. 171–192). New York: Plenum Press.

Kahn, A. S. (Ed.). (1984). *Victims of crime and violence: Final report of the APA Task Force on Victims of Crime and Violence*. Washington, DC: American Psychological Association.

Keyes, B. (1990). *Techniques of inner healing*. Unpublished manuscript.

Kilpatrick, D. G., Resick, P. A., & Veronen, L. J. (1981). Effects of a rape experience: A longitudinal study. *Journal of Social Issues, 37*, 105–121.

Kilpatrick, D. G., & Veronen, L. J. (1984). *Treatment of fear and anxiety of victims of rape*. (Final report, Grant No. R01MH2902). Rockville, MD: National Institute of Mental Health.

Kilpatrick, D. G., Veronen, L. J., & Best, C. L. (1985). Factors predicting psychological distress among rape victims. In C. R. Figley (Ed.), *Trauma and its wake: The study and treatment of post-traumatic stress disorder* (pp. 113–141). New York: Brunner/Mazel.

Kilpatrick, D. G., Veronen, L. J., & Resick, P. A. (1979). The aftermath of rape: Recent empirical findings. *American Journal of Orthopsychiatry, 49*, 658–669.

Kilpatrick, D. G., Veronen, L. J., Saunders, B. E., Best, C. L., Amick-McMullen, A., & Paduhovich, J. (1987). *The psychological impact of crime: A study of randomly surveyed crime victims*. (Final report, Grant No. 84-IJ-CX-0039). Washington DC: National Institute of Justice.

Kinzie, D. J. (1988). The psychiatric effects of massive trauma on Cambodian refugees. In J. P. Wilson, Z . Harel, & B. Kahana (Eds.), *Human adaptation to extreme stress: From the Holocaust to Vietnam* (pp. 305–318). New York: Plenum Press.

Kinzie, D. J., Fredrickson, R. H., Ben, R., Rleck, J., & Karis, W. (1984). PTSD among survivors of Cambodian concentration camps. *American Journal of Psychiatry, 141*, 645–650.

Kolb, L. C. (1984). The post traumatic stress disorders of combat: A subgroup with a conditioned emotional response. *Military Medicine, 149*, 237–243.

Koss, M. P., & Burkhart, B. R. (1989). A conceptual analysis of rape victimization: Long-term effects and implications for treatments. *Psychology of Women Quarterly, 13*, 27–40.

Krupnick, J. (1980). Brief psychotherapy with victims of violent crime. *Victimology: An International Journal, 5*, 347–354.

Laguerre, M. S. (1984). *American odyssey: Haitians in New York City*. Ithaca, NY: Cornell University Press.

Ledray, L. E. (1986). *Recovering from rape*. New York: Holt.

Lerner, M. J. (1970). The desire for justice and reactions to victims. In J. Macaulay & L. Berkowitz (Eds.), *Altruism and helping behavior* (pp. 205–229). New York: Academic Press.

Lipovsky, J. A., Saunders, B. E., & Murphy, S. M. (1989). Depression, anxiety, and behavior problems among victims of father-child sexual assault and nonabused siblings. *Journal of Interpersonal Violence, 4*(4), 452–468.

Maguire, M. (1980). The impact of burglary upon victims. *British Journal of Criminology, 20*(3), 261–275.

Mannarino, A. P., Cohen, J. A., & Gregor, M. (1989). Emotional and behavioral difficulties in sexually abused girls. *Journal of Interpersonal Violence, 4*(4), 437–451.

Martin, G. L. (1987). Counseling for family violence and abuse. In G. Collins (Ed.), *Resources for Chrisitian counseling* (pp. 54–56, 136–157). Waco, TX: Word.

Masters, R., Friedman, L. N., & Getzel, G. (1988). Helping families of homicide victims: A multidimensional approach. *Journal of Traumatic Stress, 1*(1), 109–125.

McCann, I. L., & Pearlman, L. A. (1990). *Psychological trauma and the adult survivor—Theory, therapy and transformation.* New York: Brunner/Mazel.

McCann, I. L., Sakheim, D. K., & Abrahamson, D. J. (1988). Trauma and victimization: A model of psychological adaptation. *Counseling Psychologist, 16*, 531–594.

McConnell, J. V. (1986). *Understanding human behavior.* New York: Holt, Rinehart & Winston.

Metro Dade Police Department. (1990). *Florida law enforcement handbook, Florida state statutes.* Miami, FL: Author.

Metzger, D. (1976). It is always the woman who is raped. *American Journal of Psychiatry, 133*, 405–408.

Miller, B., & Humphreys, L. (1980). Lifestyles and violence: Homosexual victims of assault and murder. *Qualitative Sociology, 3*(3), 169–185.

Miranda, J., & Storms, M. (1989). Psychological adjustment of lesbians and gay men. *Journal of Counseling & Development, 68*, 41–45.

Mollica, R. F., Wyshak, G., & Lavelle, J. (1987). The psychosocial impact of war trauma and torture on Southeast Asian refugees. *American Journal of Psychiatry, 144*, 1567–1572.

Monane, M., Leichter, D., & Lewis, D. O. (1984). Physical abuse in psychiatrically hospitalized children and adolescents. *Journal of the American Academy of Child Psychiatry, 23*, 653–658.

Myers, J. E., & Shelton, B. (1987). Abuse and older persons: Issues and implications for counselors. *Journal of Counseling and Development, 65*, 376–380.

Myers, M. F. (1989). Men sexually assaulted as adults and sexually abused as boys. *Archives of Sexual Behavior, 18*, 203–215.

Nadelson, C. C., Notman, M. T., Zackson, H., & Gormick, J. (1982). A follow-up study of rape victims. *American Journal of Psychiatry, 139,* 1266–1270.

National CASA Association Newsletter, *The Connection.* (1989, Winter). 5(1).

National Committee for Prevention of Child Abuse. (1989, April). *Memorandum.* Chicago: Author.

National Gay & Lesbian Task Force. (1984). *Anti-gay/lesbian victimization: A study by the National Gay Task Force in cooperation with gay and lesbian organizations in eight U.S. cities.* Washington, DC: Author.

National Gay & Lesbian Task Force. (1987). *Press release,* April 27, 1987. Washington, DC: Author.

National Gay & Lesbian Task Force. (1989). *Anti-gay violence, victimization and defamation in 1988.* Washington DC: Author.

National Institute Against Prejudice and Violence. (1986, October). *The Ethnoviolence Project pilot study,* pp. 1–9. Baltimore, MD: Author.

National Institute Against Prejudice and Violence. (1988). *Forum, 3*(4).

National Organization of Victim Assistance. (1985). *Bulletin.* Washington DC: Author.

National Victim Center. (1990). *Advocacy in action; Elderly abuse section.* Fort Worth, TX: Author.

National Victim Center. (1990, March). *Overview of crime and victimization in America.* Fort Worth, TX: Author.

National Victim Center. (1990, November). Crime, safety and you! *Newsletter, 1*(4). Fort Worth, TX: Author.

National Victims Resource Center. (1987, November). *Sexual assault: An overview.* Handout. Washington, DC: Office for Victims of Crime, Dept. of Justice.

Nieberg, H. L. (1972). Agnostic rituals of conflict. In J. F. Short, J. R. Wolfgang, & M. E. Wolfgang (Eds.), *Collective violence* (pp. 82–99). Chicago: Aldine Atherton.

Niederland, W. (1968). The psychiatric evaluations of emotional problems in survivors of Nazi persecution. In H. Krystal (Ed.), *Massive psychic trauma* (pp. 8–22). New York: International Universities Press.

Niles, D. P. (1990). Posttraumatic stress disorder vs. posttraumatic stress reaction. American Mental Health Counselors Association, *The Advocate, 13,* p. 9.

Norris, J., & Feldman-Summers, S. (1981). Factors related to the psychological impact of rape on the victim. *Journal of Abnormal Psychology, 90,* 562–567.

Norris, F., Kaniasty, K., & Scheer, D. A. (1990). Use of mental health services among victims of crime: Frequency, correlates, and subsequent recovery. *Journal of Consulting and Clinical Psychology, 58*(5), 538–547.

Plant, R. (1986). *The pink triangle.* New York: Holt.

Porter, S. (1989, February). New York Times. In Georgia Network Against Domestic Violence, *Newsletter, 1.*

Putnam, F. W. (1985). Dissociation as a response to extreme trauma. In R. P. Kluft (Ed.), *Childhood antecedents of multiple personality.* Washington, DC: American Psychiatric Association.

Redmond, L. M. (1989). *Surviving when someone you love was murdered.* Clearwater, FL: Psychological Consultation & Education Services.

Rencken, R. H. (1989). *Intervention strategies for sexual abuse.* Alexandria, VA: American Association for Counseling and Development.

Resick, P. A., Jordan, C. G., Girelli, S. A., Hutter, C. H., & Marhoefer-Dvorak, S. (1988). A comparative outcome study of behavorial group therapy for sexual assault victims. *Behavior Therapy, 19,* 385–401.

Rinear, E. E. (1988). Psychosocial aspects of parental response patterns to the death of a child by homicide. *Journal of Traumatic Stress, 1,* 305–322.

Roth, S. R., & Cohen, L. K. (1986). Approach, avoidance, and coping with stress. *American Psychologist, 41,* 813–819.

Roy, M., (1982). (Ed.). *The abusive partner.* New York, Van Nostrand Reinhold.

Russell, D. E. H. (1988). The secret trauma. In Wisconsin Coalition Against Domestic Violence, *Newsletter, 7*(4).

Rychtarik, R. G., Silverman, W. K., Van Landingham, W. P., & Prue, D. M. (1984). Treatment of an incest victim with implosive therapy: A case study. *Behavior Therapy, 15,* 410–420.

Saunders, B. E. (1989, January). *Treating families of child sexual assault.* Crime Victims Research and Treatment Center, Department of Psychiatry and Behavioral Science, Medical University of South Carolina. Paper presented to the Southern Unit of the South Carolina Chapter of the National Association of Social Workers, Charleston, SC.

Saunders, D. (1988, December). Fighting for child custody. *Wisconsin Coalition Against Domestic Violence Newsletter, 7*(4), 1–16.

Schlesinger, S. R. (1985). *Bureau of Justice Statistics Bulletin.* Washington, DC: U.S. Department of Justice.

Segrest, M., & Zeskind, L. (1989). *Quarantines and death: The far right's homophobic agenda.* Atlanta, GA: Center for Democratic Renewal.

Select Committee on Aging, U.S. House of Representatives. (1981). *Elder abuse* (Comm. Pub. No. 97–277). Washington, DC: U.S. Government Printing Office.

Seligman, L. (1977). Haitians: A neglected minority. *Personnel and Guidance Journal, 55*(7), 409–411.

Siegel, J. M., Golding, J. M., Stein, J. A., Burnam, M. A., & Sorenson, S. B. (1990). Reactions to sexual assault. A community study. *Journal of Interpersonal Violence, 5*(2).

Siegel, J. M., Sorenson, S. B., Golding, J. M., & Burman, M. A. (1987). The prevalence of adult sexual assault: The Los Angeles Epidemiologic Catchment Area Project. *American Journal of Epidemiology, 126*, 1141–1153.

Smith, A. (1989, September 7). Cambodian witnesses to horror cannot see. *New York Times*, p. A–10.

Snowden, K. (1988). *Satanic cult ritual abuse handout*. Richmond, VA.

Sorenson, S. B., Stein, J. A., Siegel, J. M., Golding, J. M., & Burman, M. A. (1987). The prevalence of adult sexual assault: The Los Angeles Epidemiologic Catchment Area Project. *American Journal of Epidemiology, 126*, 1154–1164.

Spitzer, (1990). *A draft criteria for the Diagnostic and Statistical Manual of Mental Disorders IV regarding Disorders of Extreme Stress Not Otherwise Specified (DESNOS)*.

Steele, K. (1989). Sitting with a shattered soul. *Pilgrimage: Journal of Personal Exploration and Psychotherapy, 15*(6), 19–25.

Steinmetz, S. (1986). Elder abuse: One-fifth of our population at risk. *Caring, 5*(1), 69–71.

Steinmetz, S. K., & Amsden, D. J., (1983). Dependent elders, family stress, and abuse. In T. H. Brubaker (Ed.), *Family relationships in later life* (pp. 178–192). Beverly Hills, CA. Sage.

Sterba, R. (1969). Some psychological factors in negro race hatred in anti-negro riots. In A. D. Grimshaw (Ed.), *Racial violence in the United States* (pp. 408–413). Chicago: Aldine.

Sue, S., Akutusu, P. D., & Higashi, C. (1987). Training issues in conducting therapy with ethnic-minority group clients. In P. Pedersen (Ed.), *Handbook of cross-cultural counseling and therapy* (pp. 275–280). Westport, CT: Greenwood Press.

Sykes, G., & Matza, D. (1957). Techniques of neutralization. *American Sociological Review, 22*, 664–670.

Symonds, M. (1980). The "second injury" to victims. In L. Kivens (Ed.), *Evaluation and change: Services for survivors* (pp. 36–38). Minneapolis, MN: Minneapolis Medical Research Foundation.

U.S. Attorney General's Task Force on Family Violence. (1984, September). *Recommendations from the final report*. Washington, DC.

U.S. Department of Health and Human Services. Office of Human Development Services and Clearinghouse on Child Abuse and Neglect Information. (1989, March). *Child abuse and neglect: A shared community concern.* Washington, DC: Author.

U.S. Department of Justice. Bureau of Justice Statistics. (1985). *The crime of rape.* Washington, DC: Author.

U.S. Department of Justice. Bureau of Justice Statistics. (1985, January). *Household burglary.* Washington, DC: Author.

U.S. Department of Justice. Bureau of Justice Statistics. (1989, April). *BJS data report, 1988, NCJ-116262.* Washington, DC: Author.

U.S. Department of Justice. Bureau of Justice Statistics. (1989, June). *Criminal victimization in the United States, 1987, NCJ-115524.* Washington, DC: Author.

U.S. Department of Justice. Office of Juvenile Justice and Delinquency Prevention. (1988, July). *Child sexual abuse victims and their treatment.* Washington, DC: Author.

U.S. Select Committee Subcommittee on Health and Long Term Care Report. (1989, Fall). As reported in The Coalition of Advocates for the Rights of the Infirm Elderly publication, *Carie Newsletter, 9*(2).

U.S. Surgeon General. (1984). As reported in *Middle Way House Newsletter,* February, 1989.

van der Kolk, B. A. (1990). The trauma spectrum: The interaction of biological and social events in the genesis of the trauma response. *Journal of Traumatic Stress, 1,* 273–290.

van der Kolk, B. A., & Greenberg, M. S. (1987). The psychobiology of the trauma response: Hyperarousal, constrictions, and addiction to traumatic reexposure. In B. A. van der Kolk (Ed.), *Psychological trauma,* (pp. 63–87). Washington, DC: American Psychiatric Press.

van der Kolk, B. A., Greenberg, M. S., Boyd, H., & Krystal, J. (1985). Inescapable shock, neurotransmitters and addiction to trauma: Toward a psychobiology of post traumatic stress. *Biological Psychiatry, 20,* 314–325.

Walker, L. E. (1979). *The battered woman.* New York: Harper & Row.

Waller, I. *Crime victims: Needs, services and reforms.* (1985). Paper presented at the 4th International Symposium on Victimology, Department of Criminology, Ottawa.

Waller, I., & Okihiro, N. (1978). *Burglary: The victim and the public.* Toronto: University of Toronto Press.

Weissman, E. (1978, August). Kids who attack gays. *Christopher Street,* pp. 9–13.

Wilson, J. P. (1989). *Trauma, transformation and healing: An integrative approach to theory, research and post traumatic theory.* New York: Brunner/Mazel.

Wolpe, J. (1958). *Psychotherapy by reciprocal inhibition.* Stanford, CA: Stanford University Press.

Wooden, W. S., & Parker, J. (1982). *Men behind bars: Sexual exploitation in person.* New York: Da Capo.

Worden, W. J. (1983). *Grief counseling and grief therapy: A handbook for the mental health practitioner.* New York: Springer.

Yassen, J., & Glass, L. (1984). Sexual assault survivors group: A feminist practice perspective. *Social Work, 29,* 252–257.